THE FAMILY JEWELS

Discovering
AMERICA

Mark Crispin Miller, Series Editor

This series begins with a startling premise—that even now, more than two hundred years since its founding, America remains a largely undiscovered country with much of its amazing story yet to be told. In these books, some of America's foremost historians and cultural critics bring to light episodes in our nation's history that have never been explored. They offer fresh takes on events and people we thought we knew well and draw unexpected connections that deepen our understanding of our national character.

John Prados

THE FAMILY JEWELS

THE CIA, SECRECY, AND PRESIDENTIAL POWER

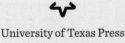

University of Texas Press

AUSTIN

Requests for permission to reproduce material from this work
should be sent to:
  Permissions
  University of Texas Press
  P.O. Box 7819
  Austin, TX 78713-7819
  http://utpress.utexas.edu/index.php/rp-form

∞ The paper used in this book meets the minimum requirements
of ANSI/NISO Z39.48-1992 (R1997) (Permanence of Paper).

LIBRARY OF CONGRESS CATALOGING-IN-PUBLICATION DATA

Prados, John.
  The family jewels : the CIA, secrecy, and presidential power /
by John Prados. — First edition.
    pages   cm
  Includes bibliographical references and index.
  ISBN 978-0-292-73762-4 (cloth : alk. paper)
  1. Intelligence service—United States. 2. United States. Central Intelligence Agency. 3. Presidents—United States. 4. Executive power—United States. I. Title.
  JK468.I6P696 2013
  327.1273—dc23   2013004240

doi:10.7560/737624

J. HIGGINS: *You were with Mr. Donovan's OSS,*
weren't you, sir?

MR. WABASH: *I sailed the Adriatic with a movie star*
at the helm! . . . It doesn't seem like much of a war
now, but it was. I go back even further: to ten years
after the Great War, as we called it. Before we knew
enough to number them.

J. HIGGINS: *You miss that kind of action, sir?*

MR. WABASH: *No—that kind of clarity.*

—LORENZO SEMPLE, JR., AND DAVID RAYFIEL,
THREE DAYS OF THE CONDOR SCREENPLAY,
FEBRUARY 3, 1975, FROM THE NOVEL *SIX DAYS*
OF THE CONDOR BY JAMES O'GRADY

☰ CONTENTS ☰

≡ ACRONYMS ≡

BNDD	Bureau of Narcotics and Dangerous Drugs
CI	Counterintelligence (CIA)
CIA	Central Intelligence Agency
CTC	Counter-Terrorism Center (CIA)
DCI	Director of Central Intelligence
DO	Directorate of Operations (CIA)
DOJ	Department of Justice
FAS	Federation of American Scientists
FBI	Federal Bureau of Investigation
FISA	Foreign Intelligence Surveillance Act
FISC	Foreign Intelligence Surveillance Court
FOIA	Freedom of Information Act
HVD	High Value Detainee
IG	Inspector General (CIA)
IOB	Intelligence Oversight Board
IRA	Irish Republican Army
IRS	Internal Revenue Service
KGB	Soviet Intelligence Service
NSA	National Security Agency
NSC	National Security Council
NYPD	New York Police Department

OGC   Office of the General Counsel (CIA)
OLC   Office of Legal Counsel (DOJ)
PDB   President's Daily Brief
PFIAB   President's Foreign Intelligence Advisory Board
PR   Public Relations
PRB   Publications Review Board (CIA)
TSP   Terrorist Surveillance Program

THE FAMILY JEWELS

≡ INTRODUCTION ≡

I n June of 2007 the mailman brought a large package to the National Security Archive, a public interest group that works for open government by advocating freedom of information and pressing for release of the sealed records of the United States government, which are then made available in several forms to anyone who is interested in them. The package contained a newly declassified document, a copy of the notorious Central Intelligence Agency (CIA) compilation called "The Family Jewels." This material was explosive because it described abuses—illegal domestic activities carried out by the CIA over a period of decades. Agency insiders aware of its sensitivity dubbed the collection "The Family Jewels." Revelation of some of its contents in the *New York Times* late in 1974 had ignited a firestorm of criticism in the United States, which in turn led to a series of investigations of intelligence activities by a presidential commission plus committees of both houses of the U.S. Congress. Those investigations progressed throughout the next year—and 1975 has come down in history as the "Year of Intelligence" in the United States.

The existence of the Family Jewels documents—the

original is really a compilation of items—had become known at the time but had forever been shrouded in secrecy. In 1991 the Archive filed under the Freedom of Information Act (FOIA) for declassification of The Family Jewels. The CIA denied the request, the Archive appealed, and the agency finally relented. Thus the package that arrived at the National Security Archive's front desk. We knew the significance of the Family Jewels documents from the storm of media coverage that followed. Archive director Thomas Blanton and I—as the senior fellow most knowledgeable on intelligence matters—spent literally seventy-two hours doing back-to-back interviews with print and broadcast journalists from all over the United States and dozens of foreign outlets spanning the globe from Latin America to Europe to Asia. The CIA itself, in the person of General Michael V. Hayden, its then-director, showed up at a conference of diplomatic historians to take credit for releasing The Family Jewels—as if this had been its idea, not the result of hard-fought pursuit of an FOIA case for nearly two decades.

The National Security Archive posted the Family Jewels documents on our website along with introductory material, plus an index that I compiled from the material. We wanted to do more. The first idea was for a document reader. Examination of the actual contents of The Family Jewels revealed them to be quite disappointing: we could see that a host of other materials—long-released documents, the CIA's own papers—describe the abuses covered in The Family Jewels in much greater depth. But our idea for an expanded reader that melded the Jewels with this other material became lost in the press of other business.

The "Family Jewels" compilation proved as explosive as it was not for its actual contents but because of the real abuses that underlay this sparse reporting. Its impact was demonstrable in the flurry of investigations that followed the press revelation. That season of inquiry took its course and led to creation of the system of formal intelligence oversight that exists in the United States today. However, the issue of abuse in intelligence activities has not gone away in the years since 1975, and in the first decade of this century it mushroomed with the excesses of President George W. Bush's war on terror. It was and still is important to engage with this problem if there is to be public confidence in the intelligence activities conducted by a democratic nation. It came to me that "The Family Jewels" really serves as a metaphor: Family Jewels designate a certain category of operations, ones that become sensitive as exuberance exceeds proper boundaries. Family Jewels are eternal. Only their specific content changes over time. I retrieved my notes and documents from the original project, and the result you see before you.

*T*he Family Jewels is *not* the story of the Year of Intelligence. My aims are broader than that. Its core is also not a review of the investigations themselves—although interactions between investigators, spooks, and presidential emissaries are central to the narrative. Nor is this book about the CIA documents known as The Family Jewels, although evidence from those figures in what is presented here. Rather, this tale begins with the sudden revelation of CIA domestic operations—the original Family Jewels—and continues through White House efforts to craft a response. The narrative then describes certain intelligence activities. The focus is the Jewels—the operations, the spooks who conducted them, the efforts to uncover them, the politicos who ordered them or attempted to stymie inquiry. Finally, the focus settles on the techniques the CIA and other intelligence agencies have used to protect their image. All of this is based on *real* records. None of it is made up. Viewed as a whole, the resulting picture of the Family Jewels in play is stunning.

This is the story of an *attitude*, a private presumption of

superiority based on the possession of secret, and supposedly superior, knowledge. That attitude led dedicated and
conscientious men and women to reach too far, do too much,
and dispense with limits to follow misguided orders. Their
cohorts worked equally assiduously to prevent the public
from learning what was happening. The result is the creation
of Family Jewels—legal and political time bombs, which can
lie dormant for years or even decades, but which eventually explode with a force that not only ends careers but can
threaten institutions and even governments. These are the
real Family Jewels. Individually, the epics each have their
discrete details, but the trajectories of the histories become
disturbingly familiar. For the sake of proper governance, it is
necessary to shine a spotlight on the Family Jewels.

In the intelligence business the standard response to revelations is to invoke national security and appeal to responsible people not to touch the emergent scandal for fear of
damaging important interests. The argument here is that the
true damage to the nation is wrought by the operations themselves—and by efforts to evade investigation of them. The
attempt to prevent public knowledge, suppress inquiry, and
avoid accountability harms essential elements of the system
for oversight and control—and ultimately public confidence
in the enterprise. Evasion corrodes the legal framework
erected to govern intelligence activities—which protects the
agencies themselves—and it undermines the political support necessary when issues of growth, reform, or mission
require forging a fresh consensus. Evasion subverts internal
morale by creating cleavages that divide officers implicated
in abusive activities from those who follow the rules, and
by throwing factions of rank-and-file and management into
what is fundamentally a conspiracy, sometimes to obstruct
justice, other times simply to avoid responsibility. Depending on the provenance of the original operations, evasion
also pulls other institutions—whether different intelligence

units, the Justice Department, or the White House—into the obstruction conspiracy. The political dangers are real. What is false is the idea that activities cannot be scrutinized. In a democracy the rule of law is central. This creates special tensions with respect to intelligence activities, which by nature work to the edge of or beyond the law. That makes public confidence vital. The uneasy relationship between secret agencies and public order requires that intelligence maintains the highest standards of discipline and accountability. Anything that challenges public confidence is harmful.

Two points are axiomatic. First, the potential for abuse is perennial. Intelligence covers a global range of concerns, and it utilizes a broad spectrum of methods. Political, military, social, and even economic concerns change over time and drive demands for action. Events alter previous perceptions of the state of nature. Presidents demand countervailing efforts. Directors devise projects. Operational logic can push projects across boundaries. The combination of purpose and circumstance leaves original goals behind. Thus are Jewels created. *The Family Jewels* illustrates this by taking a range of the abuses of the 1970s as archetypes, detailing the operations, and then showing how the same kind of activity has been replicated. Authorities sought different purposes in the later operations, they were conducted for the most part by different individuals, and the regulatory regime changed and tightened, but still the projects crossed the line.

Equally important, the temptation to avoid scrutiny has remained a constant. Both presidents and agencies succumbed. Here the narrative explores the efforts of several presidents and their intelligence agencies to prevent, curtail, or outflank investigations of Family Jewels as they are revealed. As part of this exploration I devote significant attention to the CIA's use of the media, not, as usually conceived, for such purposes as disguising agents, but as tool and object to be manipulated for the purpose of controlling knowledge—and *not* in foreign countries. A related subject, the CIA's creation and use of an apparatus to manage what its own employees can write about their experiences, is also treated in considerable detail. Manipulations of the record are made in the name of national security but in practice serve political and institutional goals.

The book makes a distinction between "The Family Jewels," the compilation of CIA documents that bears that name, and Family Jewels, the broad range of questionable or abusive CIA activities. Through Family Jewels the narrative examines the impact of the attitudes that drive the system. Nevertheless, the original document must not be denied its importance or name. In order to distinguish the two, this narrative uses the terms "Family Jewels documents," or "original Family Jewels," to denote the collection of CIA papers, but the plain terms "Family Jewels," or simply "Jewels," to signify the category of controversial operations that, both individually and collectively, lie at the heart of our inquiry. In a few places that usage may appear awkward, but the formula is necessary to establish our distinction.

The Family Jewels opens with chapters that introduce the Family Jewels documents and recount how 1975 became the Year of Intelligence. A prologue briefly revisits the journalistic revelation that set off controversy. Two subsequent chapters review how and why the Family Jewels documents were created, and what measures President Gerald R. Ford took in the immediate aftermath of the disclosure. This latter prefigures a much later discussion of the cross-cutting interests presidents have in drawing upon intelligence agencies for political cover, and conversely those of spy units in securing presidential protection.

Scandals and controversies during the Year of Intelligence

not only disclosed details of many operations covered here, they led to creation of the system of oversight that exists in the United States today. This latter apparatus became a hurdle to be overcome by the perpetrators of many subsequent Family Jewels. This accountability mechanism still has to be made to function properly for there to be effective intelligence operations in a democratic system.

A succession of chapters ranges over time. These take four of the most important issues investigated in 1975—political surveillance, eavesdropping, detention and interrogation, and assassination. They represent most of the subjects dealt with in the Family Jewels documents, but I have deliberately excluded one area—the CIA's mind-control experiments. The story here is too sensational and the declassified record even more expurgated than it is in many other areas, plus the available records appear to show the drug experiments ended in the early-to-mid-1960s.[1] The way that public sensibilities have evolved, it would be surprising had these experiments been resumed later, and in any case primary sources have hardly progressed in more than a decade. As for the Year of Intelligence itself, existing accounts focus on the congressional investigations. These treat events almost entirely as a face-off between Congress and the intelligence agencies, neglecting the White House perspective. *The Family Jewels* makes an effort to illuminate this crucial area, without which the events of 1975 cannot be understood properly. However, the congressional sources and accounts of its investigations are introduced wherever they are germane to the narrative. Nevertheless, the central concern is operations and what happened to them, not the investigations per se.

The narrative shows that charges leveled against the CIA reflected real intelligence operations and outlines how the same kinds of controversial spy activities replicated themselves in later decades. Each intervening chapter takes up the thread of one kind of Family Jewel—political surveillance, eavesdropping, harsh interrogation, or assassination—or shows the lengths to which the CIA went to cloak its daggers. A final substantive chapter brings the story full circle to the White House. The conclusion analyzes our findings and proposes a means by which Family Jewels can be more effectively monitored and—hopefully—prevented.

John Prados
Washington, DC
January 2013

≡ PROLOGUE ≡

I t all began with an astonishing headline. December 22, 1974. Those who picked up the big Sunday edition of the *New York Times* found a blockbuster story splashed across three columns of the front page under the text "HUGE CIA OPERATION REPORTED IN U.S. AGAINST ANTI-WAR FORCES, OTHER DISSIDENTS IN NIXON YEARS."[1] The story ran in other papers too. In his lead paragraph investigative reporter Seymour Hersh charged that the Central Intelligence Agency (CIA) had conducted a massive illegal domestic intelligence operation. Elsewhere he mentioned wiretaps on people's phones, break-ins, agents penetrating political groups, photographs taken at demonstrations, and a surveillance and disruption plan aimed at Americans—coordinated by the Nixon White House. All this was illegal under the CIA's charter, which prohibited activities within the United States, and many activities were also violations of existing criminal statutes. The CIA's place in the American pantheon had already become deeply controversial. The Watergate political scandal, which destroyed the presidency of Richard Nixon, added to the pot. The agency had defended itself by claiming it had been duped. These were new charges, even more serious, and Hersh's account included more Watergate news as well—of an attempt to blackmail the CIA by former agency employee, now convicted Watergate burglar, James McCord, Jr.

Several paragraphs into his account Seymour Hersh mentioned that many of the abuses he was reporting had been uncovered by a culling of CIA files ordered under former agency director James R. Schlesinger, and deep down the story mentioned that the current director, William E. Colby, confirmed that a complete investigation had in fact been conducted. Colby referred to the issues uncovered as "family skeletons." Hersh, together with *Times* publisher Abe Rosenthal, had confirmed that directly with Colby in an interview before the piece was written. When the Hersh revelations appeared, Colby knew, as did few outsiders, that the agency's file review had produced a real document—or more properly a collection of documents. The cognoscenti knew it as "The Family Jewels."

Langley might have gotten off more easily had the *Times* downplayed its disclosures. And that might have happened. There was a frantic run to make press time. *Times* bureau chief Bill Kovach edited the piece, and in the bustle let the adjective "massive," describing the CIA operations, slip by. That became a sore point for the Washington bureau chief, who worried it gave the agency an opening to discredit the story. The appearance of the *Times* revelations was like striking a match in a tinderbox.

One who saw the flicker of flame was journalist David C. Martin. A cub reporter on his first job—the night shift at the Associated Press (AP)—Martin was tasked with keeping watch on the news tickers and early editions and finding stories that could be matched or bettered by the AP. The early edition of the Sunday *Times* was obviously explosive. The Hersh story spoke to Martin, the son of a CIA officer. He began to mine the story for names and telephone people.

One name he found was that of James Angleton, chief of the agency's counterintelligence unit. Martin picked up the phone, figuring he was on a desperate mission—others would already be all over Angleton. But no, the man answered the call. Soon David Martin had his own scoops to add to the pile. Associated Press reporting gave the CIA scandal even more legs—plus wider distribution. Even more fat fell in the fire. Senator Walter Mondale was at home when he saw the Hersh story. Mondale typically set aside Sunday afternoons to read books that struck his fancy and scan a variety of newspapers. For months, Mondale recounts, senators had been hearing rumors of outlandish activities by the intelligence agencies, but the *Times* revelations were still shocking.[2] Over several years Americans had been exposed to a new, cynical vision of government—first the Pentagon Papers had shown how the United States government had misled the public into the Vietnam war, then Watergate demonstrated presidential integrity at its nadir. Now the Family Jewels scoop unmasked the CIA's nefarious doings—with Congress completely in the dark. Mondale and other legislators were incensed. Within days, Rhode Island's John Pastore rose on the Senate floor to argue the Congress could not abdicate its responsibility to investigate these matters.

WHERE DID THE FAMILY JEWELS COME FROM?

The answer to that question depends on which "Family Jewels" are on the table. At the broadest level the Family Jewels are the set of intelligence activities that are most sensitive from the political, legal, and moral standpoints. These Family Jewels evolve from the warp and woof of operations. Many projects are conceived, born, and completed without ever numbering among the "jewels." Others are noncontroversial at the outset but endure or morph in such a way that one day they become Family Jewels. Yet other intelligence activities are sensitive from the start. A project can be controversial politically where its nature challenges the public's understanding of acceptable activities. Sensitivity also arises when a project pushes the limits of legality or skirts proper approval. And operations that controvert moral standards are Family Jewels by nature. From this perspective a set of Family Jewels often exists, shrouded in secrecy, at the heart of intelligence operations. This has been true throughout the history of the Central Intelligence Agency (CIA) and the United States intelligence community—as will be shown. The problem is a thorny one and has long escaped the attention it deserves.

There is a specific set of Family Jewels that derives from a certain era of American intelligence history and a specific document known as "The Family Jewels," compiled at Langley, Virginia, CIA headquarters. The time was the early 1970s and the answer to the question can be quite specific: From a director afraid of being blindsided by revelations of the agency's past domestic activities, illegal by definition under the National Security Act of 1947. The director was James R. Schlesinger, appointed by President Richard Nixon. When he perceived political pitfalls from what he did not know about their operations, Mr. Schlesinger demanded his subordinates create a record of CIA misdeeds. The Family Jewels is the result.

It happened like this:

In 1972, during the transition before his second term, Nixon stunned the serving director and most at the agency's Langley headquarters by asking Director Richard M. Helms to resign. Sending the former spy chief to Iran as ambassador, Nixon showed his displeasure with the CIA by going completely outside the espionage business to select Schlesinger, an economist and defense intellectual who then headed the president's Office of Management and Budget. His White House job had given Schlesinger a good sense of the Nixon administration's budget problems. Almost his only experience with U.S. intelligence, other than as a consumer of reports on Soviet strategic forces (during years as a RAND Corporation analyst), had been in assembling a review of intelligence community efficiency for Mr. Nixon in late 1971. Thus Schlesinger became the boss, a post then known as the Director of Central Intelligence (DCI), with a mandate to reduce and streamline the community in general and the CIA specifically. The Vietnam war was entering a new phase without U.S. combat involvement, requiring fewer CIA field operations. Schlesinger had no particular liking for the CIA, and he detested its long-serving chieftain Helms, but that was not the root of his actions. Rather, he had a specific mandate from the president. Richard Nixon, who had trimmed CIA budgets and overseas personnel from his first year in office, wanted a director who would be his ally. Thus Schlesinger arrived at Langley determined to cut deadwood from the CIA's ranks, and he proceeded to do so.

Director Schlesinger's motives are important to the Family Jewels for two reasons. First, his firings of CIA officers put him at odds with agency professionals and affected what its rank and file would eventually be willing to report in the Jewels. Second, Schlesinger already knew that investigative journalists, Seymour Hersh specifically, were nosing into CIA domestic activities.

Note that all of this took place as the Watergate scandal began to boil over, after six months of more or less successful White House efforts to keep the lid on this potent political threat, which flowed from the Nixon presidential campaign as well as his efforts against activists opposing the Vietnam war. Scandal became a real possibility once a gang of campaign-employed burglars was arrested inside the offices of the opposition political party, the Democratic Party, on June 17, 1972. The party's offices were located in a building along the Potomac known as The Watergate, and "Watergate" became the shorthand for the whole complex of political skullduggery carried out under President Nixon. The trial of the Watergate burglars began on January 10, 1973, ten days before Mr. Nixon's re-inauguration and three weeks ahead of Schlesinger's swearing-in at Langley. Jim Schlesinger had nothing to do with the Watergate burglars or break-in, and he knew nothing about their activities for the CIA during the Helms era. In February the U.S. Senate empaneled a committee to explore the scandal in all its ramifications.

Watergate loomed as an issue that could implicate the CIA, and the agency knew of journalists' inquiries while Helms still headed it. Notes taken at the CIA director's morning staff meeting show that on January 18, 1973, senior aide John Maury told the group that Seymour Hersh had asked Representative Lucien N. Nedzi (D-MI) about allegations of extensive domestic spying. Nedzi headed a panel of the House Armed Services Committee then in charge of monitoring the CIA. Richard Helms responded by asking senior officials to see Nedzi and brief him on what the agency did and did not do within the United States. Next day Director Helms confirmed his order. Nedzi wanted CIA's presentation made to his full subcommittee. That had yet to happen when James Schlesinger took over on February 2. Six days later Maury, the CIA legislative liaison chief, reminded the group of the impending House briefing. At that point the head of CIA's analytical unit, Edward Proctor, suggested that an internal review identify what in fact the agency was doing at home. That way "marginal" operations could be eliminated and the CIA would look sharper. Thus the idea of a "Family Jewels" document was already in the wind.

Schlesinger's avowed determination to pare back the CIA alarmed its allies in Congress. They scrutinized his actions closely. Director Schlesinger was called to testify before the then-secret subcommittees of Congress concerned with U.S. intelligence—like Nedzi's—almost monthly during this interval. That put Schlesinger on notice that controversial CIA activities could threaten his entire program. Agency people knew this danger as "flap potential."

Just three months into Schlesinger's tenure at Langley, on April 27, 1973, the Department of Justice revealed in a memorandum to the judge presiding at the trial of the Watergate burglars that in the fall of 1971 the same men, then working directly for the White House, had burglarized the offices of the psychiatrist who treated antiwar activist Daniel Ellsberg. Ellsberg had infuriated the Nixon White House by leaking the Top Secret study of U.S. policy in the Vietnam war known as the Pentagon Papers. Next, on May 2, the federal grand jury considering Watergate indictments learned from a key figure in the burglaries, former CIA officer E. Howard Hunt, a White House official and then–Nixon campaign intelligence operative, that he had received CIA help on the Ellsberg break-in.

All this stunned Director Schlesinger, who summoned the acting chief of the agency's Directorate of Plans[1] and asked him what was behind the story. That man, Cord Meyer, Jr., confirmed Hunt's testimony: the agency had furnished him a camera, disguise materials, and false identification. Later investigations established the assistance had followed a telephone conversation between Nixon's domestic counsel, John Ehrlichman, and CIA deputy director General Robert Cushman, followed by a Hunt call to Cushman, both in July 1971. Director Schlesinger learned separately, at almost the same time, that CIA scientists had prepared a "psychological profile" of Ellsberg for the White House. Furious, Schlesinger ordered Meyer to review the agency file on "Mr. Edwards," the cover identity given to Howard Hunt.

As he examined the Hunt file, Cord Meyer discovered photographs of a building. They were of the sort often used to plan covert operations. The setting clearly seemed to be the American West, perhaps California. The agency's photo labs, it turned out, had developed Hunt's pictures used to prepare the break-in. Astonished, by his own account, Meyer reported this new information to an incredulous James Schlesinger.

"What else have you people been hiding from me?" Director Schlesinger retorted.[2]

Meyer's boss at the time, Deputy Director for Plans William E. Colby, was in Thailand on a Far East inspection trip. In a Bangkok newspaper, he read of Hunt's testimony and the CIA assistance on the Ellsberg break-in. As the agency's executive director in 1972, under orders from Director Helms, Colby had been point man for all Watergate-related CIA matters. Colby had briefed Schlesinger on what he thought was the whole story, but he, too, had known nothing of the Hunt problem. Colby immediately dropped his inspection and returned to Washington. He saw Schlesinger. The new director demanded the inside scoop—as Colby recounts, "We would tear the place apart and 'fire everyone if necessary,' but we had to find out whether there were any other such questionable or illegal activities hidden in the secret recesses of the clandestine past."[3] They might explode at any time.

Colby drafted an order to make Director Schlesinger's wish a reality. Schlesinger and Colby finalized the directive, which the DCI issued on May 9, 1973. The same day Schlesinger made another of his appearances before the Senate Appropriations Committee and used the opportunity to declare he was imposing fresh controls on the agency. Referring to both this Capitol Hill testimony and the press reporting on the CIA and Howard Hunt, the Schlesinger directive not only prohibited all domestic operations, it ordered all "senior operating officials of this Agency to report to me immediately on any activities now going on, or that have gone on in the past, which might be construed to be outside the legislative charter of this Agency."[4]

Every CIA officer was enjoined to contact Schlesinger's office if he or she had knowledge of such activities, and ex-employees were invited to do so as well. Anyone given an order going beyond the charter should call immediately. Mr. Schlesinger supplied his telephone number for that purpose. "With that directive," Colby recounts, "the CIA 'family jewels' were born, and led inexorably to a year of Congressional investigations and a whole new status for American intelligence."[5]

Bill Colby took the lead in assembling The Family Jewels. He was assisted by CIA Inspector General (IG) William V. Broe and his staff. A second Schlesinger order demanded information on any contact between any CIA employee and any of the individuals implicated in Watergate. The IG staff ranged back over the minutes of the CIA director's daily meetings and extracted items that seemed to fill the bill. Each CIA directorate or division chief wrote a paper recounting activities that fell within the scope of the directive, and provided attachments that illuminated their summaries. Here fear played its role—fear of falling to Schlesinger's ax—as well as CIA officers' disdain for the director, inclining agency barons to report only the bare bones of many escapades. "Down in the directorates," Bill Colby recalled, "they were upset that this could drag out a lot of things."[6]

Thus the actual, original Family Jewels amounted to a flawed product, merely scratching the surface on key points. Bill Colby surveyed the reports and asked for amplification where he felt it necessary. Here again The Family Jewels suffered because a number of activities it detailed had peaked during the 1960s, when Colby had been preoccupied with Far Eastern matters; or in the period from 1968 to 1971, when he had actually been in South Vietnam, assigned to run pacification programs. In important instances Colby did not know what to ask for. The various submissions were bound together to create the final document, a massive compendium of 693 pages. The Family Jewels went to the CIA's executive management committee on May 17. Despite its length, Colby was unimpressed: "I remember my impression after looking at the whole set of items was that they were pretty small potatoes. They really were."[7] But not having pursued knowledge of the underlying programs, and with little sense of American public attitudes, Colby actually missed the full implications of what he held in his hands.

It turned out that CIA activities with "flap potential" were many, not few. They included activities to thwart journalists and to sway opinion; an intrusive operation that built files on Americans based on physical surveillance, or on opening their mail; hostile CIA interrogations; drug experiments on Americans, witting or not; infiltration of political groups opposed to the Vietnam war, plus assistance to other federal agencies performing similar roles; CIA subsidies to Nixon White House political operations; and more. Agency intelligence circulated to other government bureaus such as the FBI had fueled further domestic intrusions. Some activities, such as assassination programs, were entirely excluded. The CIA employed tactics including telephone wiretaps, illegal under the 1968 Omnibus Crime Act; spying on Americans inside the United States; break-ins; coordination with local police units; and the specific techniques required for the political surveillance programs. All of these activities were explosive in themselves, the compendium more so. The Family Jewels is probably the most sensitive secret document ever produced by the Central Intelligence Agency.

In the meantime Watergate upheavals brought William E. Colby to the head of the CIA. The resignation of Attorney General Richard Kleindienst at the end of April led Nixon to shift his secretary of defense over to head the Justice Department. The president then named James R. Schlesinger to lead the Pentagon. Colby was promoted to Director of Central Intelligence. Thus it was Bill Colby who would deal with the fallout from The Family Jewels and answer the questions that arose from the projects the documents revealed.

Before the change of command, Jim Schlesinger and Bill Colby agreed that the results of their inquiry should be shared with congressional overseers. Colby, who faced confirmation hearings and whose last Vietnam tour had been contentious (due to assassination charges connected to the notorious Phoenix program), was especially concerned to smooth his way on Capitol Hill. Consequently he took up The Family Jewels with key senators and congressmen. Most were content to listen to the CIA officer's basic briefing,[8] but Lucien Nedzi wanted more. On May 23 Colby and Inspector

General Broe met with Nedzi for two hours and described the data on CIA illegalities in detail, including the most sensitive sections. By Broe's account, Colby described the compendium as "descriptions of activities (especially involved in the domestic scene) that had flap potential." Colby and Nedzi discussed the material item-by-item, "and in most cases [Nedzi] actually read the text."[9] The congressman had many reactions—some no doubt unprintable—but also not detailed in Broe's record. He demanded a copy of the original order to compile The Family Jewels plus more information on ten issues raised in the documents. Nedzi also suggested making the information public. Obviously, from 1973 until 2007 the CIA resisted doing that.

With one exception Congressman Nedzi agreed to follow the CIA's lead in keeping quiet about the Family Jewels. The exception was Watergate. Nedzi was holding hearings to investigate the agency's role in the political scandal. He was especially interested in the CIA's handling of a series of letters it received from White House Plumber (and former CIA officer) James McCord during the months after his arrest in the Watergate burglary. Nedzi demanded testimony on that. A hearing was held. Colby had Howard Osborn, CIA security chief, swear out a deposition on the letters and the agency. Osborn, Broe, agency General Counsel Lawrence Houston, and other officials duly appeared. Nedzi went ballistic over the failure to report McCord's letters to FBI Watergate investigators.[10]

Apart from taking testimony on the letters, however, Nedzi and his secret CIA subcommittee took no action other than to report on the agency's Watergate issues.[11] In particular they did nothing in public. Relieved it had "informed" legislative overseers while successfully keeping the lid on the Family Jewels, the CIA did nothing further. Director Colby did promulgate orders confirming prohibitions already issued on the underlying CIA abuses. Until that fateful day in December 1974 when Sy Hersh published the first of his articles in the *New York Times*, nothing was known of the Family Jewels, including at the White House. Schlesinger apparently rejected informing the president, and Colby never thought of it. The question, he recalled, "Just never arose; never answered the question, never even posed the question."[12] The several investigations of the Central Intelligence Agency that proceeded through the year 1975 would result from the combination of a blindsided president, CIA reporting that merely dipped into the programs, and the public outrage that followed revelation of some of the abuses.

THE FAMILY JEWELS
The White House Reacts

Director Colby knew of the December 1974 *New York Times* story that revealed The Family Jewels. Seymour Hersh had approached him to ask questions, and later for comment on the allegations. The spy chieftain attempted to dissuade the journalist from submitting the story as he had it, arguing that Hersh was mixing very different elements into the same stew: the CIA investigating whether foreign nations controlled the antiwar movement, its efforts to plug leaks, and its work to counter espionage. Hersh was not impressed, nor were his editors. The *Times* went with the story they had, and added to it over succeeding days. Once the series was published, not only did the reporter's take seem justified, but more abuses surfaced: the CIA mail-opening and its drug experiments on unwitting Americans. The charges were explosive. Coming on top of Watergate, controversy over CIA complicity in the 1973 Chilean coup, long disquiet over the CIA's role in Vietnam, and, starting from the Bay of Pigs fiasco, years of gradual exposure of covert adventures, the Hersh articles created a public uproar.

Some CIA veterans believe the real mistake lay in creating The Family Jewels in the first place, that without this compendium of nefarious misdeeds, there would have been no controversy and the spy life could have gone on as usual. This was an illusion. The improprieties hung like a sword of Damocles. The only question was how long it would take for the weight of what had been so secret so long to reach the point where the sword's edge cut the restraining ropes of CIA secrecy. The underlying abuses, not the flap potential of the document, controlled the outcome.

The original Hersh story mentioned suspicions that much shredding of documents had occurred at CIA when Schlesinger demanded The Family Jewels be assembled. That may or may not be true, but certainly the Jewels collection amounted to less than the sum of its parts. Moreover, in writing his stories Hersh did not actually have access to The Family Jewels. He worked from tips and the accounts of officials he confronted with information gleaned elsewhere. Only in the last days did the agency confirm the document existed. In short, excesses had reached the point where bits of the story were popping out of troubled employees in many places. It only required a good investigator to put the pieces together—and that Sy Hersh did very well.

The simple revelation of The Family Jewels led to a full year of investigations of the Central Intelligence Agency and the entire U.S. intelligence community—the "Year of Intelligence," as 1975 has become known. This story involves some individuals very well known today—Richard Cheney, Donald Rumsfeld, and Henry Kissinger—and it shows that the machinations during George W. Bush's administration were the work of persons with long practice.

Foremost among them was the man who would reach the pinnacle of his career as vice president of the United States. During President Gerald Ford's time, it was Richard Cheney who served as deputy chief of staff in the White House, his boss being Donald Rumsfeld. That weekend in 1974 President Ford was headed for a ski vacation in Vail, Colorado.

Rumsfeld went with him. Ford intended to set time aside only to meet economic advisors for ideas on his upcoming state of the union address. Cheney held the fort at the White House when the alert came of the impending *New York Times* revelations. Staff were left to craft a response to the CIA flap in Ford's absence. Their solution was for the president to create a commission to conduct a limited review of aspects of the charges. Gerald Ford agreed—and selected his vice president, Nelson A. Rockefeller, to lead it. The presidential commission ultimately failed to head off separate investigations by both houses of Congress.

Richard Cheney—who has always styled himself "Dick" in a bid for informality—played the central role in contriving the White House strategy to meet the crisis. Cheney initially sought to clamp down a lid of secrecy, protecting President Ford by heading off any congressional inquiries into the abuse revelations and ensuring that only approved information should emerge, and that under controlled conditions. He was not successful. There would be investigations by not one but two congressional committees in addition to that of the Rockefeller Commission. Cheney is oddly circumspect on this period in his memoir. He simply writes that "Jack Marsh kept me apprised of the Rockefeller Commission's progress and the work of the two committees on the Hill."[1] This threadbare passage conceals Dick Cheney's central role in the entire Ford strategy. While presidential counselor John O. Marsh did indeed watch the investigations closely, a host of aides were involved, and Dick Cheney stood at the tip of the spear. More than that, the deceptive language stops short of recounting that it was Dick Cheney who concocted President Ford's strategy in the first place.

The story begins with Bill Colby, who certainly awaited the Hersh articles with trepidation. Colby did not simply sit mum. The day before the *Times* began to run its revelations, Colby saw Acting Attorney General Lawrence H. Silberman

and agreed to refer to the Justice Department any allegations deemed worthy of investigation. Colby also phoned the
White House and warned deputy national security advisor
Brent Scowcroft of the imminent appearance of the disclo-
sures. Scowcroft's boss, Henry Kissinger, contends the news
had the effect of a "burning match in a gasoline depot."[2] He
also claims the White House was blindsided by the story, that
Colby never told the NSC staff he had had an interview with
Hersh, and that the first inkling President Gerald R. Ford had
of the breaking news came with the initial article, when the
CIA director phoned the president aboard Air Force One.[3]
Kissinger may be right that Colby did not tell the White
House of his interview with Hersh—but it was hardly a standard practice for CIA to report every journalistic contact to
the White House, and in any case, Colby's aim in meeting
with Hersh had still been to somehow head off the stories.
When Colby phoned Air Force One, he knew they were coming. Ford was en route to Vail.

Whatever the state of play, on the first day the White
House did nothing. Don Rumsfeld phoned the NSC offices
looking for Kissinger or Scowcroft but could not reach either.
In his own memoir, incidentally, Rumsfeld passes over this
entire affair. His Ford White House story jumps from putting his stamp on the staff to the days of the 1976 presidential
campaign. But the CIA flap, in between, mushroomed into a
full-blown political crisis. The second morning, in Hersh's
follow-up story, he began to discuss Central Intelligence
Agency officials involved with some of the domestic spy programs, particularly Richard Helms and James Angleton. This
time Kissinger was out of the starting gate immediately, calling Rumsfeld about "the Helms matter." Insisting he knew
nothing and that no such activities had been reported, Kissinger demanded that Director Colby provide an immediate recitation of the facts. Ford's press secretary could then
fairly say the president had asked for a report and leave it at

that. Five minutes later Kissinger spoke to Colby. The CIA chief agreed to submit a review, said the White House could have it by the next day—possible only due to the existence of the Family Jewels documents—and gave Kissinger a brief description of the projects at issue.

Bill Colby himself raised the possibility of an outside panel, commenting that the president "would be well advised to put some independent investigator on it after he looks at what I tell him to assure him that what I am telling him is right."[4] Late that night a cable from Vail arrived at the White House Situation Room. It contained President Ford's instructions, relayed by chief of staff Rumsfeld. The CIA was to address the matter in writing within forty-eight hours. Mr. Ford considered turning the Colby Report, as this document became known, over to the President's Foreign Intelligence Advisory Board for an opinion. Rumsfeld's cable also introduced a new character: he asked that materials about to be sent to the president be shown first to his own deputy, Richard Cheney.[5] Rumsfeld's cable made Cheney Ford's point man on the affair.

Meanwhile, Dr. Kissinger had already begun to spin the CIA story. After his phone conversation with Colby, the good doctor, in his White House capacity as national security advisor to Ford (Kissinger also served as secretary of state), prepared a memorandum for Rumsfeld on public handling of the allegations. Here Kissinger went back on his advice that press secretary Ron Nessen comment, now recommending that no statement be issued. Nessen should confine himself to answering questions. Kissinger supplied a list of anticipated queries and suggested replies.[6] Privately, Kissinger had another phone conversation, that same morning, with television journalist Ted Koppel. Kissinger insisted—he said it twice, and added that this was "to my almost certain knowledge"—the CIA had only dealt with "the degree to which foreign countries were infiltrating foreign student movements."

Seconds later Kissinger added, "I am so sick of these things. They have been in the newspapers thousands of times."[7] To the contrary, the reason the Hersh articles proved so explosive was precisely *because* they documented charges—of CIA infiltration of American political groups—that the government had long denied. In 1967 there had been a previous wave of public concern when it emerged that the CIA had funded an American private group, the National Student Association, and the Johnson administration had issued assurances that domestic spy activities were prohibited. The new disclosures showed not only that domestic spying had continued, but that CIA operations were much broader and more intrusive than anyone imagined.

In his conversations with reporters on Christmas Eve, Henry Kissinger repeatedly took the position that his role was merely to collect a report from the CIA and forward it to President Ford. He told journalist Marvin Kalb there would be some sort of investigation. "We want something that brings out the facts," Kissinger said. "What the mechanism is, we've not decided."[8] To Barry Schweid, Henry maintained he had not read the Colby Report carefully.[9] Not true, of course. Colby's paper arrived at the White House the same day as these conversations. By the next morning Kissinger had written a five-page distillation, sent to Vail by courier along with Colby's brief. The Kissinger summary is striking as much for what it *does not* say as for what it does: his précis works hard to place as many CIA excesses as possible in the Johnson presidency, often citing the Nixon years in the context of reining in runaway programs. There is no mention at all of the Huston Plan (see Chapter 3). That project's product, an interagency intelligence committee coordinated by White House counsel John Dean, is given the same context Kissinger used in his telephone conversations—foreign links with foreign dissidents. Telephone taps, physical surveillance of journalists and others, and a series of additional excesses during the Nixon years are preemptively consigned to a category of items that Kissinger maintained were "erroneously" connected to CIA domestic activity. Kissinger carefully attributed this to Colby's report, not his own judgment. The memo also says something *absent from* the Colby Report: that among the 9,944 files the CIA had compiled on Americans, it had opened 14 on members of the United States Congress.[10]

Meanwhile, Colby had also informed Representative Lucien Nedzi, who already knew of the Family Jewels. Nedzi played down the CIA abuses when first asked, telling *Newsweek* magazine, "You might call it illegalities in terms of exceeding their charter, but it certainly wasn't of the dimension . . . of what has appeared in the newspapers."[11] Nedzi proved dead wrong.

Even as the Ford administration gathered its facts, the political flames the Hersh revelations had ignited burned hotter. More disclosures from Sy Hersh and others filled the media. CIA abuse became an issue on which politicians staked out positions. On Christmas Eve, as Kissinger read the Colby Report, Illinois congressman Paul Findley sent a letter to President Ford recommending that he appoint an independent special prosecutor to look into the CIA question, much like the Watergate prosecutor (or, later, the one who investigated the Lewinski affair during Bill Clinton's administration). Findley's voice was only one among a growing chorus. The Ford White House paid attention. On December 24 political advisor John O. Marsh sent President Ford his own memo advocating a blue ribbon panel to examine the complaints and recommend safeguards. A simple referral to the Foreign Intelligence Advisory Board would be inadequate to still these troubled waters.

The day after Christmas, when President Ford received the Colby Report, couriered to Vail, the CIA scandal became a political headache at the highest level. The blue ribbon commission idea was already being bruited about, not just by Marsh but also Dick Cheney, and he had a commentary ready that very day. Cheney's memo already mentioned the possibility a commission might forestall "less desirable" congressional inquiries. Staff were not sure of the scope to be given such an investigation—Kissinger argued forcefully that any inquiry be limited to what the press had already mentioned. Possible members were discussed, including whether to select some from Congress. Cheney's handwritten notes are replete with lists of potential members and pros and cons of each. Whatever the choice, staff foresaw, action must be taken promptly.

Dick Cheney went further. The White House deputy chief of staff spent a few days looking at the Colby Report, the flow of paper, and the Hersh stories. He pulled his thoughts together in a December 27 note that remains one of the most significant—and completely ignored—artifacts of the Year of Intelligence.[12] Cheney's note reveals an acute instinct for the jugular, one fully developed at that time. He shows the White House was aware of vulnerabilities inherent in the CIA scandal beyond those Kissinger had identified: Cheney clearly referred to the Huston Plan, he connects Huston's Nixon White House project with Helms of the CIA, and he adds the notation "Helms, et. al.—possible perjury." And Cheney argues that any congressional investigation would take place in the context of Watergate and the Ellsberg case, plus knowledge of Richard Nixon's White House tapes.

Mr. Cheney laid out four goals for the president. The first was simply to examine the charges. The second was key: "Ensure proper presidential posture; avoid being tarnished by controversy." After that came the installation of safeguards on intelligence. Finally, Cheney wanted to insulate the CIA from anything that could inhibit its ability to operate.

There were several ways to get there. Cheney's first option was simply to accept the Colby Report as accurate, but he doubted "Congress & the Nation will accept such a report as valid and consider the matter closed." That course practically guaranteed congressional investigation. The second possibility was to remain neutral—a "do nothing" stance that would also ensure congressional inquiry. Cheney's third option was to *"Take Action* by having the executive branch take the lead in the investigation and by accepting the responsibility for making certain the CIA is adhering to its charter." Cheney envisioned public release of all or part of the Colby Report, a Justice Department role in prosecuting any real abuses, and a "special group or commission" to do the uncovering. Mr. Cheney's logic clearly favored the third option, and he says so. That course was preferable because it enabled President Ford to avoid defending Colby's report; it could minimize supposedly unwarranted or irresponsible attacks on the CIA; it would demonstrate presidential leadership; and it "offers the best opportunity for convincing the nation that gov't does indeed have integrity." Dick Cheney presented one more reason for his preferred option, one that will be familiar to observers of the later Cheney in the Iran-Contra affair, as secretary of defense, and as vice president: "It offers the best prospect for heading off Congressional efforts to further encroach on the executive branch." After the 9/11 attacks, staying in character, Richard Cheney would oppose congressional hearings on intelligence failures leading up to the day of the tragedy, and he would resist requests that he, along with President George W. Bush, should appear before the bipartisan national commission established to explore all aspects of this disaster.

President Ford accepted the blue ribbon commission immediately. Thus, within seventy-two hours of the submission of the Colby Report, the Ford White House had settled on a strategy. Days of frantic phone calls and letters, and pages of Dick Cheney's scribbling, detail the push. Governor Ronald Reagan of California quickly accepted. Dean Rusk was asked but turned down the Ford White House. Representative Samuel Stratton volunteered but was not chosen—in fact, no one from Congress was selected. Lawyer Lloyd Cutler was mentioned favorably but not chosen. General Andrew Goodpaster was considered but rejected on grounds he would need protection from the Left. Generals Matthew B. Ridgway and Maxwell D. Taylor both passed the first muster, but neither was selected; the White House went instead with retired general Lyman R. Lemnitzer. The intended chairman was former solicitor general of the United States Erwin N. Griswold. President Ford's fingerprint is visible there, for the actual chairman would be Vice President Rockefeller, who appears on none of the candidate lists. Griswold would be a member but not the chairman. The others would be labor leader Lane Kirkland, financier C. Douglas Dillon, and political figures John T. Connor and Edgar F. Shannon, Jr.

By New Year's Eve the Ford White House had a list of prospective members of a commission and a draft executive order establishing it. The Rockefeller Commission would have narrow limits on its inquiry and a short interval in which to conduct an investigation. Everything was arranged for a whitewash. Another plank was laid that day too, when CIA Director Colby and his chief counsel met anew with Justice Department officials to lay out the extent of CIA's vulnerabilities, which were significant.

Two conversations with Gerald Ford are especially significant. The first took place between the president and Henry Kissinger, who spent the morning of January 4, 1975, closeted with him, going over the allegations. "What is happening is worse than in the days of McCarthy," Kissinger complained, "worse for the country than Watergate." Kissinger added that former CIA director Richard Helms had warned him "the stuff out in public represented just the tip of the iceberg," that if the rest came out "blood will flow."

Reaching for a specific instance, the national security

advisor added, "For example, Robert Kennedy personally managed the operation on the assassination of Castro." Here Kissinger expressed a personal opinion best calculated to convince the president that Ford's next guest, Richard Helms, would require protection. In his brother's administration, Bobby Kennedy had been careful not to leave records of any murder plotting against Fidel Castro, and the truth about Kennedy's involvement remains murky to this day. Kissinger next speculated on why charges regarding the CIA's covert operation to overthrow the government in Chile were *not* among the disclosures rampant in the media. The national security advisor had been widely credited with being a leading proponent of that effort. Chile's absence from the public discussion, Kissinger thought "sort of [a] blackmail on me." Bill Colby had been "a disgrace," and once the ill winds had subsided, he ought to be moved and replaced by someone with "towering integrity." Kissinger worried the CIA could be emasculated.[13]

The other crucial encounter is President Ford's talk with former CIA chieftain Richard Helms. As early as Kissinger's initial phone contacts, he had been asked whether Ford would summon Helms, now ambassador to Iran, for consultations. Kissinger opposed that move. But by December 27 President Ford had told Cheney he wanted to see Helms, and the meeting was arranged. To prepare the president for this encounter, the previous day Deputy Attorney General Lawrence H. Silberman had sent Ford a memorandum regarding "certain items that may come up" during his conversation with the former CIA director. Silberman was careful to note that the Department of Justice had not yet begun to look into most of these matters and that he himself had not made up his mind about them. The sensitive issues included allegations of violations of United States postal laws, charges of illegal break-ins and entries, and possible violations of U.S. wiretapping strictures. One issue, "which, to say the least, present[s] unique questions," lay in "plans to assassinate certain foreign leaders." Another—which Justice had already begun investigating—was "the possibility that Mr. Helms may have committed perjury during the confirmation hearings on his appointment as Ambassador to Iran."[14]

President Ford and former CIA director Richard Helms met on January 4, immediately after the chief executive had finished with Dr. Kissinger.

"You and I have known each other for a long time," Ford told Helms. "I have only the most admiration for you and your work. Frankly, we are in a mess." The president informed the CIA veteran that he was going to appoint a commission and invited Helms to say anything he wanted. The spy chief first questioned why the shenanigans of the Federal Bureau of Investigation were being excluded. President Ford said he would consider it.

"I hope they will stay within their charter," Ford said of the Rockefeller Commission, "but in this climate we can't guarantee it." Ford pleaded with Helms to understand his position.

"I have been in the service 32 years," Richard Helms replied. "At the end all one has is a small pension and a reputation—if any." The basic charges, he reported, stemmed from orders to him to discover foreign connections to American dissidents. The spook then put an implied threat on the table. Though he felt deeply for the president, remained a member of his team, and, Helms said, did not intend to foul the nest if it could be avoided, "If allegations have been made to Justice, a lot of dead cats will come out. I intend to defend myself.... I know enough to say that if the dead cats come out, I will participate." Helms felt the mood in the country was ghastly, but he had no intention of taking the fall for CIA actions carried out on his watch.[15]

President Ford announced the Rockefeller Commission the next day, January 5.[16] The commission held its first

hearing a week later with current and former agency directors William E. Colby, James R. Schlesinger, and Richard
Helms as witnesses. Vice President Rockefeller took aside
Colby, who would testify at many of these sessions, and asked
him not to divulge so much. Colby, under oath with a legal
responsibility to be fully responsive, was startled. The direction of this "investigation" is evident.

But Congress was not to be mollified. Its own suspicions
led the Senate to act. Senator John Pastore and Senate
Majority Leader Mike Mansfield of Montana put together
a resolution creating a select committee to study the whole
expanse of U.S. intelligence activities. On January 27 the Senate passed that legislation by a vote of 82 to 4.[17] The House
of Representatives followed suit on February 19.[18] President
Ford—and Dick Cheney—got their Year of Intelligence after
all. And the point of departure for these new investigations
would be the CIA Family Jewels. In the Senate, Idaho Democrat Frank Church, a member of that august body for almost
two decades without ever leading a major committee, would
be Mansfield's selection for chairman. Walter Mondale asked
to be a member. "This wasn't just a matter of a few little spy
capers," Mondale recalls. "This was a question of whether
large, powerful agencies of the executive branch and even
the White House were going to obey the law and make themselves accountable."[19]

DOMESTIC SURVEILLANCE

Protecting its college recruiters had been a concern of the Central Intelligence Agency since the 1950s. This function belonged to its Office of Security. The rise of Vietnam antiwar protest made enrolling trainees more sensitive, to the point agency recruiters ceased to meet prospective candidates on campus. Worried about the agency's access to campuses, in February 1967 the Office of Security conducted a nationwide survey of potential challenges to CIA enlisters. Managers decided that Langley needed to know more about the antiwar movement. Project Resistance followed that December, assigned to Howard Osborn's security office. The idea was to study campus dissidence on a systematic basis. Within months the project had accumulated so much material that chiefs created a Targets Analysis Branch to sift the data. Had the project been limited to inquiries, and simply related to facilitating recruiters' campus visits, this might not have been so egregious. At a certain level recruiting could be seen as a support to foreign intelligence operations. The agency could argue that domestic activity intended to facilitate recruiting was entailed in its mission. But Project Resistance viewed potential threats with a wide-angle lens, and it moved from simple research to field operations directed at Americans. By law and by custom the CIA was prohibited from carrying out domestic activities. The agency crossed that Rubicon without much thought for the consequences.

Questioning standard agency contacts at the universities, the CIA learned the names of individuals opposed to its activities, looked at those persons' contacts and found organizations with which they were affiliated, and then investigated those groups to discover more organizations and individuals deemed hostile. Langley recruited informants to dig deeper. Project Resistance ended up opening files on between six and seven hundred American persons and organizations and indexing twelve to sixteen thousand more individuals' names. Resistance was not supposed to infiltrate CIA personnel into political groups, but offers from local police and even directly from police informants soon induced it to accept this kind of help. On at least two occasions, in May 1968 and November 1969, Project Resistance was *ordered* to collect intelligence on specific persons or groups. In early 1970 CIA managers were commenting favorably on the project's use of its existing contacts and new informants.

By year's end Langley worried that its field units were going too far. On January 6, 1971, security division chief Osborn issued specific orders that "No attempts should be made to recruit new informants or sources such as campus or police officials for the express purpose of obtaining information regarding dissident groups, individuals or activities."[1] Nevertheless, an entirely new stream of data developed as a result of CIA's Nixon-era assistance program for local law enforcement. Under this government-wide initiative, training and equipment were furnished to police entities (for example, CIA trained a dozen New York Police Department officials in the use of computerized data processing to build case files). Grateful police officials then tipped off the

CIA to developments in their localities. The temptation for agency officers to ask for more, in effect tasking police informants, became enormous. Evidence is lacking for how often they succumbed, but the Osborn directive indicates this had become a problem.

Project Merrimac was another Office of Security initiative. This was simply supposed to help secure CIA facilities, warning of protests that might threaten headquarters. Merrimac began in February 1967 when division chief Osborn assigned a CIA proprietary to seek advance information, first regarding a march on Washington that took place that April, then a broader effort to monitor four "target groups": Women Strike for Peace, the Washington Peace Center, the Congress on Racial Equality, and the Student Non-Violent Coordinating Committee. Four CIA contract employees—none a professional—later expanded to a much larger force. Again the quest for information led to infiltrations of domestic political groups.

The CIA surveilled meeting places and members, took photographs, looked into financial support for the organizations, collected license plate numbers, attended meetings, and more. On September 14, 1967, the CIA's top operations boss, Thomas Karamessines, ordered Merrimac to utilize "available covert assets" to "very discreetly determine" this kind of data for the National Mobilization Committee to End the War in Vietnam, then planning an October protest at the Pentagon, *not* the CIA. At that demonstration CIA security personnel staffed a Special Activities Division Duty Office to assist Johnson administration security officials. There would be CIA participation at almost every major subsequent protest event, including the Chicago Democratic Party convention in August 1968, the Fall 1969 marches on Washington, and the Cambodia protests of May 1970. In each case the CIA provided sophisticated technical equipment plus personnel to run it. In the Family Jewels documents only *one* of these operations is mentioned—one that bothered agency rank and file, who were likely unaware of the wider effort. That was the help provided to federal security forces at the Chicago convention. Top agency officials Karamessines and his boss, Director Richard Helms, professed ignorance of this involvement. With that act, CIA operational security rose to the level of officials lying to their own employees.

As for the sequestering of the "take," to be expected in an activity designed merely to ensure the safety of CIA facilities, security chief Osborn conceded the opposite: "Over the course of this project we reported pretty much . . . everything we got."[2] Mission creep widened in pace with the growing controversy in America over the Vietnam war. Agency documents indicate the CIA placed an informant within the Washington public school system to warn of black militants, and it infiltrated such African American events as the 1968 Resurrection City encampment and a rally for Malcolm X Day.[3] According to the Church Committee investigation, Project Merrimac continued through September 1970. Supposedly terminated, in fact it went on. That October 3, division chief Osborn told Helms at the morning staff meeting that Weatherman dissidents had decided to launch a fall "offensive" and were thinking of targeting the agency. CIA personnel again worked to counter protesters at the May Day event of 1971. Then the CIA lent a Miami safe house and film equipment, provided technical expertise, and furnished false identity material to the Secret Service for use at the political conventions in that city during 1972. There is also at least one instance of the CIA passing intelligence regarding an American to Washington-area (Fairfax County) police, and another of a CIA officer actually participating in a Montgomery County police raid. All of these were prohibited domestic activities. Merrimac operations were not finally prohibited until August 1973.

By far the most extensive domestic spying was that carried out by the CIA Counterintelligence Staff. James Angleton's staff here functioned under instructions from Director of Central Intelligence Richard M. Helms. The Church Committee established that Helms acted "in response to White House pressure."[4] Although the director issued no written order, the next day, August 15, 1967, a memo from Thomas Karamessines, Angleton's direct superior, shows that both men conferred with Helms about the project. In the memo Karamessines instructs Angleton to create a unit for domestic surveillance and discusses its mission as well as candidates to lead it. Most important, top CIA officials clearly anticipated operational activity—not mere intelligence analysis—and detailed a mechanism to conduct it, with the counterintelligence unit furnishing guidance while field activity would be carried out by CIA area divisions. The project was given the cryptonym MH/Chaos the following year. An update for management two weeks into the initiative reveals that Chaos had been given priority equal to that with which the CIA went after Russian and Chinese spies—in other words illegal domestic activity was *as important as the CIA's main Cold War mission*. This high priority combined with very tight security. Domestic spying, in CIA parlance, became a "special access program." Chaos offices were located in a secure vault in the basement at Langley headquarters.

The first tasking to stations overseas went out on August 31, 1967. A November cable from the new unit shows the surveillance program up and running. Agency stations and other CIA staffs were told Chaos was developing information on whether American individuals and groups had foreign connections. The field effort was considerable. For example, CIA operatives followed Black Power advocate Eldridge Cleaver in Conakry, Guinea, and elsewhere, as The Family Jewels acknowledges. Unacknowledged were attempts to infiltrate the Black Panther organization in Algiers, the attention paid to various Panther activists during their trips to Europe, and the huge effort to track Americans' contacts with Vietnamese in Europe. Eldridge Cleaver may or may not have noticed CIA surveillance in Sub-Saharan Africa, but his colleague and competitor Stokely Carmichael did. In and out of Conakry at the time, and also at Dar Es Salaam in Zanzibar, Carmichael notes: "In my experience, in Dar people and things were not necessarily who or what they seemed. . . . from the moment I got there all kinds of people are in my face. Some I now know to have been sent by the CIA."[5] Project Chaos officer Frank Rafalko confirms Langley's interest in Conakry, Dar Es Salaam, and Algiers.

Chaos tapped elements throughout the CIA. Agency reporting to President Johnson in 1968 clearly indicates close surveillance of American peace activists visiting the North Vietnamese mission in Paris. Indeed, Chaos first came to the attention of the CIA Inspector General when a routine IG survey of the European Division disclosed that this surveillance was absorbing a significant portion of the division's labor effort. The same was true of the East Asia (then Far East) Division in Hong Kong, Japan, and even Saigon. When American activists Jane Fonda and Ramsey Clark visited North Vietnam in 1972, the Foreign Broadcast Information Service put a round-the-clock watch on Radio Hanoi.

The Chaos staff was known as the Special Operations Group. Angleton selected Richard Ober, among those first mentioned at Helms's meeting, to run the project. An eighteen-year veteran with service in Germany and India, Ober was an experienced CIA operations officer. Director Helms liked him as a third-generation oarsman at Harvard. With a master's in international relations from Columbia, just finishing the course at the National War College, Ober also offered potential as an analyst. Best of all, Ober had headed the CIA's *Ramparts* magazine investigation (see Chapter 8), whose files were bequeathed to Project Chaos. By Summer 1967 Ober had collected hundreds of names for additional case files—he put the number at 50 to the Church Committee, but other data indicate the agency assembled at least 127 files from the *Ramparts* investigation alone. Ober began to build a computerized database. In short, he became the CIA's recognized in-house expert on American political dissent.

Although housed in James Angleton's Counterintelligence Staff, Ober's unit had an unusual dispensation to report directly to Helms. Angleton, a notorious micromanager who rode herd on his subordinates, ordinarily would never permit the existence of such a channel. Associates of the Great Counterspy later told Chaos officers they believed Angleton was attempting to distance himself from Special Operations Group activities. Personally quite close to Helms—they often drove together to work—Angleton may have reasoned that if a big issue came up the director would tell him about it, while the less Angleton had to do with the Chaos operation the better it would be for him if something went wrong.

Frank Rafalko, who joined the unit two years later, mounts a spirited defense of Project Chaos in the only extant insider account of this operation.[6] Rafalko repeats the standard formula that the Special Operations Group had the simple purpose of collecting and disseminating information and maintaining a database. This is a misleading claim. Rather, the very first paragraph of Tom Karamessines's founding directive specified that the unit would be the focal point and coordinator for operational activity. Dissemination of intelligence came second. To give Ober's unit its due, most of what it accomplished *was* in the creation of files and circulation of "intelligence," but that was how the story unfolded, not the unit's purpose, which was to target "subversive student and related activities." Equally to the point, where the directive attempted to stay within the bounds of the CIA charter, explicitly noting operations were to be overseas,[7] the major focus quickly became domestic instead, and the Group's main customer the Federal Bureau of Investigation (FBI). Ober's unit not only provided general information, it responded to specific FBI queries, targeted protesters as per those calls, and added names to its lists or opened files in accordance with FBI requests. Each of those activities was illegal.

Rafalko's defense is that there was a real security problem (he cites huge numbers of bombings and other incidents), that counterintelligence work necessarily entails compiling large-scale files, and that the CIA acted in accordance with presidential orders. But his raw bombing statistics lump together all manner of incidents beyond war protests and differ significantly from Justice Department figures given at the time. Moreover, the agency possessed no police powers whatever, yet its reporting aimed to assist federal and local authorities in suppressive efforts against American citizens—also off-limits to the CIA. No presidential "order," as such, exists. Lyndon Johnson's "directive" was oral. In his memoirs, Richard Helms cites LBJ's constant pressing for proof the antiwar movement was financed and directed from abroad, and President Johnson's rejection of the CIA director's objection that this task would take the agency beyond its charter.[8] This would not be the only time Helms took a presidential concern and turned it into a CIA program. The most notable other case was Chile—and there Helms's effort to shield his agency project from oversight led to the destruction of his career.

As for presidential demands, the question of their legality continues to intrude. CIA officers take an oath to defend the Constitution of the United States, not the power of a chief executive, whether Lyndon Johnson or Richard Nixon. The FBI knew, even if CIA did not, how thin the ice was. When Ober's unit opened a dedicated communications net and began sending the FBI messages regarding its assignments, Frank Rafalko quickly got a phone call from a Bureau counterpart begging CIA not to put any of this on paper. The FBI man couched his plea in terms of Bureau director J. Edgar Hoover exiling people to Siberia—in this case, Fargo, North Dakota—if he saw any of the message traffic.[9] There was a very good reason why Hoover would not want any paper records. Investigation without probable cause was as improper for the FBI as was domestic spying for the CIA.

The episode of the Huston Plan illustrates Hoover's concerns perfectly. An aide in the Nixon White House in the summer of 1970, Tom Charles Huston proposed a mechanism to unify government action against dissenters. Legal obstacles were to be revoked or ignored, and a wide variety of measures taken: break-ins, wiretaps, mail-opening, infiltrations, and more. The program would be implemented under the aegis of an interagency committee. Mr. Nixon approved verbally. He, too, did not want his signature on a written order of this kind, or to have a session with security agency chiefs and openly demand action. Nixon had his chief of staff put his verbal approval in a personal memo. The FBI's Hoover scuttled the Huston Plan by complaining to Attorney General John Mitchell. Wiser heads at the White House put this scheme to rest. Richard Helms, on the other hand, commented favorably during the meetings where Huston sounded out the agencies on his proposals, and Helms designated Richard Ober as his man on the interagency committee. Its creation became the sole result of Huston's machinations.

Antiwar activists, student leaders, and black militants were the quarry in all this. To keep Chaos small, Director Helms demanded it use data processing, which involved another CIA unit, the Office of Computer Services, located in the support directorate. Rafalko, who had signed on as a specialist on black radicals, ended up as the wizard behind the Chaos computer system called "Hydra." The data went to the Office of Current Intelligence, in the Directorate of Intelligence, which formulated a series of reports—all of which found no trace of foreign (read Soviet, North Vietnamese, or Chinese) control over the protesters.

Failure to discover control by some enemy was not for lack of effort. Ober's group formed part of the Directorate of Operations. Its European Division was heavily embroiled with Project Chaos due to the fact that numerous international events opposing the war took place there. Spying on the North Vietnamese and People's Revolutionary Government (National Liberation Front) missions in Paris was undoubtedly the single most productive source of leads, since any American activist who visited became a target. That was no problem for John L. Hart, a former station chief in Saigon, who led the division at the time. Like Karamessines and Ober, he believed in the mission. The Near East Division, when it was under David Blee, resisted Ober's taskings at least until 1971, an annoyance since black militants were forging links with the Palestine Liberation Organization.

Many Chaos collection demands went to the directorate's Soviet Bloc Division. That unit's reporting mentioned various expressions of Soviet solidarity and affinity with protesters, and occasional evidence of concrete assistance, as in furnishing Soviet aircraft to carry delegations of American antiwar activists on visits to North Vietnam. Except for that last, all the information was perfectly apparent to anyone who read the newspapers. There was at least one instance in which the Communist Party of the United States of America paid for the airline tickets activists used to attend an international conference. There were indications that Cuban intelligence assisted black militants in moving to Algeria. But there was no evidence of actual control.

In June 1968 a cable sent over Karamessines's signature asked European CIA stations to enlist host country spy services in the quest for data on American dissidents. This represented an advance over his orders the previous year, which had recognized the potential value of data from foreign allies but issued no order. Former Canadian intelligence officers also affirm that their "D Operations" group was in regular contact on these matters, primarily with the FBI but with the CIA as well. Another question was American draft resisters fleeing north. The Canadian Secret Intelligence Service kept a general watch on them. During periodic visits to Langley, the Canadians exchanged information with all agency elements. Jim Angleton would have had his counterintelligence matters to discuss, Richard Ober his Chaos business.[10]

Project Chaos was given its cryptonym at this time, when separate channels for intelligence on antiwar activists and black nationalists were merged. Ober seconded Cord Meyer, Jr., as Langley's liaison to the 1968 Kerner Commission on civil disorders. Group staff were also on the telephone to the National Security Agency (NSA) constantly to confirm persons' identities and related information, and occasionally in touch with a liaison officer regarding assignments and an exclusive series of NSA reports about its Project Minaret (see Chapter 4), a parallel domestic activity. The NSA reports were hand-carried to the Ober group, which received an average of two a day, more than 1,100 pages in all. The CIA added thirty Americans' names to the Minaret "watch list," but also those of seven hundred foreign individuals or groups.

Richard Ober discussed the possibility of a direct channel to the State Department with Director Helms, but nothing ever came of it. The Justice Department requested access to the CIA name file on several occasions in 1971, including when Weatherman radicals bombed the Capitol Building, in the Catonsville Eight case, and in the Pentagon Papers leak. There was also case-by-case contact with the Secret Service and the Naval Investigative Service (now the Naval Criminal Investigative Service, or NCIS). Ober wanted to build a relationship with the Bureau of Narcotics and Dangerous Drugs (now the Drug Enforcement Administration), but that never went beyond preliminaries. On the other hand, the Special

Operations Group and U.S. Army intelligence jointly ran agents against the antiwar movement.

The Family Jewels documents convey the impression that only a handful of reports on political dissent were candidates for "flap potential." The first, for which Chaos coordinated the flow of information from the operations directorate and the FBI, was "International Connections of the U.S. Peace Movement," completed on October 31, 1967. Its principal author was Office of Current Intelligence (OCI) analyst Paul Corscadden. The focus on American citizens was plain. The CIA cable requesting data for this report, sent on November 2, 1967, provided that "COVERAGE SHOULD BE LIMITED TO CONTACTS BETWEEN ELEMENTS OF US PEACE MOVEMENT AND FOREIGN GROUPS OR INDIVIDUALS. VIETNAM PROTEST ACTIVITIES IN YOUR AREAS SHOULD BE REPORTED ONLY INSOFAR AS DIRECT CONNECTION WITH US ORGANIZATIONS OR CITIZENS IS INVOLVED."[11]

There were other reports too. The key one was the September 1968 OCI paper "Restless Youth." A CIA note covering this paper openly admitted to its sensitivity, "because of its subject matter, because of the likelihood that public exposure of the Agency's interest in the problem of student dissidence would result in considerable notoriety . . . and because . . . the author included in his text a study of student radicals in the United States, thereby exceeding the Agency's charter."[12] That coverage had been at the request of the White House, but it was the Central Intelligence Agency that had agreed to the assignment.

There were many, many more reports, some from OCI, others from Chaos itself. In June 1969, Project Chaos began producing its own analyses, starting with the special paper "Foreign Communist Support to Revolutionary Protest

Movements in the U.S." In January 1971 came "Definition and Assessment of Existing Internal Security Threat—Foreign."

None of the reports found any evidence that Moscow, Hanoi, or other communists actually controlled American protesters. But this did not stop CIA analysts from pushing the evidence as hard as they could, repeatedly construing the simple fact of contact between Americans and communist officials as something more sinister. The value-laden reporting retailed what the administration wanted to hear. In mid-October 1969, when Richard Nixon was secretly considering a massive bombing campaign to coerce Hanoi, the antiwar movement held a Vietnam Moratorium protest in Washington. Project Chaos, after conceding that the protest would be bigger than anyone had anticipated, reported that it was

[l]ed by persons and organizations, whose names are familiar in the annals of dissent, a great number of people will be involved in the Washington-area . . . actions. Supported in large part by long-time dissidents, many whose motivation is suspect, it is debatable whether this . . . can have any favorable impact on an administration which must be as desirous of peace in Vietnam as the pacifists, and ironically, appears to be making noticeable progress towards a settlement with honor, despite the damaging effect on negotiations wrought by the domestic agitation for termination of U.S. involvement. That [Vietnam Moratorium Day] will be a comfort to Hanoi seems self-evident.[13]

A month later came even bigger antiwar protests. The CIA already had doubt that as many Americans would turn out in the colder weather of November. The agency's anticipatory special report led off, "In spite of the past performance of Indo-Chinese communism, characterized by blood bath tactics and terrorism, the antiwar element somehow chooses to believe, or at least chooses to state, that an immediate U.S.

pullout would not result, necessarily, in wholesale slaughter of hundreds of thousands of innocent Vietnamese." The report pictured the protest as a manifestation of classic leftist "united front" tactics, expressed a belief that the movement would fail to meet its goals—especially for promised subsequent demonstrations—and insisted that support for Nixon's policy was growing in the wake of the president's November 3 "great silent majority" speech. The CIA predicted the protest would be violent and might muster perhaps some 150,000. In a follow-up analysis Chaos predicted that "the previously estimated number of participants (150,000) can probably be revised downward" and repeated its estimate that "potential for violence continues high."[14] In actuality, the number of protesters who turned out in *San Francisco* is variously counted at between 100,000 and 250,000. Those in Washington numbered more than half a million. Violence was minuscule. The protesters included senior diplomats, CIA officers—even Bill Colby's wife. Analysts with the Office of Current Intelligence (OCI) may have repeatedly and accurately rejected charges of foreign control over the movement, but reporting from Chaos itself had a distinctly different flavor.

Director Helms had already given the White House fresh copies of the earlier OCI analyses finding no foreign control. The reaction from Nixon and Kissinger was that Langley was not trying hard enough. Prodded by the administration, Helms reviewed CIA activities aimed at American dissidents late that summer. Here he had the chance to do what he told the Church Committee he would normally have done—tell the president this was wrong. Instead Helms issued a directive in September 1969 specifically claiming, "we have the proper approach in discharging this sensitive responsibility, while strictly observing the statutory and *de facto* proscriptions on Agency domestic involvements."[15] Helms found that "several components" of the CIA had "legitimate operational interest" in the "radical milieux," and he referred approvingly to Ober's Chaos group, which Helms found needed "skilled analysts," plus "experienced operations officers." Ober had begun with just one single assistant. And Chaos needed "sophisticated computer support" to break down the backlog of undigested information. Helms also directed ("I expect") Howard Osborn's office to share its Merrimac and Resistance data with Ober's unit.

Though he did not order it, the director encouraged CIA components to give up "a select few" skilled personnel to Chaos, and the agency's Office of Computer Services to provide "on-line capabilities and other facilities" not only for data storage and retrieval but for a "link with certain other elements of the security community." In the offices of the Counterintelligence Staff, Angleton for the first time developed an organizational chart for Project Chaos and decided that it needed thirty-six officers. At this time, too, Ober's unit began to develop unilateral assets, going beyond its previous role as command center for domestic collection. Until then it had relied on collateral reporting from other CIA agents or the U.S. Army.

A security scare occurred during the summer of 1971 when the White House Office of Management and Budget conducted a review of CIA spending. Fearing the budgeteers might catch wind of Chaos, Ober obtained the agreement of top management to instruct agency personnel not to mention the project to examiners—then led by the selfsame James R. Schlesinger, who would one day order compilation of The Family Jewels. Given President Nixon's antipathy for the agency, and continuing White House pressure for CIA budget cuts, fencing off Chaos by itself indicates the priority accorded this illegal domestic spying.

In fact, Chaos actually grew. The size of the Special Operations Group had been set. But Ober felt he needed sixty people. At the time, the CIA's Counterintelligence Staff had about two hundred, so it is evident that domestic surveillance consumed a substantial proportion of Angleton's complement. The Ober unit increased to more than forty, with others on temporary duty. By 1972 Chaos accounted for over 20 percent of the entire counterintelligence staff.

Before it was all over the Hydra computer system listed 300,000 Americans, and CIA had opened files on nearly 10,000 citizens, among them 14 members of Congress, including Representatives Bella Abzug and Patsy Mink.[16] The CIA's Central Reference Service also maintained informal "snag files," unclassified collections of open source materials, primarily press clippings, on Americans who visited Cuba and other political activists. In promoting this data to outsiders, senior officials actually made exemplars of Chaos files on Black Power advocates H. Rap Brown and Eldridge Cleaver. Beatles musician John Lennon also figures in CIA records. There were a thousand more files pertaining to private organizations.[17] Chaos incorporated information from NSA monitoring and wiretaps. And it funneled unverified FBI data into the files, some months as many as a thousand items, making them all the more incendiary when Chaos then generated reports for the FBI, recycling the Bureau's own information, now sanctified as CIA material.

More intelligence came from agency units. The Domestic Contact Service, for example, provided Chaos more than two hundred reports between 1969 and 1973. In the latter part of 1973 it contributed to wiretaps by collecting phone company records listing U.S. phones originating overseas calls. The Foreign Broadcast Information Service supplied translations from news sources abroad. The Directorate of Science and Technology furnished technical services. Then there was the CIA's mail-opening project (Chapter 4). MH/Chaos utilized over 130 agent sources and developed 7 agents who infiltrated the antiwar movement. In addition, Chaos used sources referred to it by the FBI. A separate "Project 2" under the pseudonymous "Earl Williams" sought to insert CIA agents into movement groups to establish cover credentials for further spy assignments. One pseudonymous agent, "Bob Finch," was prebriefed to seek out specific movement leaders in whom the FBI was interested who were involved in the May Day protest of 1971. Thus Project 2 agents also collected intelligence.[18] Frank Rafalko, whose initial job was to work against black radicals, debriefed agents in hotel rooms. Chaos had about 30 agents on the books at any given time. And Project Chaos initiated at least two wiretaps that, if in the United States, were illegal. Mission creep again.

According to the late Angus Mackenzie, a California academic who made an extensive inquiry into CIA domestic activities, one of Ober's key agents was a Chicagoan named Salvatore J. Ferrera. This fellow's trajectory suggests how insidious Chaos could be. Recruited at Loyola University in Chicago, Ferrera first made friends with leftist writers, who introduced him to people interested in creating a movement newspaper, *Quicksilver Times*, of which he became a founder. Ferrera helped engineer an editorial revolt after which, for a time, *Quicksilver* was actually run by FBI undercover agents. With cover as a journalist, Ferrera reported on the paper, on the Youth International Party (Abbie Hoffman's "Yippies"), on the National Peace Action Coalition, on movement plans for what became the May Day protests, and more.

The actual CIA operation to infiltrate agents into the movement was known as Project MP/Lodestar. Several operatives were inserted and relied upon over extended periods. Four more were used on single missions. They were among forty sources referred to Chaos, slightly over half by the FBI, the rest from other CIA branches. Reporting from a hundred additional agents topped off the Chaos files. As for Sal Ferrera, after May Day he went to Paris and used his background to insinuate himself into groups there. Ferrera then took up with CIA whistleblower Philip Agee (see Chapter 8) and actually supplied the agency periodic progress reports on Agee's book exposing CIA Latin American activity.[19]

Ober used the wide variety of data to generate special intelligence analyses plus spot reports. The latter bore formulaic text observing no evidence of protesters' international links, then went on to cover dissident activities in considerable detail. Americans might be startled to learn some of what the CIA thought it knew. Chaos analysts seem to have loved the image of fire, and often wrote of the "fire" driving the movement or the "hot" disputes among various protest groups. In early 1972 Chaos intelligence went into high gear to report on protesters' preparations to demonstrate at that year's political conventions, matching technical aid Project Merrimac was simultaneously giving the Secret Service. As late as the end of 1972, when America underwent an actual firestorm of controversy over the Nixon administration's Christmas Bombing of Hanoi, Chaos opined the upheaval reflected the "dying embers" of the movement. But the CIA reports were not mere recapitulations; many took the form of listing upcoming events, for which authorities could then prepare, or analyzed the momentum and support for future protests. All this went beyond simple domestic spying.

When the reports could cite some actual international event, Chaos positively gushed. On July 26, 1972, a CIA report mentioned that representatives of a Swedish peace group would participate in protests, and that a delegation of Americans was going to meet Vietnamese representatives in Paris. The report grouped these as "new indications of foreign plans or efforts to inspire, support, influence or exploit activities designed to disrupt or harass the Republican National Convention," where Richard Nixon would receive his party's nomination for a second term as president a month later.[20]

Activists opposed to the Vietnam war did not know anything specific about Project Chaos, protected by its own secrecy "compartment" at the time, but they were also not unaware of CIA interest. When Vietnam Veterans Against the War (VVAW) came together in Detroit at the end of January and beginning of February 1971 to present testimony about the nature of the conflict—what they called the "Winter Soldier Investigation"—the subject of the agency and the movement came up when someone asked about the CIA in Laos. "Take a look at your own antiwar movement," said VVAW organizer Mike McCusker. "You'll find the CIA in there somewhere."[21] McCusker had no idea how right he was. VVAW would be among major groups at the 1972 Republican convention, and it duly figured in Chaos reporting.

Mr. Ober's unit prepared detailed briefings on its activities in June 1972. These showed that the 1969 Helms directive had indeed strengthened the Special Operations Group. Chaos had added several branch chiefs that fall and reached its full complement in mid-1970. Despite overtime, there were not enough staff to cover the material. In the spring of 1971 the CIA decided to add another eighteen staff to the domestic spy unit. It never reached that level. On June 2, 1972, actual Chaos personnel numbered forty-two. Several more field sources were informants seconded by the FBI to work under CIA control. In each of the years 1970 and 1971, the FBI had furnished over ten thousand data items to Chaos. Ober's unit itself had originated more than two thousand messages in each of those years, received as many cables, plus over a thousand dispatches by hand. It had put out some 1,457 spot reports and generated 51 memos, studies, or estimates. The briefings pictured MH/Chaos as a "low-cost collection program." But in July 1972 CIA headquarters sent a cable to its stations reducing the priority for data on American dissidents. Officials attempted to reorient Project Chaos with a bid to make it the CIA focal point for international terrorism. That gambit again hints at the agency's basic mind-set. Comments on the legality of domestic spying in the Ober briefings, if there were any, have been deleted in declassification.

Despite—or because of—its extensive activity, the CIA domestic spy project became increasingly controversial *within* the agency—long before revelation ignited the major public firestorm that led to congressional investigations. In the spring of 1971 the agency's Management Advisory Group expressed serious concern over "possible repercussions which may arise as a result of CIA's covert domestic activities." These senior managers believed that fine-grain explanations for how such activities might be legal "will be lost on the American public," and that "there is probably nothing the Agency could say to alleviate a negative reaction from Congress and the U.S. public." Any flap threatened serious damage to the agency's relations with Congress, as well as its real intelligence mission.[22] CIA leadership rejected these prescient warnings. That spring Director Helms, speaking to the American Society of Newspaper Editors, insisted, "We do not target American citizens," and in the fall at Langley, speaking to employees during the agency's annual awards ceremony, he assured them, "You can rely on those denials." The charges were "silly ideas" perpetuated by "jokes." Agency officers should speak up when they had occasion to do so "and set the facts straight."[23]

On December 21, 1971, the Management Advisory Group met with Deputy Director Karamessines again. He spent more than an hour insisting CIA responsibilities "make it mandatory for us occasionally to take an interest in American citizens overseas." Karamessines denied the "scuttlebutt" that Project Chaos had a function "to keep book on Black Power adherents." Ober's unit had precisely such a function. The management advisors stuck to their guns and took their case to agency executive director William E. Colby, because their concerns went beyond the clandestine service. He too attempted to quiet their fears. On April 21, 1972, Mr. Colby sent a memo to all CIA directorates purporting to explain the domestic activities. Colby avoided discussing the spying against African Americans or the antiwar movement.[24]

Still under budget pressure, the CIA sought places to cut dollars and slash staff positions. The Special Operations Group was one possibility. In 1972 Cord Meyer, Karamessines's deputy, assessed this project. The Chaos briefings referred to here were compiled to document its mission for Meyer, who had once been a candidate to head the unit. In the early days Ober had been instructed to consult Meyer for leads. They had been colleagues in dealing with the Kerner Commission, and Meyer was not inclined to cut Chaos now. Despite its own analytical opinion that American protest had burned down to dying embers, the project sailed through. In his memoirs Meyer would write, disingenuously, that due to its highly compartmented nature the project "did not come before me for review," and that "I had only marginal knowledge of the specific activities undertaken by the Special Operations Group."[25] The cult of secrecy ran deep.

In the fall of 1972 CIA Inspector General (IG) William V. Broe conducted a periodic review of the operations directorate's European Division. The IG team preparing its survey discovered even before its inspection trip that Chaos accounted for a good deal of the workload, though Archie Roosevelt, the new division chief, did not seem to mind. When the IG team asked Ober for a briefing, he resisted on grounds they had no "need to know." This backfired. The IG inspectors were sensitized. In Europe they encountered bothersome Project Chaos paperwork, found physical surveillance of Americans a drain on staff, and discovered that appeals to foreign intelligence services were ticklish at several CIA stations. According to inspector Scott Breckinridge, a member of this team, "As we moved about from post to post, we found the MHCHAOS operational burden excessive. . . . We began to conclude that there was an indiscriminate character to the names on the Bureau's lists, which seemed to have been accepted indiscriminately by the MHCHAOS people. . . . The apparently indiscriminate nature of the program raised broader concerns on the part of personnel in the field as to whether the agency was being made part of some sort of thought police program."[26]

After completing the European survey, Broe, on November 9, sent Colby a separate letter raising questions about Chaos. This went beyond complaints by CIA management advisors and forced Helms into a specific review. Colby and Karamessines discussed the results with the director on December 5. Helms agonized over flap potential. He wanted Chaos continued, but in a way that avoided controversy. On December 20 Colby ordered Karamessines to redirect Project Chaos toward terrorism: "This should bring about a reduction in the intensity of attention to political dissidents in the United States not, or not apt to be, involved in terrorism."[27]

This marked the beginning of CIA's shift away from domestic spying. On August 29, 1973, William Colby, having himself become CIA director, issued an omnibus order on domestic activity that imposed fresh restrictions, including strict definitions of who could be targeted by Chaos, and a prohibition on agency personnel taking the lead in physical surveillance abroad. Seven months later Colby terminated Chaos altogether.

Three staffers were trained in procedures for destroying the Chaos records at a cost of $60,000 ($310,000 in 2012 dollars). Over a long, frustrating summer, their instructions changed repeatedly. Though files may have been liquidated, reports were not. Indeed, reams of the original Chaos reporting on antiwar groups survived to be declassified. When the Hersh revelations broke the dam, senior officials ordered the destruction—now of evidence—terminated. Then the Year of Intelligence almost swept away the agency. At the point when the Rockefeller Commission was about to disclose its findings regarding domestic surveillance, the CIA's General Counsel suddenly ordered the destruction of files regarding "dissidents."

What is it that made CIA domestic surveillance a Family Jewel? First, the operations were clearly illegal under the law that created the agency and the regulations supposed to govern it. In addition, the operations were acknowledged, in-house, to fall in that category, but were excused by appeal to higher authority. Many intelligence operations are unlawful on their face because that is the nature of the business, but in most situations of conventional espionage, the activity lacks the quality of being offensive to society or of serving the interests of the political leadership. Equally important, the goal of domestic spying was information-gathering that infringed on the constitutionally protected rights of citizens. In addition, opportunities were afforded to change course, but agency leaders rejected doing so. Next, the CIA tried to protect itself through secrecy, eventually extending to the destruction of records. Family Jewels are characterized by activity that goes beyond boundaries, refusal to rein in the operators, and then covering up the behavior.

Unlike some other matters in the Family Jewels documents, the Central Intelligence Agency's operations against American citizens are fairly well represented, *except* that the papers only touch the surface. The truth is that CIA aimed at the antiwar movement in America widely enough and deeply enough for this to become controversial within the agency itself—at the time, not later on. Top management repeatedly resisted change until the Paris ceasefire agreement in 1973 extracted the United States from active combat in Vietnam. By then war protests had largely ceased. The record of domestic surveillance is a cautionary tale demonstrating a real problem.

A preliminary point directly bears on what is covered here. This was not Indians off the reservation or a few bad apples. The CIA had multiple programs aimed at Americans. They were conducted by both the intelligence and operations directorates of the agency and cut across traditional boundaries. Infiltration of agents occurred under several programs. The Office of Current Intelligence of the Directorate of Intelligence produced the reports most often cited when CIA analysis of the antiwar movement is discussed. But Directorate of Operations reporting clearly had the same purpose. The term "mission creep" emerged in the 1990s to describe how programs begun for one purpose subsume different goals. Mission creep certainly affected the CIA's domestic spying of the 1960s.

Another point: these kinds of activities are so intrusive and controversial by nature that government has an almost irresistible temptation to lie about them. Director Helms would be indicted on perjury charges in the late 1970s, but the bill of particulars concerned his statements to Congress on CIA covert operations in Chile. Yet Helms's testimony regarding CIA domestic surveillance had been equally mendacious. At a congressional hearing on February 7, 1973—*before* the Seymour Hersh revelations and the Year of Intelligence—Senator Clifford Case (D-NJ) asked Richard Helms about Nixon White House demands that U.S. intelligence agencies "pool resources to learn more about the anti-war movement." Helms said he could not recall whether *any* president had ever asked the CIA to spy on Americans, then he continued: "We were not involved because to me that was a clear violation of what our charter was." *And* Helms added that, if asked, he would have told a president that such activity was not "advisable."[28] But CIA domestic spying had not started with Nixon. In his memoirs, Helms himself records that President Lyndon B. Johnson had listened to his protestations against involvement for about fifteen seconds before ordering action.[29]

Disclosed for the first time in the declassification of the Family Jewels documents—and apparently noticed by no one even then—the CIA also lent itself to a crass Nixon White House attempt at open manipulation of American public opinion. At the time of Nixon's 1970 invasion of Cambodia, the president gave the usual speech justifying his action, which was predictably followed by a flood of mail to the White House. Officials organized an effort to answer that mail. The Nixon White House then asked Langley to *pay for this program*. An administration hostile to the agency, gleefully cutting its budget, here demanded the CIA's money as a token of its loyalty. Helms acquiesced. The political mail caper was not only a domestic intrusion on CIA's part—and thus a charter violation—it represented an instance of a line agency caving to White House demands to act in a directly political role, a breach of *any* ethical understanding of separation of powers, administrative practice, or constitutional role. The CIA compounded this transgression when it permitted Nixon officials to dip at this well a second time, to the tune of more than $33,000 (over $195,000 in 2012). The CIA understood this move was beyond bounds: telephone call transcripts show that agency officials strove to get the Nixon White House to submit paperwork in a form that would not reveal the purpose of these payments.

Today, the CIA's illegal domestic snooping seems an artifact of a bygone age. Except . . . so much of what has happened in the war on terror remains shrouded in secrecy. The situation with respect to government accountability and public knowledge, comparing the Vietnam era with now, is stuck somewhere around the 1969 time frame. Certainly the temptation is there. As with the mass of protesters and militants then, the United States now has a large resident population of individuals—the cleavage this time being ethnic and religious—that government has deemed suspect. And we know that in other ways the Vietnam experience has been repeated. The United States military, local police, and FBI operatives have infiltrated a wide variety of activist groups in the guise of counterterrorism. Muslim social groups and mosques have been put under watch. The FBI's "national security letters" have been abused in the same fashion as were its investigative powers in the 1960s and 1970s.

As army intelligence did during Vietnam, the military resumed domestic spying. Donald Rumsfeld's Pentagon created an entity called the Counterintelligence Field Activity (CIFA). The army's intelligence chief argued in a November 2001 memorandum that, "contrary to popular belief"—a breathtaking sally—"there is no absolute ban on [military] intelligence components collecting U.S. person information."[30] Deputy Secretary of Defense Paul Wolfowitz ordered establishment of the unit in February 2002, and by the end of 2003 it had expanded like Topsy into a proliferated entity with directorates, staffs, and a database called "Talon," into which CIFA funneled data on a variety of Americans exercising their constitutional rights. As with Project Chaos, the Pentagon unit enjoyed access to data from all federal agencies—and it got reports from local police as well.

Counterintelligence Field Activity agents infiltrated local chapters on both the east and west coasts of a university group advocating gay and lesbian rights and Quakers who sought to discourage military recruiting and thereby oppose the Bush wars. CIFA even demanded videotapes of academic conferences to identify persons who seemed of Middle Eastern origin. Other times operatives took their own pictures, as during a public protest in front of the headquarters of Halliburton, the corporation formerly headed by then–vice president Richard Cheney. Thus military security was helping protect a private business. This does not seem to have bothered Field Activity officials. Investigation by the Pentagon's inspector general found that CIFA had compiled data on 180 organizations, and that if subsequent demonstrations were included the number reached 263. Talon became an embarrassment when it turned out that, contrary to the military's own regulations, old information was not being purged from the files, and CIFA was eventually abolished. The only good aspect to all this was that the intrusive security never attained the scale of that of the Vietnam era. But its similarity to those abuses is evident—and the military effort was exceeded by that of local police and the FBI.

Who can say that there has been no CIA involvement in any of this? Indeed, there are indications that suggest the opposite. A 1981 presidential directive permits agency technical assistance to police forces. The creation of an array of dozens of so-called "fusion centers," which bring together federal and local security officials for purposes of sharing information and conducting counterterrorism operations, has certainly involved CIA input, especially in the wake of widespread accusations that Langley's failure to share intelligence and "connect the dots" was a factor in the tragedy of the 9/11 attacks. These charges were substantiated by a major commission investigation whose recommendations included precisely such intelligence sharing.

It is a fact that a senior CIA official, David Cohen, left the agency to take charge of the intelligence unit of the New York Police Department (NYPD). The Reagan-era order that authorized CIA help to local police also required that such assistance be approved by the agency's general counsel, at this time Scott Muller. But the counsel's office never sanctioned Cohen's move to the NYPD. David Cohen began at Langley as an economic analyst—he was a principal in estimates of Soviet oil production in the late 1970s and '80s—but ended as chief of the CIA's clandestine service. Cohen had a penchant for operations, plus many agency contacts to draw upon. And Cohen's NYPD unit has subsequently been accused of high-handed tactics in its activities. Relations between FBI and the New York police, long delicate, deteriorated with Cohen at the head of the Intelligence Division. The CIA was an obvious alternative. At first the idea was that the New York police would obtain better access to CIA intelligence, but Cohen quickly went beyond that to create field teams, dispatch officers to scenes of major incidents all over the world to gather data firsthand, spy on citizens in their neighborhoods and mosques, and conduct NYPD sting operations like the infamous "red squads" of the 1960s. By 2005 the NYPD was good enough to be supplying data to Langley.[31] The FBI now refuses to participate in NYPD stings.

In the wake of 9/11, then–CIA director George Tenet attached an active officer, one Larry Sanchez, to the NYPD to help strengthen its counterterrorism capabilities. In that case Sanchez trained NYPD officers in intelligence tradecraft. Sanchez also selected an NYPD detective to undergo the full agency instructional program at Camp Peary in Virginia. Sanchez became Cohen's deputy in 2004. Until then he had continued on the CIA's payroll, and even now only took a leave of absence, resigning several years later after conflict of interest protests from CIA's own New York base chief. Sanchez remained with the New York police until 2010. His job as police Intelligence Division assistant director was then filled—wait for it!—by a new undercover officer seconded from the Central Intelligence Agency, reportedly one of its most senior men. Langley's General Counsel never approved the Sanchez assignment either.

During this period the New York police undertook an aggressive program of monitoring Muslim groups as potential subversives. Its "Demographics Unit" supposedly simply mapped neighborhoods. But officers listened in on conversations and attended local events, and the merest whiff of suspicion was used to open investigations. In fact, the most recent terrorism conspiracy case in New York, in which citizens were arrested in an alleged bomb plot, was so heavily infiltrated by NYPD that the FBI refused to participate. What this says about agency domestic activity is not clear.

The most serious terrorist attack attempted in New York City after 9/11 was a car bombing in Times Square, averted in May 2010. Nearby vendors called in as suspicious a parked sport utility vehicle that turned out to be rigged with a bomb. Standard police work traced the license plate number to its owner and led to the apprehension of the perpetrator. Federal Bureau of Investigation special agents quickly took over the investigation. The NYPD Intelligence Division had little role to play. On the other hand, the police spooks and the FBI were very active in gathering data on the "Occupy" Movement, whose march on Wall Street and encampment there in the fall of 2011 sparked a wave of national—and even international—protests against corporate greed and collusion. The protests were activities shielded by citizens' First Amendment rights. To the degree that CIA fed NYPD intelligence to other fronts of the "Occupy" protests, or relayed data gathered elsewhere to the New York police, the agency had arguably engaged in domestic activity.

What is crystal clear is that CIA practices aroused concern. Thirty-four congressmen addressed a letter to Attorney General Holder requesting action. The House Permanent Select Committee on Intelligence held a hearing. In October 2011 Michael Morell, acting as CIA director until the swearing in of David Petraeus, ordered an IG inquiry. The Inspector General, David Buckley, conducted a two-month examination and cleared Tenet and the agency of any impropriety for the NYPD relationship. But early in 2012 Langley informed the New York Police Department that its officer's assignment would be terminated come spring.

From what can be gleaned so far, the Vietnam-era surveillance remains the high point of CIA domestic activity. But the record today remains murky. Meanwhile, the act of spying on citizens is as unacceptable today as it was before. Thus abuses during the Bush era are a potential Family Jewel that cannot be dismissed until the relevant records are released. So far, the documented instances of military domestic spying already raise suspicions. As for U.S. intelligence writ large, a huge Family Jewel—a real one and closely related—exists in the form of National Security Agency electronic surveillance of Americans. That represents an evolution of a different CIA program from the bad old days. Together with the Jewels of CIA renditions, torture, black prisons, and assassination, these are the real scandals that secrecy now protects.

SURVEILLANCE II
Private Communications

At the time James Schlesinger demanded that CIA create the Family Jewels documents, its mail-opening figured in a minor key. Intelligence officers understood the chilling aspect of their infiltration of political groups quite well, while the opening of personal mail drew on classic techniques of espionage tradecraft. Yet there were specific prohibitions in law against anyone—the CIA included—tampering with the U.S. mail. During the 1975 Year of Intelligence, mail-opening emerged as a huge scandal: an acknowledged illegality and one that touched the hearts and minds of citizens—ordinary people committing their private thoughts to paper and entrusting them to the sacrosanct U.S. Post Office. The spooks somehow missed the point that this activity, more than a technical violation of law, struck at Americans' personal feelings and expressions. Socially reprehensible, legally criminal, the mail-opening became an instant Family Jewel.

For citizens today, this monitoring of private communications deserves to be regarded as even more sinister. In the 1950s and 1960s, when this surveillance was underway, mail served the same functions as today's cell-phone calls, texts, and e-mail.[1] Monitoring the mails meant, then as now, Big Brother peering into the citizenry's major form of casual—and formal—communication. In addition, as a supersensitive project—and this is a problem with today's high security phone monitoring as well—the mail-opening was kept outside the normal project approval process, making abuse that much easier. The more secret the activity the greater the temptation to evade safeguards.

In the spring of 1952 the CIA's operations staff, more specifically its Soviet Russia Division, first suggested a mail-opening program. The avowed purpose was psychological warfare. By opening letters to and from the Soviet Union the spies hoped to discover what bothered Russians. Those raw sores could be picked at by incorporating them into the themes of U.S. propaganda, both overt and covert. No consideration was given to the fact that obstructing the mails, tampering with the mails, and so on were criminal offenses (under Title 18, U.S. Code §1701 and following, and Title 39, §4057). That July a CIA office chief suggested a feasibility study be conducted in conjunction with the Post Office Department.[2]

The project moved from experimental to full-scale activity in February 1953. Here the Post Office acquiesced, in effect, to a criminal violation of law, subject to the understanding that there would be *no* tampering with the mails "beyond the minimum necessary for an exterior examination."[3] Exterior examination meant looking at the envelope and recording sender and addressee. The Soviet Division's cryptonym for this project was SR/Pointer. Agency inspectors later observed that SR/Pointer could not be considered a true "project" because *it had never been put through the CIA's formal approval process.*[4]

The Post Office's limited sanction came at a high point of

the Cold War, when President Dwight D. Eisenhower initiated all manner of covert operations to combat the Russians and their supposed Third World clients. Despite enjoying Eisenhower's favor, the Central Intelligence Agency never sought his permission for this initiative. No doubt believing he was preserving Ike's plausible deniability by not obtaining authorization, CIA Director Allen W. Dulles foolishly ensured by this means that CIA mail-opening was never blessed by higher authority.

Post Office guidelines permitted CIA to track who (or, more properly, what addresses) sent mail to or received it from the Soviet Union, but nothing of the contents. The Post Office's "minimum necessary" also meant restricting intelligence officers to making handwritten notes of addresses. The procedure did not afford the speed CIA sought and made it impossible to handle more than a fraction of the mail. The program was still in its infancy when, in September 1953, the Soviet Russia Division pressed to go beyond this restriction by photographing rather than noting the "covers" (envelopes) of *all* the mail addressed to Russia. The Post Office refused.

Director Allen Dulles and then–chief of operations Richard Helms of the Soviet Russia Division met with Postmaster General Arthur E. Summerfield on the afternoon of May 17, 1954. They tried to break the logjam. The Soviet Russia Division also wished to move beyond covers to copy the actual contents of letters. Dulles did not mention that the CIA wanted more than covers. The CIA director spoke of photographing covers of U.S. mail, but, the agency's notetaker recorded, "also said we wanted very much to be able to review first-class correspondence of this same sort directed to *Latin America*."[5] Mr. Summerfield *did not comment specifically*," but, according to Helms's record of the meeting, nevertheless gave the impression "he was in favor of giving us any assistance which he could." The CIA took those assurances to the bank. It immediately ordered expansion of the SR/

Pointer project. The very next day a postal official went to New York, the mail transit point and locale for SR/Pointer, to check on the necessary arrangements.[6] In 1975 Church Committee investigators established that the CIA had deliberately *avoided* mentioning its larger goals in discussions with postal officials.

The CIA project proceeded. But virtually all the letters examined contained no real intelligence. The agency's Soviet Division tired of investing resources in a project that yielded so little. A key change took place late in 1955. At that point James Angleton of the Counterintelligence Staff made a bid to take over the action, with the fieldwork to be done by the Office of Security. Angleton's proposal memorandum reveals the agency was *already opening* letters, noting, "The only added function . . . is that more letters will be opened," as opposed to the "very limited number" already being processed. Angleton also frankly added, "Presently letters are opened without the knowledge of the Post Office Department on a completely surreptitious basis" in a CIA office in New York, and that so far no one in the Post Office suspected the truth. The revised project would be known as HT/Lingual. Its purpose would be counterintelligence. The CIA aimed to identify possible Russian spies or their accommodation addresses so as to detect enemy agents. Richard Helms, now risen to assistant deputy director for operations, approved this scheme on a fateful day—December 7, 1955. The directorate consented to Lingual's budget several months later.

Project Lingual functioned smoothly for a very long time. Mail transiting the Port of New York was handed over to CIA by the bagful. The work took place after-hours, when post offices were closed. An agency facility in a secure room at LaGuardia Airport photographed the covers. Letters selected for interior examination were carried to a CIA office in Manhattan. There the letters were steamed open—the CIA never found a better way to do this than over boiling water from a teapot—and the letters themselves photographed and checked for such esoterica of the spy trade as microdots or secret handwriting. They were then replaced and the envelopes closed with an iron on an ironing board. Letters from both Manhattan and LaGuardia were then reinserted into the U.S. mail.

Volume increased tremendously: 832 pieces of mail got the heavy-duty treatment in 1956, but there were 8,000 a couple of years later. The first bump in the road came in January 1958 when the FBI, wanting to start something similar, discovered CIA was already opening mail. Instead of turning in the agency, the FBI wanted in on the take, which the spy service was happy to share. Project Hunter became the FBI's name for its collection effort on the mail, and it received 57,000 items from the CIA over the period of the program. In all but three years, the FBI received more spot reports from agency mail-opening than any CIA component. Over twenty years, the mail-opening program in New York alone (there would be several lesser adjuncts) handled 28,322,796 letters, which works out to slightly fewer than 4,000 *a day*.

The development that sharpened Project Lingual's challenge to constitutional rights occurred at this time. The CIA created a "watch list" to improve efficiency. This document was not permitted outside the Office of Security. Agency officers memorized it there and used the list to cull mail. They received no other guidance on what to select for the steam bath. Only one step separated watch-listing Russian spies and doing the same for Americans, and since the Communist Party of the United States of America (CPUSA) was already an FBI target, that barrier fell immediately. From there it was but a short step to watch-listing other American political groups and citizens. Updates to the watch list were made every few months at first, but demand accelerated so much before the end that the lists were being changed twice a month. The watch list contained three to four hundred names.

In late 1960, when Lingual was photographing roughly 1,800 covers and examining 60 letters a day, the CIA Inspector General (IG) did its first project evaluation. According to Thomas Abernathy, one of the team on this review, the IG did not discuss legality. Its report observed that Project Lingual had not been formally approved, its cost could not be established with precision (expenses were split among CIA units and there was no overall budget line), and "no tangible operational benefits had accrued . . . as a result."[7] The IG report recommended that the DCI take a deeper look and have CIA ready a cover story for the moment when Lingual's existence was revealed. Allen Dulles took no action. His successor, John McCone, *was never even told about Lingual*. The only response to the IG report, after the passage of a full year, was a memorandum from James Angleton's deputy on the CI Staff, Raymond Rocca, which frankly admitted: "Since no good purpose can be served by an official admission of the [CIA criminal] violation, and existing Federal statutes preclude the concoction of any legal excuse for the violation, it must be recognized that no cover story is available."[8]

In the meantime the CI Staff had requested—and Richard Helms approved—an *expansion* of Project Lingual under which the CIA's Technical Services Division established a laboratory at Idlewild (soon Kennedy) Airport that enabled both more letter examinations and chemical tests on those opened. The lab was up and running by early 1961. That year 14,000 letters were subjected to intrusive examination.

It is worth pausing a moment to comment on Helms's role. His fingerprints are all over Project Lingual. The only declassified CIA documents approving any aspect of Lingual bear his signature. Helms attended the original—and subsequent—meetings between CIA directors and postmasters general, approved the initial Lingual budget, and sanctioned its expansion. Helms would be at the center of the action later as director in his own right. Allen Dulles obviously knew

70

about Lingual, but the Church Committee established that neither of his immediate successors—McCone and William F. Raborn—ever did. As for postmasters general, the Summerfield meeting record—Helms's record—is ambiguous. A Raymond Rocca memorandum for the CI Staff on January 27, 1961, contended, "There is no record in any conversation with any official of the Post Office Department that we have admitted to opening mail."[9] Soon afterwards Helms was among the group who met with President Kennedy's Postmaster General, J. Edward Day, and recorded that "no relevant details" were withheld.[10] But a decade later the Lingual project chief commented on this same record, "The wording of this memo leaves some doubt as to the degree to which Day was made witting."[11] The Church Committee concluded that between 1961 and 1971 *no* Post Office chief was informed of the CIA mail-opening. Similarly, no attorney general knew of Lingual except for John Mitchell in the Nixon administration, and no president of the United States ever knew of or approved the CIA mail-opening. Suggestions inside the CIA in 1965 to tell Lyndon Johnson were rejected. This gives new meaning to Thomas Powers's view of Helms as "The Man Who Kept the Secrets."[12]

It is in the period of the Vietnam war protests that Project Lingual began to run flat out. In 1967, the year Helms ordered creation of the Chaos domestic surveillance unit, the mail-openers reached their peak volume, prying open 23,617 letters.[13] In 1969 Project Chaos chief Ober actually solicited the FBI for names of Americans to include on the Lingual watch list. An Ober memorandum argued that "'the Bureau should not overlook the utilization of the agency's Hunter project [the FBI name for Lingual] for the development of leads in the New Left and Black Nationalist fields.'"[14] It was also during 1969 that the CIA dispensed with the inconvenience of shuttling mail in and out of Manhattan, doing all its processing work in Building 111 at Kennedy Airport. By the end of

1972 the FBI had added 289 more names. A third of the 600-odd people on the list by then were nominated by the Bureau. It is difficult to avoid the impression that by this point *the main focus* of CIA mail-opening was on Americans exercising constitutionally protected speech.

Richard Helms would later defend himself variously. With the Church Committee he actually prevaricated—or came preciously close to that—telling the inquisitors that he *assumed* that Allen Dulles had made some arrangement with Arthur Summerfield regarding legality, and that his place was not to question Mr. Dulles, a lawyer, on a matter of law.[15] But Helms had been present at the only meeting with Summerfield, he *knew* what had been said, and he had made a contemporaneous record. And in any case Summerfield had no power to waive federal criminal statutes. As with J. Edgar Hoover and the Project Chaos records, there was a reason why Dulles never put his name to a Lingual approval. He *was* a lawyer. Only Helms's signature appeared. And Helms stuck to the Soviet spy rationale. But the mail-opening went far beyond that, as will be seen shortly, and Helms himself (in his memoirs) could credit Project Lingual with uncovering no more than *two* Russian agents. That is not much to show for CIA's invasive prying into 215,820 pieces of first-class mail plus recording over 28 *million* covers. In his memoirs the former spy chieftain presents the Department of Justice's decision not to prosecute agency officers for mail-opening as an *affirmation* of his course, and continues to maintain that Lingual had been "cleared" by the postmaster general.[16] Justice's reluctance to serve up a criminal indictment in the superheated atmosphere of Watergate and the Year of Intelligence should not be mistaken for a judgment of innocence.

O thers, including officers at the CIA, had a much different impression of Lingual's value. "We got no benefit from it at all," observed Howard J. Osborn, whose Office of Security actually ran the mail-opening. "The product was worthless."[17] In 1969 Osborn went to CIA Deputy Director Karamessines to shut it down—budget reductions had him under pressure and Osborn wanted to preserve other valuable staff slots. Jim Angleton showed up to support Lingual. Karamessines sided with Angleton. By then the illegality and domestic surveillance aspects had reached the point where they were contentious within the CIA itself. In an agency oral history, Director Helms countered those who objected: "[On] mail-opening and a couple of other operations, these young people [that is, agency junior officers] didn't know anything about them, so there was no basis for their criticizing."[18]

The Inspector General, meantime, conducted a fresh review of the CI Staff in 1969 and "came across" Project Lingual, which he proceeded to examine. John Glennon headed the team for Inspector General Gordon Stewart. Glennon found that hardly anybody at Langley was actually using the Lingual material; its main consumer was the FBI—for domestic surveillance purposes. The IG report explicitly noted: "'Most of the officers we spoke to found it occasionally helpful, but there is no recent evidence of it having provided significant leads or information which have had positive operational results.... The positive intelligence derived from this source is meager.'"[19] Glennon told the Church Committee that his team never mentioned legality, "because we assumed that everyone realized it was illegal." Gordon Stewart agreed, adding that when briefing the IG report he told Helms the project had no legal basis and recommended the CIA get out of mail-opening, handing it over to the FBI.[20] Only Angleton disagreed.

In 1971 the CIA team screened 4,375,000 pieces of U.S. mail at Building 111. They chose about half (2,269,000) to examine, culled 25,000 of those for covers and 10,500 for recording of contents. A quarter (6,500) of the letters taken for photography (thus *about 60 percent of those recorded*) were selected on the basis of the watch list. Over 80 percent of the intrusions were exploited for "intelligence" purposes, with two thousand reports sent to the FBI and five thousand circulated within CIA. The statistics for 1972 are similar: 2,308,000 letters selected (out of 4,350,000 that passed through CIA hands), 33,000 covers photographed, 8,700 letters recorded, 5,000 of them based on the watch list. About half the 1972 disseminations went to the CI Staff, a high proportion of them to Project Chaos, and a quarter to the Soviet Bloc Division. Project Lingual prying was nothing if not massive.

The Office of Security tried to drop mail-opening again during 1971 with no success. Karamessines took its side this time, but Director Helms overruled him. Neither Howard Osborn nor Gordon Stewart were naïve young intelligence officers. But not only did Richard Helms refuse to shut down Lingual, in exchanges with the FBI over the next two years he extolled the mail-opening project as one of the CIA's major contributions to domestic intelligence. The CIA's official history of Helms's tenure as director observes that the man almost always agreed with Jim Angleton—and it offers Project Lingual as an example.[21]

The Church Committee eventually concluded that "a significant—perhaps the primary—portion of the product related to domestic, rather than foreign, intelligence concerns."[22] Mail-opening watch lists had doubled in size and were modified frequently. They were compiled by the CI Staff, which meant major inputs from Richard Ober's Chaos staff. Again from the Church Committee: "The Watch List, in short, originated with a relatively few names which might reasonably be expected to lead to genuine leads for intelligence or counterintelligence information, but soon expanded well beyond the initial guidelines into the area of essentially domestic intelligence."[23] Among those turning up on the list were congresswomen Bella Abzug and Patsy Mink—again—writers John Steinbeck and Edward Albee, religious groups like the American Friends Service Committee, peace groups and political activists, scientific groups like the Federation of American Scientists, even a former deputy director of the CIA, Herbert Scoville. Anyone who had visited the Soviet Union or Cuba was fair game. (That included a member of the Rockefeller family.) A curious inclusion was that of the publisher Frederick A. Praeger, a participant in CIA-subsidized book projects intended to purvey agency propaganda. Between a quarter and a third of the mail CIA opened belonged to the people and groups on the watch list. The rest was selected at random—an equally distressing proposition.

Stopping Project Lingual proved impossible, at least while Helms led the CIA. Inspector General reports in both 1960 and 1969 were ineffectual. The 1962 realization that concocting a cover story would be pointless had no impact. The CIA had a near-death experience in the mid-'60s when its illegal program came near to being revealed by a congressional inquiry—the episode that led managers to consider telling President Johnson—but that had no effect either.

What finally cracked the nut was the possibility the Post Office might move against Langley. In April 1969 William Cotter, a former CIA person, now the chief postal inspector, complained to Jim Angleton's special assistant about Project Lingual. Cotter was an experienced agency officer with eighteen years' service, ending at the Office of Security. He was not some neophyte, and he knew all about the mail-opening. Cotter's predecessor as postal inspector had known only of photographing envelopes, and nothing regarding actual mail tampering. But Cotter agreed to consult the CI Staff before going to the postmaster general, and Angleton, according to the Church Committee, persuaded Cotter that his CIA secrecy agreement precluded his telling the postmaster general of the mail-opening.

That understanding held for about a year and a half. Then, early in 1971, Dr. Jeremy J. Stone, president of the Federation of American Scientists (FAS), filed an inquiry with the Post Office—in fact directly to Cotter—specifically asking whether FAS mail was being tampered with. Of course, FAS was on the Lingual watch list. The "flap potential" was obvious. On May 19 Director Helms convened the officials concerned. They tried to figure out how Jeremy Stone could have found out and decided he must have been warned by Herb Scoville, a former CIA deputy director, who was on the FAS board. Since Scoville had left the agency in the mid-'60s, that is an indication of how long CIA had been watching the Federation. Tom Karamessines expressed "grave concern" that "any flap would cause the CIA the worst possible publicity and embarrassment." An inspection by Bill Cotter raised that danger. To head off that possibility Director Helms met with Postmaster General Winton M. Blount on June 2, 1971. The evidence on how much Helms told Blount about the mail-opening is disputed.[24] Helms nevertheless sought to impress him by citing letters from Black Power advocate Eldridge Cleaver.

Jim Angleton argued that handing mail-opening over to the FBI would not work: the Bureau would not meet CIA's needs, and the activity was about *foreign* intelligence. He insisted the game was worth the candle. On June 1, the day before the CIA director met with Postmaster General Blount, he saw Attorney General John Mitchell. A reading of the documents clearly indicates Helms sought Justice Department protection, then informed Blount of CIA's illegal operation—and *only at the point when it was in serious danger of compromise*. Thus Helms *protected* the mail intrusion project.

Director Helms's instructions after these briefings reinforce this interpretation: he told responsible officials that in the event of a security flap or danger of a leak, Lingual was to be folded up instantly and its personnel absorbed into the agency's New York base. Almost immediately a fresh problem arose. In August 1971 the mail-openers selected a letter at random that turned out to be from Idaho Senator Frank Church. There was no Church Committee at that point, so this was not a factor, but the act of intercepting a United States senator's correspondence threatened an enormous flap. That should have triggered action according to Helms's edict. Instead, Jim Angleton merely ordered that elected officials be taken off the watch list, and any of their intercepted mail be put in a "Special Category Items" file. Angleton kept this in his personal safe. By 1973 the file contained not only the Church letter, but one from Senator Edward Kennedy, mail from a governor, another from a congressman, and a half dozen other "items."

The power of secret knowledge can be extremely seductive. One wonders if Angleton succumbed, since there are multiple testimonials to Lingual's minimal intelligence value. His determination to keep mail-opening going in the face of mounting obstacles requires explanation. In presenting Lingual to Helms's successor, Schlesinger, Angleton made extravagant claims as to its effectiveness in identifying Soviet exchange students as Russian spies, but Lingual was hardly necessary to make that discovery.[25] The other logical explanation is the utility of the mail intercepts in monitoring American citizens, both in their own right and as trading stock for dealing with the FBI. (In today's context we have to wonder what the National Security Agency and others do with the intercepts they must have acquired of officials and prominent citizens.)

Meanwhile, Postal Inspector William J. Cotter's discomfort continued to rise. In 1972 Cotter let it be known he no longer felt bound by his CIA secrecy agreement and intended to rescind Post Office Department understandings with the agency. This raised hackles at Langley, since neutralizing Cotter now required Helms to approach the postmaster general and renegotiate the original arrangement. Then James Angleton lost his benefactor when President Nixon sent Helms to Iran as ambassador, appointing James Schlesinger as the Director of Central Intelligence. Angleton's bid for redemption, assembling the most comprehensive overview of HT/Lingual yet put to paper, argued the CI chief's case solely on the basis of counterespionage against the Soviets, mentioning "radicals" and "dissidents" only in the context of alleged Russian connections. Agency executive director William E. Colby used this paper in February 1973 to brief Schlesinger and his deputy, showing them samples of the "take." Director Schlesinger was not impressed and said so. Rather than go back to the well at the Post Office, he ordered that CIA induce the FBI to take over the mail-opening, or, failing that, terminate it.

This proved the end of HT/Lingual—except for the investigations, inquiries, and history. In the after-years, despite Church and all of that, Langley remained sensitive to its legal jeopardy from this excess. Agency censors used their authority to protect Langley. Restricted to deletions of information damaging to national security when they declassify documents, the censors instead deleted so as to hide the CIA's liability. During the Year of Intelligence, William Cotter indeed testified before a panel of the House Judiciary Committee. Langley's Office of Legislative Counsel reported on March 20, 1975, that Cotter's testimony on Project Lingual was about to be released, and that the Post Office official had furnished "a complete picture of the mail intercept program," which revealed which senior officials had been aware of it. As late as 2005—thirty years after the fact—the CIA censors still pretended that the fact Mr. Cotter had spoken out, and the sparse details the congressional liaison office had included of what he said, were proper national security "secrets."[26]

Langley's Project Lingual files were destroyed in 1990 on instructions from CIA's General Counsel. When the John F. Kennedy Assassination Records Review Board sought them later that decade, the CIA could find only a few working files that survived.

It is obvious why mail-opening became a Family Jewel. Even the agency acknowledged its flap potential. In addition to criminality and social reprehensibility, the mail-opening illustrates other dangers inherent in intelligence activity. Project Lingual moved through the classic stages of a covert operation: begun for discrete purposes it expanded, became routinized, attracted even less oversight, pushed beyond original boundaries, and ended up as another surveillance program threatening constitutional rights. The communications surveillance projects also demonstrate the tremendous difficulty of bringing secret operations back under control. Senior officials repeatedly resisted terminating—or even cutting back—the project. It is hugely significant that operatives disdained matters of legality—almost as an afterthought, one related merely to the viability of their cover story. But the projects were certainly illegal. From Day 1. And the CIA knew it. That is a black thought.

Finally, the surveillance evolved with the technology: at the beginning, when letters were a primary form of communication, while another was cables and telegrams, the CIA served as the intrusive agent for the letter operation, while the National Security Agency monitored the electronic forms, as will be seen shortly. When communications monitoring returned, the public had shifted to the computer and cell phone for its vehicles, and the spooks followed suit. Recent monitoring has been NSA all the way. The Family Jewel would be polished anew in the aftermath of the September 11 attacks.

Here may be the place for a general point about CIA's internal controls, specifically on the function of the agency Inspector General. This treatment of an assortment of CIA activities, Project Lingual not least among them, reveals details of a good half dozen IG reviews of projects. Two concerned Lingual, another the assassination plots, others the agency's chemical experiments or the drug trafficking in Southeast Asia. In all these inquiries the focus remained on CIA *efficiency*, not the legality of operations. Though the IG's investigators took pains later to argue they had called for termination of various activities, never once was their expressed aim to eliminate illegalities. And actions often proved less than advertised. With Lingual the recommendation was not to terminate the project, but to pass it along to the FBI. On assassinations (see Chapter 6) the aim of investigation was purely to assess flap potential.

The IG had no authority to enforce his recommendations or to review their implementation, except as authorized by the CIA director. Worse, completion of an IG inquiry was often represented as certification that some episode had been "covered," whereupon the underlying records were destroyed. This happened with evidence of both CIA assassinations and interrogations before the Year of Intelligence. Agency arguments at that time that its programs were monitored effectively by the internal apparatus were disingenuous at best.

Not until the 1990s, when a system of presidentially appointed Inspectors General replaced the internal mechanism, was there a significant advance in this area. Some of the most valuable oversight work accomplished in recent years resided in the IG's investigations, some retrospective, some current, of drug trafficking, the Guatemalan hit squads, the shootdown of American missionaries by the Peruvian air force under a CIA project (not covered here), and its inquiries into Bush-era rendition and interrogation programs.

But the independent Inspector General still has important limitations. Most important is that the IG is seen as an adversary by operators. An Inspector General seeking to preserve a modicum of comity is thus tempted to get along by going along. Next is the IG's limited investigative capability. Line agency officers try to avoid assignment to the IG, where they are obliged to challenge colleagues—who may be their superiors later on—about controversial matters, with potentially career-ending consequences. The most experienced officers with the deepest current knowledge are in short supply whereas an IG tour is not "career enhancing." The solution of rotating line officers through the IG has limitations, since the careerists' recourse is to pull punches during investigations. Less effective field officers, young lawyers plus senior field officers on their final tours, round out the IG complement. The operating units believe IG inquiries are one-sided efforts to take them down. Tension abounds in these inquiries.

A CIA director has the ability to compel the excision of sensitive information from an IG report to Congress. This sets up a dynamic reinforcing the Inspector General's incentive not to be seen to be off the reservation, thus limiting the effectiveness of investigations. The spooks' counterattack against the IG would be seen during the war on terror, when a spate of leaks divulged details of CIA rendition and interrogation programs (Chapter 5). Senior line officers suspected the IG's office as the source. In May 2007 CIA Director Michael Hayden put an aide, Robert Dietz, to work on an inquiry into the Inspector General's office. The agency instituted more than a dozen measures to prevent the IG from going too far, and created an ombudsman to handle the cases of officers who felt the IG had dealt unfairly with them. It is noteworthy that the inquiry began when the Inspector General delivered an opinion that CIA's destruction of evidence of illegal methods in prisoner interrogations might constitute an obstruction of justice. This sally constituted a disturbing shot across the bow. The conclusion must be that the effectiveness of CIA Inspectors General remains limited.

Meanwhile, the technology continued to advance. In the mid-1960s telephone electronic switching came into widespread use, supplanting older manual systems and greatly improving the speed and convenience of phone service. More and more communications began to move by these means, to include both the phone and written communications—in the form of cables and telexes—that passed by wire or microwave. In the United States it is the National Security Agency (NSA) that has responsibility for this intelligence work. The NSA, too, had its domestic programs—ones revealed only in the heat of the Year of Intelligence. To put that differently, NSA domestic intrusions would have evaded any accountability at all but for the fact that U.S. intelligence was already under scrutiny. Of all the investigations of this season of inquiry, *only* those on electronic monitoring led to new law to regulate intelligence activity.

Actually the National Security Agency had *two* major programs. The first was known at Fort Meade, NSA headquarters, as Project Shamrock. It had been born in the fires of World War II when the United States was anxious to learn what German, Italian, and Japanese representatives in the U.S. were reporting home. Intelligence officers simply went to the major companies and asked that extra copies of cables be made for authorities. Following the war the United States persisted. So Project Shamrock had been underway even before the National Security Agency existed. Created in 1952, the NSA inherited Project Shamrock.

The transmission companies—Western Union International, RCA Global Communications, and ITT World Communications—continued to participate. Literally millions of private communications changed hands. Like tampering with U.S. mail, accessing these cables was a criminal offense. The companies were assured by senior Pentagon officials in 1947 and again in 1949 that they were in no legal jeopardy from their participation. Under the Communications Act of 1934 (47 U.S. Code §605, and 18 U.S.C. §952), the cable companies, as common carriers, had a duty to protect traffic, and federal employees who furnished or published any code or material between a foreign government and its diplomatic mission in the United States were also subject to criminal penalties. Congress had made an exception for demands from lawful authority, but this was never defined to include NSA codebreakers, and the law had never been clarified by court case.

After the war the U.S. government actually considered seeking amendment of Section 605, but avoided this until 1968, when an exception was written into the Omnibus Crime Control and Safe Streets Act (18 U.S.C. §2511 (3)). NSA lawyers gave congressional staff their opinions when lawmakers were drafting this legislation. In addition, in 1950 the United States enacted amendments to the Espionage Act (18 U.S.C. §798) that recognized communications intelligence as a government activity—but that statute merely provided for punishing individuals who divulged information, remaining silent on the legality of this type of intelligence collection per se. Thus, for most of this period Project Shamrock proceeded secretly and on shaky legal grounds. The ITT company actually dropped out of the program in 1969. The FBI involved itself too—"G-men" physically carried the telegrams starting in 1963.

By one account pairs of men, one FBI, the other NSA, would visit the cable companies very early each morning to pick up stacks of accumulated cables. Cooperating employees were paid fifty dollars a week. Technology evolved. The cable companies switched from punched paper strips to magnetic tape recordings. They were happy to continue cooperating, but reluctant to relinquish the tapes. The code-breakers suddenly needed to make copies of the tapes, which meant a physical presence in New York City. Deputy Director Louis Tordella of NSA met with CIA's Tom Karamessines on August 18, 1966. From September 1 until August 31, 1973, the CIA's Project LP/Medley furnished NSA with corporate cover and office space in lower Manhattan. There the code-breakers made their copies. The FBI also continued to bring NSA "drop copies" of cables until 1973. The NSA finally canceled Shamrock in May 1975.

The second NSA initiative was known as Project Minaret. This activity aimed to intercept telephonic conversations, not written communications. It began under President Kennedy as an effort to collect information on individuals talking to people in Cuba. Minaret expanded. Following the Kennedy assassination, the Secret Service asked NSA to monitor the phones of persons it considered threats to the president. So NSA created its own watch list. Instead of simply tapping phone circuits to Cuba, with the advent of electronic switching, microwave relay, and satellite transmission, Fort Meade could program its computers to eavesdrop on calls from specific telephone numbers and pull the signals right out of the air. On October 20, 1967, during an antiwar demonstration at the Pentagon, army intelligence asked the NSA to listen in on the calls of political activists. Lieutenant General Marshall S. Carter, who had been John McCone's deputy when Minaret began, and who had then moved over to head the NSA, received the request. He agreed. The army added its own names to the watch list.

Political dissenters were suddenly major targets. The FBI became one of Fort Meade's best customers. It put 1,000 Americans on the Minaret watch list—almost 60 percent of the total—along with 1,700 foreign persons and groups. An NSA criterion was that one side of the phone conversation had to be abroad. There were few, if any, antiwar protests planned by transatlantic telephone. Despite the wide net, as with mail-opening, the take proved paltry. FBI intelligence chief W. Raymond Wannall later told investigators, "The feeling is that there was very little in the way of good product as a result of our having supplied names to NSA."[27]

Meanwhile, new clients lined up. The Defense Intelligence Agency added a small number of persons to the watch list. The CIA's Project Chaos made contributions too. The Secret Service's slice of the pie, which peaked in 1970–1971, included 180 Americans and another 525 foreign individuals or groups. Individuals were added or removed from the watch list under criteria that remain secret even today. At any given time the denizens of Fort Meade were eavesdropping on about 800 Americans. By July 1969, just before Carter left, Minaret business had become substantial enough that he promulgated a formal charter for it. Minaret, like Chaos, was above Top Secret, in this case handled over signals intelligence channels even though no codebreaking was involved. The take included both phone material and Shamrock messages that seemed relevant. Minaret reports were hand-carried and went out with no mention of the National Security Agency. They were supposed to be used for background only. But the breadth was extensive—NSA was to collect information on individuals or organizations whose activity "may" lead to civil disturbances or in any other way "subvert" national security.[28]

The Nixon administration supplied a new element. Richard Nixon was the president who first declared war on drugs, and he created the Bureau of Narcotics and Dangerous Drugs (BNDD) to conduct that campaign. Nixon expected the CIA and NSA to cooperate. At Fort Meade that meant Minaret should add American drug traffickers to its list. At CIA, Project Chaos was supposed to identify the traffickers, and NSA began to send Langley data on the pushers beginning late in 1972. The CIA, uncomfortable that action against drugs being sent to the United States might be seen as a domestic operation, which implicated its charter prohibitions, stopped work on the drug networks after about six months. Not so Fort Meade. The BNDD put 450 Americans and over 3,000 foreign nationals on NSA's watch list. At any given time drug suspects accounted for about a third of the names on the watch list. National Security Agency officials later claimed credit for helping to capture several major drug shipments, but provided no details, making such assertions impossible to check.

Vice Admiral Noel S. Gayler followed General Carter at the helm of the NSA. In January 1971 he extolled NSA's Minaret collection ability to Defense Secretary Melvin Laird and Attorney General John Mitchell. Gayler's summary of the points covered is eloquent on the subject of NSA's pretext for eavesdropping on American activists: they represented "foreign-related subversive activity."[29] It was the same excuse the CIA used for Project Chaos. A week later a senior subordinate, NSA assistant director Benson K. Buffham, met the same two officials and obtained approval of the notes Gayler had made. On February 5 Mitchell attended a meeting of the President's Foreign Intelligence Advisory Board, where he told the group that electronic surveillance was being applied to "violence-prone groups," that there were more wiretaps in place than when the Nixon administration took office, that the NSA was advocating resumption of break-ins, and that all this lay within the scope of routine presidential power.[30]

But it was on Gayler's watch that the bottom fell out on Minaret. This followed an attempt to prosecute several antiwar protesters for alleged conspiracy to destroy government property, including one man who had aimed at CIA recruiters visiting the University of Michigan. In legal maneuvers preceding trial it emerged that the government case was based on warrantless wiretaps. The defense moved to exclude the evidence. The 1968 Omnibus Crime Control Act had specifically required proper warrants for eavesdropping.

Moreover, the phone taps here had been in place far longer than was typical, as if authorities had listened in until they could find something, anything, with which to charge the defendants. The dispute went all the way to the Supreme Court. The Nixon administration based its case precisely on the "national security" exception in the 1968 act—also the only legal basis for NSA monitoring. On June 19, 1972, the Supreme Court in the "Keith decision" ruled unanimously that warrants were necessary before commencing a wiretap even where national security issues were involved.[31] All Minaret phone monitoring was, of course, warrantless.

Vice Admiral Gayler's successor, Lieutenant General Samuel Phillips, did not immediately halt Minaret or Shamrock. Secrecy became the sole protection. As with the CIA's mail-opening, halting an activity was much harder than initiating it. Fortunately for the NSA, the Vietnam war was winding down, reducing demand for intelligence on protesters. The CIA also helped indirectly with its decision to terminate work on narcotics trafficking. That suggested the need for an equivalent Pentagon review. There officials were also becoming more squeamish—by this time the secretary of defense was none other than James R. Schlesinger. On July 5, 1973, the assistant secretary responsible for intelligence matters asked the Pentagon's general counsel to rule on whether the NSA eavesdropping was lawful. At Fort Meade the NSA performed its own review. Air force Lieutenant General Lew Allen, taking up the reins in August, huddled with NSA lawyers to pick up the pieces. The codebreakers stopped taking nominations for their watch list and halted certain support for the BNDD. Then it put Minaret reporting on hold. On September 17, Allen asked government agencies to recertify their intelligence requirements. Attorney General Elliott Richardson responded on October 1, taking the FBI out of the game and questioning the propriety of requests from the Secret Service to boot. In that letter Richardson specifically cited his need to better understand the implications of the Keith decision. Shortly thereafter General Allen terminated Minaret, except for intercepts gleaned from overseas monitoring. There is, however, some evidence from a January 1976 exchange of correspondence between the president and attorney general, by then Edward Levi, that telephone intercepts continued in the guise of the NSA monitoring *Soviet* interception of Americans' telephone calls.

When the Year of Intelligence began, all this NSA domestic spying remained under wraps. Therein lies a story too. Investigators for the Church Committee encountered immense difficulties in discovering anything about the NSA. The Congressional Research Service knew nothing, the Senate committee staffers with jurisdiction over the codebreakers had little more than budget information, and former NSA employees kept their comments at the level of disputes over parking spaces at Fort Meade. The investigators, L. Britt Snider and Peter Fenn, then approached General Allen and simply asked to be briefed on agency activities. Lew Allen arranged the briefings, but they were all vanilla. Meanwhile, the Rockefeller Commission had wound up its inquiry, and the Church Committee pressed for access to its documents. After weeks of appeals—and impelled in good part by intense public concerns over alleged CIA assassination plots (see Chapter 6)—the White House handed over the records. These files included a copy of The Family Jewels. There Snider and Fenn found just two references to NSA, but each led directly to Fort Meade's sensitive activities. One mentioned LP/Medley, the CIA's cover office lent to NSA for Shamrock. The other concerned Project Minaret. The fat was in the fire.

Britt Snider asked NSA for explanations. Nothing happened for weeks. Yet it was at precisely this moment, after thirty-four years, that the NSA suddenly terminated Project

Shamrock. By July 1975 a frustrated Snider made his request formal, crafting a set of written questions sent to Fort Meade as an interrogatory from Senator Church. The NSA responded that these matters were so sensitive they were willing to talk only to Frank Church and his Republican vice-chairman, Texas senator John Tower.

But, like the White House attempting to avoid Church Committee inquiries into CIA covert operations, in the climate of 1975 there was no possibility the National Security Agency could evade investigation. Leaks followed NSA's gambit. On July 22 the *New York Daily News* broke the story that "for at least five years" the NSA and FBI had routinely monitored commercial cable traffic to and from the United States.[32] The story hinted this practice was much older than that. Follow-up reporting in the *Daily News* forced the Church Committee into an acknowledgment that the National Security Agency had confirmed the program existed. Intelligence chief Bill Colby, testifying before the Pike Committee on August 6, found himself forced into an admission that the NSA had, in fact, monitored not only cables but phone calls. Colby attempted to get the House committee into closed session, but was repeatedly blocked from going off the record. Then Director Colby represented the activity as "incidental," asserting that it flowed from other monitoring and had been "technically impossible to separate." It was supposedly "too random for warrants." By that point, however, Congress had already taken the testimony of a senior Pentagon official who affirmed that the NSA had supplied Project Chaos with many hundreds of pages of communications intelligence.[33]

This history is not well known. But what has never been reported is what transpired inside the Ford administration. Late the previous year Attorney General Saxbe had been pressing for *new* permission for foreign intelligence surveillance. On September 18 Director Colby had concurred—

siding with NSA advocates of "surveillance which requires installation of a microphone by trespassory means." Colby had added that CIA would conduct no electronic surveillance within the United States without prior personal approval of the attorney general.[34] Deputy National Security Advisor Brent Scowcroft had counseled President Ford to go slow—even a Republican congressional task force on privacy had objections. In late December Ford had nevertheless renewed his authorization. But Scowcroft was right. By May 1975, two months before the Shamrock-Minaret revelations, *a dozen* bills had already been introduced in Congress aiming to restrict electronic surveillance even for national security purposes. The CIA protested that no "probable cause" standard would work, because the utility of an intercept could not be discerned in advance, and it objected to courts "introjecting" themselves. The agency wanted a free hand and recommended Ford stand on his "inherent foreign intelligence gathering powers."[35]

Then, on June 23, 1975, in another federal case (*Zweibon v. Mitchell*, D.C. Circuit No. 73-1847), the Court of Appeals reversed a lower court decision favoring the government. The court ruled that prior warrants must be obtained "even if the surveillance is installed under Presidential directive in the name of foreign intelligence gathering for protection of the national security."[36] Within days the Church Committee raised questions with the Department of Justice, the CIA, and NSA. By July 1975 it was clear that President Ford's own approval of eavesdropping, barely six months old, required revision. The matter had become a high-profile political issue. White House lawyer Philip Buchen advised Attorney General Levi to refuse to discuss eavesdropping when he appeared before the Church Committee on July 16. Levi took that advice, but it remained clear that the administration had to respond. Buchen assembled a working group from Justice,

CIA, NSA, FBI, and the State Department to cobble together an agreed joint briefing to which all could adhere. It was following Levi's refusal to comment on government eavesdropping that the leak of Project Shamrock occurred.

Once Director Colby had been mousetrapped into open admission of warrantless NSA eavesdropping, there could be no question but that the congressional inquisitors would follow the threads. At the Church Committee, staffers divided the turf so that Britt Snider took the lead on Shamrock while Peter Fenn looked into Minaret. Late in August Snider, who had been stymied by stonewalling at Fort Meade, was suddenly asked to NSA for a Shamrock briefing, delivered by a clean-cut, earnest agency man. The agency admitted that it had access to most cables moving through New York, that a courier went to the city every day to bring back the latest, and that the system had long been in place. The code name was Shamrock. The briefer reported it had been terminated on orders from Secretary Schlesinger, but attributed this to a sense Shamrock produced little, not to the fact it had been discovered. The NSA briefer punted on whether Fort Meade had been reading Americans' private messages, claiming analysts had their hands full merely with official cables. The briefer could not—or would not—say how long Shamrock had been underway, who had approved it, or how it began.

Not satisfied, Britt Snider sought a meeting with NSA's recently retired deputy chief, Louis Tordella. In that exalted position since 1956, Tordella would have the backstory if anyone did. They met at his home on a Sunday afternoon in September. Sure enough, the NSA man had the goods and laid out his account into the evening. Tordella conceded that Americans' cables were monitored, but maintained this concerned only a few persons and had not been a primary objective. Snider returned to his office. The NSA suddenly set up a briefing for committee members where it related the

same facts. Senator Church summoned cable company officials and took testimony, after which Snider prepared a staff
report on Shamrock.

The next step was for the Church Committee to decide
whether to hold a public hearing. No senior NSA official had
ever appeared before Congress. The committee was split,
partly but not entirely along party lines, with Church and
some favoring a hearing and Tower plus others opposed.
Senator Church convened a private meeting to hammer out
a plan, inviting Secretary Schlesinger and General Allen to
make their case against public discussion. The showdown
took place on the afternoon of October 2. Schlesinger, returning from a NATO ministerial conference in Europe, was
late and tired. Staffer Loch K. Johnson recalled the scene:
"He sounded like Moses speaking from the mount, engulfed
in swirling clouds of pipe smoke."[37] Grave and somber,
Schlesinger spoke in a low voice. Lew Allen nodded at his
points. It was all too sensitive. Hearings might inadvertently
disclose information to America's enemies. Schlesinger
seemed to have no sense of crisis, the political values at stake.
An NSA congressional aide, James G. Hudec, listened in
mounting horror as Schlesinger, who seemed tired and may
not have understood what he was asked, offered alternatives
that kept Fort Meade in control: the committee could hold
closed hearings, then write a report the NSA would edit; or it
could assemble a report that NSA would vet, and then could
have a hearing based solely on that material. Frank Church
had heard enough and dismissed the officials. Once they left,
the senators thrashed it out, and Church wore Tower down
until the committee agreed to proceed.

The Ford administration, well-informed by Republican
members and staff of the inner workings of Church's investigation, now became desperate. Attorney General Levi,
who had refused to discuss the issue previously, specifically asked to speak about the NSA. The administration was

momentarily in a stronger position because Senators Church and Walter F. Mondale, in appearances during the intervening days, had made statements disclosing certain other testimony taken privately. But Levi's appearance proved a disaster. The attorney general held his hand against his face and spoke dismissively. Staffer Johnson thought Levi looked like he was nursing a toothache. Levi held up the specter that after a public hearing corporations would no longer cooperate with government, denying NSA a valuable source. Why that should matter for an operation that had been terminated he did not say. As for those Americans on the watch list, they were suspicious individuals. Levi could not answer questions from Senators Mondale and Gary Hart. He then repeated that a public hearing would damage American security and refused to say anything more. Heated debate within the committee followed. Senator Church lost support for a full NSA inquiry, but members came to focus on Shamrock and Minaret.

President Ford counterattacked the same day, announcing that he himself would reform U.S. intelligence by fiat, issuing an executive order to revamp the system (something that did not happen until three months later). He followed up with telephone calls to Church and other committee members imploring them to back off. But the hearings on CIA mail-opening took place at this time and reinvigorated public demands for broadened investigation. Though Frank Church was buffeted by administration pressure plus rising concerns on Capitol Hill, he was also driven by the storm of public anxiety. So far as the NSA was concerned, this turned into a look at Minaret, but a consensus to go lightly on Project Shamrock. The administration came to the same place. It had to make a decision. Ford had failed to prevent any airing of dirty laundry, and the alternative was to disclose Project Minaret while minimizing attention to Shamrock. Among so many abuses being pursued, this seemed smaller, its fallout more manageable.

On Capitol Hill the Church Committee met on October 28 to make final arrangements for General Allen's testimony the next day. Under committee rules Church obtained a consensus to release Britt Snider's report even if Shamrock was not discussed. President Ford intervened with another round of telephone calls imploring senators to reconsider. Meanwhile at the White House, Phil Buchen massaged Allen's prepared testimony, already in draft. The Pentagon and NSA each proposed versions that mentioned Project Shamrock without revealing much. Allen went to the Hill armed with a White House–approved statement plus instructions to demand the committee go into executive session if it wished to discuss Shamrock. The general was prepared to talk about Minaret and the watch lists. As it played out, the focus stayed on the NSA eavesdropping on the antiwar movement.

The basic attitude that marked these NSA programs was revealed when Walter Mondale questioned Deputy Director Benson K. Buffham. Mondale asked if the NSA had been concerned about Minaret's legality, and its expert at first reacted as if he did not understand.

"In what sense?" Buffham countered, then posed his own question, "Whether that would have been a legal thing to do?"

Mondale simply said, "Yes."

"That particular aspect didn't enter into the discussion," Buffham answered.

Senator Mondale pressed his inquiry. "I was asking you if you were concerned about whether that would be legal and proper."

Deputy Director Buffham's reply went to the heart of the government's disdain for the rights of Americans: "We didn't consider it at the time, no."[38]

Senator Church dealt with Shamrock primarily from the podium by discussing some of his staff findings. A few days later he released Snider's Shamrock report. The Ford White House would be pleased at its success with the committee, but furious at the release of the report. But all it had accomplished was kick the can down the road. In the House, Representative Bella Abzug chaired the Subcommittee on Government Information and Individual Rights of the Government Operations Committee. Abzug, a New York Democrat, enjoyed a much more stable majority. She had also been a target of both CIA's Project Chaos and the NSA eavesdropping. The congresswoman seized on the NSA issue with her usual bulldog ferocity. Until mid-October all her subcommittee's requests of the Ford administration had focused on the FBI. Suddenly they began to aim at the NSA as well. The subcommittee planned a hearing with the cable company representatives scheduled to take place even before Church's better-known encounter. Abzug asked General Allen to testify. Just before the event, John Marsh of the White House appeared together with Lew Allen and senior aides to Levi and Schlesinger, attempting to head it off. At that point the NSA used the Church investigation as a screen, maintaining it was dealing entirely with committee investigators. Officials also argued that taking testimony might provide the cable companies immunity against subsequent criminal prosecution. On the morning of the scheduled hearing, Attorney General Levi took Abzug aside and personally appealed to her. The congresswoman responded by radically reducing the scope of her meeting. With release of the Senate's Shamrock report, however, the administration's strategy collapsed. Abzug renewed her determination to explore it.

General Allen, in correspondence with Representative Abzug, accepted the request to appear for a hearing and then fussed over dates and availability. Several times the Abzug hearings were scheduled, then postponed. They finally occurred in March 1976. Again Lew Allen was not available. The subcommittee issued subpoenas to the cable companies and NSA. This time Abzug found an official to provide Fort Meade's viewpoint. Now the administration invoked executive privilege. President Ford, in a letter to Secretary Schlesinger and Attorney General Levi, instructed them to reject the subpoenas. At Fort Meade, agency officer Joseph J. Tomba received a letter from Schlesinger's deputy with orders not to supply documents the Abzug subcommittee had demanded. In the hearings Tomba then refused to testify. The cable companies had no such protection, however, and they spoke before Congress. In the end, Shamrock was pretty well documented after all, despite the fact that Gerald Ford continued to claim executive privilege against provision of evidence, as when the Senate Interstate Commerce Committee sought a further look during the summer of 1976.

Meanwhile, the Ford White House was left with the problem of legal authority for electronic surveillance. Bills that had been tabled on Capitol Hill the previous year returned to the fore. The NSA testimony on Minaret, and the revealed breadth of the Shamrock intrusions, made it plain that citizens were indeed vulnerable to government spying. Rather than permit legislation to be hammered out by others, Ford now cooperated on a law to cover electronic surveillance. In February, while informing Congress of his executive order on intelligence, the president declared he would work with it on new legislation. Coincident with the Abzug hearings, President Ford hosted a lunch at Blair House bringing together Edward Levi with his codebreakers and the President's Foreign Intelligence Advisory Board, feeling out what needed protection. Levi had already met that morning with Henry Kissinger, Donald Rumsfeld, and George H. W. Bush, now, respectively, heads of the State Department, Pentagon, and U.S. intelligence community. Representing the White House were Brent Scowcroft, Philip Buchen, and Jack Marsh.

By then a draft bill existed—acceptable to Levi, Buchen, and Marsh—and Levi had already begun feeling out members of key congressional committees. Talking points prepared for this meeting make explicit that the purpose was to get a statute enacted before the courts further narrowed executive freedom of action. Kissinger resisted language abridging any presidential authority over intelligence gathering. He wanted a provision that would permit warrantless wiretapping of persons who were not American citizens or resident aliens, and he wanted to lower the threshold at which statutory warrantless provisions kicked in—to information the government considered merely "important," as opposed to the "essential" standard in the draft legislation.[39] On March 23 President Ford had thirty-six congressional leaders to the White House to unveil his proposal. Walter Mondale was included. Frank Church was not. Jack Marsh reported that Massachusetts Senator Edward Kennedy had been especially helpful. Kennedy had, in fact, indicated his willingness to introduce the bill in the Senate.

Herein lies the origin of the Foreign Intelligence Surveillance Act (FISA). Ted Kennedy indeed championed it. The vagaries of election year politics, the changeover to the presidency of James Earl Carter, and the debate over an even more ambitious project for a statutory charter to govern the entire intelligence community delayed action for a long time, but FISA passed in 1978 and became law. One key provision created a federal court, its judges named by the Chief Justice of the Supreme Court, to hear applications for wiretap warrants. Another clause required a showing of probable cause for the warrant, with even more stringent rules on evidence if the suspects were American citizens. It is worth noting that both provisions governing the Foreign Intelligence Surveillance Court—deemed inadequate after the September 11 attacks—formed parts of the original, *Republican*, proposal for the Act.

Electronic eavesdropping on Americans and the monitoring of cable traffic made a classic Family Jewel. The

wiretapping began on shaky legal ground that was demolished by the courts. It continued past the end of the Vietnam
war and stopped only when top officials concerned with liability called a halt. The cable interception was criminal on its
face. Both operations ultimately relied upon secrecy for their
protection. Shamrock, the cable project, continued until its
cover had begun unraveling. The Ford administration's ultimate response was to craft new legislation to permit electronic eavesdropping to continue, albeit under some regulation by the courts.

L eap ahead a quarter of a century. By then FISA had been
enacted, and the Foreign Intelligence Surveillance Court
had become established and well practiced. The law survived
court challenge in 1982 when a trio of Irish Republican Army
supporters had disputed it when nabbed for running guns to
the IRA. The National Security Agency had regulations governing who could be targeted, and providing for "minimizing" information collected about American citizens. In any
case of doubt, NSA employees were to seek the counsel of its
lawyers. The criterion that one side of a phone conversation
had to be located abroad was firmly in place. The executive
had even learned to navigate the politics of modifying FISA—
during the Clinton administration, it had gone to Congress,
twice, to obtain modifications that would modernize the
system, with new provisions for physical searches and for
data related to computer addresses and Internet communications. In short, the system had become routinized and was
periodically updated. In addition, the existing legal strictures
posed little obstacle to government investigation. More than
ten thousand times, United States authorities had applied to
the court for electronic surveillance warrants. On just four
occasions were they denied. At the end of Bill Clinton's presidency, the arrangements for ensuring that NSA could collect

intelligence through electronic surveillance while safeguarding American citizens' constitutional rights seemed to be working smoothly—and in the government's favor—without major difficulty.

The National Security Agency director at the time, air force General Michael Hayden, was said to be a stickler for regulations, and in 2000 he gave a speech extolling NSA's virtuous protection of the public's rights. Then came the attacks of September 11, 2001. At Fort Meade, Hayden immediately implemented a special watch on communications into or out of Afghanistan, where the Al Qaeda perpetrators were located. He then softened the parameters for his "minimization" procedures, moving to a wartime footing. The director had once told a congressional committee, by way of illustrating how well citizens were protected against eavesdropping, that if Al Qaeda leader Osama bin Laden crossed into the United States at Niagara Falls, the NSA would have to stop watching him. That now seemed unacceptable.

General Hayden went to George J. Tenet, the Director of Central Intelligence, to say he needed fresh orders. About the same time, Vice President Dick Cheney asked Tenet if the National Security Agency could do more. Tenet and Hayden then went to see Cheney, and the vice president took their message to President George W. Bush. The chief executive convened both officials in the Oval Office. General Hayden told Bush the nation was "flying blind without a warning system." He wanted a setup to monitor communications into and out of the United States without FISA warrants. President Bush was ready for that. By his account he asked presidential counsel Alberto Gonzales and the Department of Justice whether he could properly authorize such a measure. Both replied in the affirmative.[40] On October 4, 2001, Bush approved the aggressive NSA eavesdropping known as the "Terrorist Surveillance Program," one far beyond Project Minaret. Later Bush okayed even more activities, all highly classified. The surviving restriction was that one side of a call be outside the United States.

Meanwhile, General Hayden told a congressional committee that he was interpreting his original authorities aggressively, then clammed up. When Representative Nancy Pelosi, a California Democrat who was then chairwoman of the House Permanent Select Committee on Intelligence, wondered what Fort Meade was up to, and set her staff to find out, the codebreakers stood mute. Pelosi and Hayden exchanged letters. The NSA chief simply reiterated his original comment. In early October, Hayden assembled top staff at Fort Meade, informed them of the new surveillance regime, and emphasized the need to move forward, with an appropriate genuflection to privacy rights.

That marked the beginning of what has already been more than a decade of intensive NSA eavesdropping on Americans and others, the details of which remain largely masked. The surveillance must inevitably vacuum up huge amounts of data on Americans—much more than in Vietnam days. Some estimates of the number of messages stored in NSA computers rise to the tens of *trillions*. Though unknown even now, the way these projects have been shielded, the zealousness with which the executive sought to avoid inquiry, the several instances in which the tips of these icebergs have surfaced, and the (not secret) technological processes through which this kind of electronic monitoring functions, give good reasons to suspect that the Terrorist Surveillance Program (TSP) shields a massive intrusion into Americans' lives. The TSP is very likely one of today's Family Jewels.

Consider first the quality of executive branch interaction with the congressional committees that oversee U.S. intelligence. Unlike in the Vietnam era, today a system of oversight committees—established precisely as a result of the Year of Intelligence—exists to monitor the clandestine agencies. Under established regulations, the overseers are supposed to be kept fully and currently informed on every significant secret activity. But Bush officials attempted to hide the Terrorist Surveillance Program. "This program was too important and too highly classified for briefings to the whole committees," Dick Cheney contends, "which, given the rotations of members into those slots [on the oversight panels], would have resulted in dozens being briefed."[41] Vice President Cheney's objections are misleading. The members of those units have been cleared for every aspect of the intelligence business. The impression the vice president gives of turnover on the panels is exaggerated, and their function was specifically to monitor *all* government activities.

The maneuver to keep electronic surveillance out of the oversight arena was based on a 1983 executive order under which President Ronald Reagan governed U.S. intelligence. The Reagan order defined "special activities"—long a euphemism for communications intelligence and covert operations. The loophole emerged when the executive and Congress, wrangling in the wake of Reagan's Iran-Contra affair, agreed that knowledge of the most sensitive operations could be restricted to a "Gang of Four" (the chairmen and vice-chairmen of both houses' intelligence committees) rather than being shared with the full committees. The second Bush administration handled the eavesdropping that way. Thus, George Tenet makes a point of noting that "senior congressional leaders" were called to the White House and informed within a couple of weeks of TSP's inception, and that a dozen such meetings (seventeen actually) were hosted by Vice President Cheney, usually in his West Wing office, before the program leaked. But the Gang of Four were sworn to silence, and no one else knew. "Oversight" became impossible.

Meanwhile, an important feature of the Bush administration's goal in obtaining the USA Patriot Act was to secure provisions to legalize this eavesdropping, approved without Congress being able to consider its classified realities. The administration obtained this legislation in the heat of 9/11, receiving congressional approval in October 2001. Richard Cheney, darkly hinting that opponents of the legislation would be aiding and abetting terrorism, stoked the frenzy in which this law passed within hours of its appearance on the floor. Most members of Congress did not even know the Terrorist Surveillance Program existed, and the congressional vote took place two days *before* the Four were first briefed on it. The president signed the law the same day the senior legislators were informed.

That marked the onset of a high-handed approach in this matter heartily encouraged by the vice president. But despite the administration's best efforts to shield the program in a compartment above Top Secret, as with the original Family Jewels it is inevitable that secret operations become known, in particular where they involve controversial elements. In due course the White House discovered the *New York Times* had the story and pressured the newspaper to spike it. Editors did respond, holding James Risen's story for more than a year. The TSP was revealed in Risen's December 16, 2005, *Times* article. President Bush confirmed its existence. At that point Bush officials hastened to claim the sleuthing had been under proper oversight all along, asserting that Congress had been briefed on it thirty times (the correct figure is given above). But almost all those briefings, by the Bush administration's own listing, had been of the Gang of Four only, so secret that both rank-and-file overseers and the gang's own staffs remained in ignorance. In 2003, when one of the Four, West Virginia Senator Jay Rockefeller IV, wrote Vice President Cheney to complain about certain aspects of the TSP, including the administration's neglect of its duty to inform the full oversight committees, Rockefeller had had to put his letter in longhand, because no one in his office had the requisite security clearances to type it.

The administration's attitude is more clearly revealed in what happened in the immediate aftermath of the revelation. Predictably, the House Permanent Select Committee on Intelligence asked for a full briefing on the eavesdropping and scheduled a secret hearing to receive General Hayden's testimony. That had to be canceled when White House chief of staff Andy Card forbade Hayden's appearance.

Secrecy did not only apply to Congress. On January 23, 2006, Hayden appeared at the National Press Club for a speech specifically regarding what the NSA had been doing to protect the nation. Of the Terrorist Surveillance Program Hayden said, "That authorization was based on an intelligence community assessment of a serious and continuing threat to the homeland. The lawfulness of the actual authorization was reviewed by lawyers at the Department of Justice and the White House and was approved by the attorney general." General Hayden added that he had asked the three most senior lawyers at NSA for a further review and they had also come out in its favor—"Supported, not acquiesced," was Hayden's language.[42]

Several of General Hayden's assertions to the American public were inaccurate or misleading. Within the administration, TSP measures were initially screened only by NSA lawyers, then passed to the White House. Fort Meade's experts spoke to General Hayden, who worked in tandem with Cheney attorney David S. Addington and presidential counsel Alberto R. Gonzales. At the Department of Justice (DOJ), only John Yoo was read into the program. According to later investigation by the inspectors general of a range of agencies, including DOJ, CIA, and the NSA—and contrary to both Hayden's and Mr. Bush's versions of this story—Yoo prepared his analysis *after* the program was in place. In keeping with his other opinions, Yoo based this one on an unrestrained reading of presidential power. Superiors learned of

Yoo's work from reading about it in the newspapers, years later. At the White House, however, his paper was represented as the official Justice Department position.

No other Justice legal expert looked at the Yoo paper until late 2003, and then DOJ officials found serious flaws in his arguments. Presidential counsel Gonzales asked DOJ to supply a memorandum agreeing the agency had operated within the law. The White House considered it important to obtain a retroactive approval, much like the controversial "retroactive" covert action finding that figured in the Iran-Contra affair. Similarly, vice-presidential counsel Addington challenged Deputy Attorney General James Comey to examine all of Yoo's opinions and declare which ones Justice still supported.

The TSP's electronic eavesdropping was sensitive enough that, even with the sweeping orders Bush had given the NSA, he needed to recertify it every forty-five days. Each request was accompanied by a report on current activity and on what had been learned during the last period. By 2004, the National Security Agency wanted to widen its collection effort with the next reauthorization. According to press reports, the NSA sought to add a broad data mining feature to its basic interception operation.[43] This led to a crisis. James Comey informed the White House that Justice could not approve continuance. At another meeting—with the legal authority due to expire on March 11—Vice President Cheney thundered that Comey would be endangering "thousands" of lives if DOJ did not comply. President Bush ordered an emergency briefing for the Gang of Eight (the Four plus the senior congressional leadership). There congressional leaders raised serious objections. Inside the White House, Alberto Gonzales represented the Gang of Eight as having approved.[44] Dick Cheney also asserts in his memoir, "It was unanimous: Every member agreed that [TSP] should continue."[45]

The day had come when it was necessary to secure

Attorney General Ashcroft's approval, or at least his acquiescence. Gonzales and Addington viewed this as superflu-
ous. Cheney maintains that Ashcroft had already approved
the program twenty times, and that the DOJ objection, from
inexperienced people, was merely to one aspect of collection. At that moment Ashcroft was at George Washington
University Hospital being treated for pancreatitis. On March
10 White House officials tried to induce Ashcroft to sign off
from his hospital bed. He had been in intensive care for a
week, without food or drink, and was grouchy. Alberto Gonzales, Bush chief of staff Andrew Card, and David Addington
appeared at his bedside and demanded Ashcroft's signature.
No slouch when it came to aggressive security measures—
he had approved the dubious FBI "national security letters"—Ashcroft recognized a legal morass when he saw one.
He refused. Ashcroft delegated his authority to Jim Comey.
The latter had rushed to the hospital too, when he learned the
Gonzales group was headed there, and told the attorney general he would resign if DOJ agreed. Actually *eight* senior officials at Justice were in revolt, ready to leave as well. So was
FBI chief Robert Mueller. Cheney later blocked the promotion of one of the DOJ officials who had objected to the shaky
legal foundation for this surveillance.

The White House went ahead with reauthorization, substituting Alberto Gonzales's approval for that of the attorney general. This meant relying upon a personal aide with
no institutional authority whatever in place of the nation's
top legal official. The Gonzales paper asserted, according
to the joint inspectors general, that DOJ's earlier approvals
were valid (despite being based on inaccurate information).
Deputy Attorney General Comey learned this at the White
House the next day, when Bush signed the certification.
Afterwards Comey buttonholed NSC counterterrorism specialist Fran Townsend in the hallway, the six-foot, eight-inch
lawyer towering over the diminutive staffer. Comey began

to explain, but Townsend was not cleared for the program and did not recognize the code word he used. She stopped Comey, then went to national security advisor Condoleezza Rice and alerted her. "I had known Comey as an attorney who had earned a distinguished record as a New York prosecutor," Rice relates. "If he was reaching out to someone who might not have been read into the program, it was clear to me that something must be wrong."[46] Condi Rice went to President Bush on March 12 and recommended he speak to Comey. The two met in the Oval Office for fifteen minutes. Rice reports that White House attorneys had been aware of the misgivings at Justice for weeks, but had not told Bush until the morning he was to sign the reauthorization—and then the president faced the dilemma of whether to approve or halt the entire TSP in its tracks.

After meeting with Comey, President Bush ordered that the NSA eavesdropping be modified to meet the Justice Department objections. Justice would rework its legal opinion on that basis. Vice President Cheney minimizes this crisis, claiming the dispute centered on one small element in a huge operation. He also asserts that Ashcroft had told Bush he would approve and then reversed himself. But the entire top echelon of officials at the Department of Justice plus the director of the FBI were prepared to resign over this. The issue had to be more than a tiny cog in the machine. On March 23 James Comey and Dick Cheney met privately. Justice approved a fresh paper. This episode of controversy demonstrates the White House's determination to pursue its invasive surveillance program.

For his second term President Bush elevated Alberto Gonzales to attorney general, replacing the departed Ashcroft. In moving to the Justice Department, Gonzales took with him the notes he had made of that contentious meeting with the congressional leaders, scribbled in a spiral notebook a few days later, after Bush spoke to Comey and then instructed

Gonzales to make a record. Gonzales took the notes home in his briefcase and kept them there for an undisclosed interval. Later he brought them back to work, and placed the papers in a private safe outside his office rather than in secure storage at the Justice Command Center, required for a document that noted operational aspects of the TSP as well as its classified code name. This was not an inadvertent act—Mr. Gonzales was found to have mishandled seventeen other documents as well. Highlighting the dangers of disclosure, at one point officials responding to an FOIA request searched that safe paper by paper. When called to testify before Congress on the eavesdropping, Gonzales gave rather opaque testimony. Legislators also subpoenaed the program certifications and accompanying Justice Department memos. These were held by Vice President Cheney, who claimed executive privilege for them and denied the summons in toto. "This program is one of the things of which I am proudest," Cheney writes. "If I had it to do over again, I would, in a heartbeat."[47]

Then there is the Foreign Intelligence Surveillance Court, empaneled specifically to deal with these kinds of questions. It too was, and is, extremely compliant. At last report there have been nineteen thousand executive requests for surveillance warrants since the 1970s, with only those four rejections already noted. Put differently, *no* Bush administration demand for a warrant was ever rejected. By one count this FISA eavesdropping has aimed at seven thousand foreigners and five hundred Americans.[48] The Court tried to *modify* two warrants, which the administration appealed and won in both cases. Despite this degree of cooperation, and the system's smooth functioning for many years, Bush officials not only demanded warrantless eavesdropping, refusing to take TSP cases to the Court, but rejected briefing it on the program. Only the chief judge was informed, and not until

January 2002, roughly during the TSP's *third* reauthorization period. Later, a chief judge of the Court resigned in protest of the administration's manifest arrogance.

That action became just another hiccup in this sorry story. Starting with the Patriot Act, the Bush administration repeatedly sought and obtained amendments to FISA, to the point where it tried to eliminate most standards for granting warrants. In a bloody political fight in 2007, the administration secured fresh amendments to permit warrantless interception on persons merely thought to be outside the United States who could be construed in some way as being of interest to intelligence investigators. The information collected could be retained for up to a year without referral to the Court.

Technical aspects of surveillance operations add to the worry that a Family Jewel exists here. As everyone knows from dealing with the Internet, it is not at all difficult for hackers to penetrate messages, and Fort Meade has some of the best hackers around. A huge proportion (90 percent) of Internet traffic passed over fiber optic cables accessible to the NSA. The cable aspect was discomfiting from the legal side because FISA provisions defined "transmission by wire" as the point where warrants became necessary (the essence of 1970s "wiretapping"), but the cables posed no technical impediment to NSA experts, and the legal restrictions were dismantled by amendments. Wireless communications are even easier to penetrate, and technology has favored the codebreakers because, since the dawn of the intercept program, more and more communications—both Internet and telephone—have moved to radio transmission. Fort Meade has pretty much been free to intercept wireless since the beginning of eavesdropping.

Reportedly the NSA merely collected information from the "externals" of communications—the emitting and receiving addresses, the titles of e-mails, their timing, and so on.

But under current conditions it is difficult to associate a device with a particular person, or more specifically, to identify his or her citizenship. This reduces the possibility of excluding, a priori, communications purely between American nationals. To perform electronic surveillance *aimed at foreign targets*, gathering everything is necessary, including Americans' messages.

In addition, the old NSA "minimization" rule—that one end of a communication had to be abroad—is increasingly less reflective of reality. Not only are there many computer servers so located—a ready-made excuse for intercepting Americans' transmissions—but until recently the vast majority of all *foreign* traffic at some point transits servers in the United States. This feature, facilitating NSA access to foreign traffic, unfortunately also means that Fort Meade's operators routinely data-mine transmissions across servers moving Americans' messages. As long ago as Project Minaret, the NSA already had computer software that could key on specific words, then pull down the contents of phone calls containing them. This technology is so widely distributed today that hackers use it. The story of what happened in the donation of the personal papers of former CIA officer Phil Agee (Chapter 8) demonstrates that in fact the NSA *is* reading beyond the externals. In summary, there are purely technical reasons to expect that the Terrorist Surveillance Program and its adjuncts, once investigated, will be found to involve the same kinds of domestic intrusion as those of the Vietnam era, ones that were ruled illegal in the courts and against which law was enacted.

M ail surveillance, whether or not one accepts that it represented the 1960s version of today's warrantless electronic intercepts, was a chilling activity. Today the Terrorist Surveillance Program holds Americans' attention. Very few are aware that on December 20, 2006, President Bush attached a "signing statement" to his approval of a Post Office reform bill asserting that the U.S. government "shall construe" a section of that law to permit the opening of mail—to protect life, guard against hazardous materials, or conduct "physical searches specifically authorized by law for foreign intelligence collection."[49] Years after the bad old days of Vietnam, the Bush administration arrogated to itself the power to carry out illegal activities that were an acknowledged Family Jewel, claiming them authorized by "law" that consists entirely of a statement made by the president.

That little detail in a sense completes this cycle. Intelligence operatives believe in product. Projects are initiated to obtain that product, information. In a democracy those projects can infringe on the rights of citizens. The hard thing is to guard the rights of citizens while providing for the requisite intelligence. There is a balance to be struck, but the need to do that is obstructed by the operational logic of intelligence. In the clandestine world, it is frequently the case that collection projects fall short. Few—though with significant exceptions—prove to be the gold mines their advocates promise at the moment of approval. So intelligence officers fall back on the formula that they collect small pieces that someday might solve a big puzzle. At the same time, they expand collection, which often turns it to purposes other than the original ones. If that happens to magnify the threat to individual rights, the intelligence mavens would prefer that the public not know.

This is not a coincidental development: it is a cycle, a pattern. The CIA's Project Lingual turned into a vehicle used against political dissent, was thoroughly defrocked, and three decades later the specter of mail-opening is revived. The NSA's Project Minaret, also aimed at political dissent, was specifically outlawed. The Terrorist Surveillance Program overrode those controls, and it, too, expanded. How far TSP

went remains shrouded in secrecy. Insiders in the 1970s recognized such programs as Family Jewels. They still are.

As for the particular collection efforts surveyed, at the
end of the day Richard Helms bears direct and substantial
responsibility for the CIA abuse in Project Lingual. Helms
not only approved James Angleton's proposals for the mail-
opening, he rode shotgun thereafter—backing expansions,
turning aside complaints, keeping a weather eye for outside
challenges, intervening with Cabinet officers when the project came under fire, and ordering measures to reduce visibil-
ity—and flap potential—all the while pushing for action. And
all of this in service of something CIA acknowledged as illegal from the start. Helms's superiors failed to act when questions were raised, and he himself championed an effort that
yielded minimal results in a context where the flap potential
remained astronomical throughout.

Even if the original aim of catching Russian spies is seen
as legitimate, the failure to fully air the ramifications of mail-
opening outside the CIA, and to seek a conscious authorization by the president, ensured it remained a booby trap waiting to explode. Every boundary was exceeded when Lingual
began to surveil Americans. By then Helms was the CIA
director and ought to have shut it down forthwith. Instead
he continued Lingual and linked it with other CIA efforts
to monitor American dissenters. In short, Richard Helms
encouraged abuse. This puts a stark light on his implied
threat to President Ford, when the CIA domestic activities
were revealed, that he would defend himself by letting all the
"cats" out of their cages. Indeed, there were many. This is one
reason the original Family Jewels were so explosive.

With the National Security Agency projects, there is no
simple thread of responsibility. Shamrock started early, continued a very long time, and appears never to have undergone
significant scrutiny. No doubt the take was much greater than
from the CIA's mail-opening, and officials were enamored

with communications intelligence following the successes of World War II, but this enterprise, too, was illegal. Private corporations were repeatedly given assurances their cooperation carried no criminal liability—promises that were probably also illegal. The NSA's effort to put a statutory foundation underneath Shamrock in a 1968 law was thrown out in court. Meanwhile, Project Minaret had already begun, and widened the security agency's culpability. Fort Meade's codebreakers were lucky in 1975 that the CIA and FBI attracted so much public attention, but nevertheless NSA methods were to be explicitly proscribed by law.

The jury must remain out on the Bush administration Family Jewel until the Terrorist Surveillance Program is finally reviewed in a systematic fashion. But from what appears so far, it seems the TSP story is one of systematic effort to evade existing strictures. Dick Cheney's fingerprints on this are at least as prominent as those of Helms on the mail-opening. But the roles of White House attorney Alberto Gonzales and DOJ official John Yoo, as well as those of NSA personnel, were also significant. On electronic surveillance Bush officials continue to enjoy the benefits of secrecy—and therein lies an important reminder: secrecy serves not just to protect national security but also to hide abuse. And abuses damage national security. The truth is that national security is also served by limiting secrecy. Just how abuse has flourished in the dark—and what damage can be caused by secrecy—are evident in the case of CIA detention and interrogation programs, where evidence has emerged that puts the iceberg in plain view.

DETENTION AND INTERROGATION

T he story of Yuri Ivanovich Nosenko appears in the original Family Jewels in a single paragraph of Howard Osborn's cover memo and a short paper of slightly more than one page. For Americans today, indeed for a world concerned about CIA "black prisons" and aggressive interrogation methods (read: torture), this tiny fragment cloaks a huge story. Even for the Central Intelligence Agency of the 1960s, the Family Jewels documents afforded barely minimal coverage of an issue that put the CIA beyond the borders of legality. Equally disturbing, the sparse Family Jewels text hid internal warfare that nearly tore the agency apart. As with the war on terror, the central focus of this fight was counterintelligence—finding out about the bad guys and their plans— a necessary function, but one highly susceptible to abuse.

Yuri Nosenko was a Russian spy, or, more properly, an officer of the Soviet intelligence service KGB. After initially approaching the CIA in Geneva in early 1962, Nosenko defected, again in Geneva, in February 1964. Coming in the immediate aftermath of the Kennedy assassination, Nosenko's was an important defection, because he claimed to have been a senior officer in the KGB directorate responsible for

working against Americans in Russia, and therefore knowledgeable about Kennedy's presumptive assassin, Lee Harvey
Oswald, who had spent two and a half years living there under
the KGB's gaze. There was also the question of what Nosenko
might know about possible Soviet spies inside the CIA.

After a short period of simple debriefing, Nosenko's CIA
handlers subjected him to more than three years of hostile
interrogation. This amounted to CIA operating inside the
United States, and to the agency exercising police powers by
incarcerating an individual—both violations of the agency's
charter and the reason why the Nosenko affair appears in the
Family Jewels documents. The Central Intelligence Agency's
creation of a secret prison on American soil, and its interrogation techniques, resonate with a public now faced with the
conundrums of the "war on terror."

Some background will help in understanding the Nosenko
affair. Defector Yuri Nosenko, first known by the cryptonym AE/Foxtrot, appeared in the midst of agency fears of
a spy in its own ranks, a mole hunted by CIA counterintelligence chief James J. Angleton. The climate was heavily influenced by a previous KGB defector, Anatoli Golitsyn, whose
information helped identify several Russian agents in Eng-
land and nail down the culpability of the KGB's British spy
Kim Philby. Golitsyn went so far as to charge that the KGB
had a "Monster Plot" under which much that happened in
the world—right down to the Sino-Soviet split—formed part
of a grand design intended to deceive the West. Angleton fell
under Golitsyn's spell and permitted the KGB defector to
read CIA case files. Robert de Niro's 2004 movie *The Good
Shepherd* contains a sharply edged, fictionalized portrayal of
this relationship. Where certain officials considered the Russian a provocateur, Angleton followed Golitsyn's suggestions,
initiating security investigations that wrecked the careers

of a number of highly capable CIA officers. Golitsyn insisted the KGB would try and discredit him by sending false defectors. He feared Nosenko. Angleton played Golitsyn's game there too.

No masterspy, Yuri Nosenko did not help himself with his shifting stories, fabrications and exaggerations, vague and implausible accounts of his career in Soviet intelligence, and party animal antics. Yet even before being permitted into the United States, Nosenko provided information that led to the apprehension of a Russian spy in Britain and an American turncoat at NATO headquarters, and the uncovering of massive KGB bugging (fifty-two microphones) in the U.S. embassy in Moscow. But Nosenko's CIA handlers were already suspicious. At length the agency decided to bring this Russian to the United States and question him in detail.

On April 2, 1964, Richard Helms, by now the CIA's deputy director for operations, met with Justice Department officials, who agreed that Nosenko's legal status could be left undefined. Rather than admit the defector to the United States as a resident or grant him political asylum, the Department temporarily "excluded" Nosenko but paroled him to the custody of the CIA. Helms later relied upon this ambiguous immigration status to maintain that Nosenko's detention was legally justified.[1] The case, Helms would record, "was the most frustrating operation in my experience, and was to plague me from my post as deputy director ... through much of my service as Director of Central Intelligence."[2]

The Soviet Russia Division of Mr. Helms's directorate had primary responsibility for the care and feeding of Yuri Nosenko, and its agents' frustrations increased as the man's stories failed to add up. Tennent H. ("Pete") Bagley, the case officer the Russian had originally approached, confronted his boss with the need to interrogate Nosenko more thoroughly. Soviet Division brass decided to sequester the Russian spy. Division experts and CIA Counterintelligence set out to "break" Nosenko, and they did it inside the United States. Richard Helms reflected the agency's increasing doubts. He privately approached Chief Justice Earl Warren, lead investigator on the Kennedy assassination, to tell him the CIA would not vouch for Foxtrot's information and warn him the Warren Commission should not take Nosenko seriously.

The inquisitors decided to subject the Russian to a lie detector examination and then, no matter what the polygraph said, impugn him for lying. That took place two days after the CIA's meeting with the Justice Department, and immediately upon Nosenko's return from a vacation in Hawaii. The inquisitors had no need to accuse falsely—the polygraph showed strong evidence of deception. An inquisitor immediately screamed at Nosenko, yelling that he was a phony. Guards entered the room. The captive was stripped naked. After that the Russian was kept in the attic. This proved the start of seven months of intensive questioning. A bare light-bulb and a narrow cot were the only furnishings. Nosenko was not allowed to keep a toothbrush or toothpaste and could shower and shave only once a week. A pair of guards in the hall kept him under constant watch.

The "KU/Bark Manual," the CIA inquisitor's bible, discusses at length how friendly relations with a subject are best suited to eliciting accurate data. It specifically finds strong-arm methods counterproductive. This official doctrine on intelligence interrogation was in force at the time of the Nosenko affair. The manual lays down a relatively sophisticated position, cautioning, "*it is vital that this discussion not be misconstrued as constituting authorization for the use of coercion*" (italics in the original), notes that "intense pain is quite likely to produce false confessions," and adds that "the threat of death has often been found to be worse than useless," warning that unauthorized use of coercive techniques can put both interrogators "and KUBARK" in "unconsidered jeopardy." Effective technique was to build affinity with the subject.[3]

Nosenko's interrogators threw away the book.

James Angleton's Counterintelligence (CI) Staff spearheaded analysis of the Nosenko data, with a unit known as the Special Intelligence Group producing leads for the inquisitors. That was under Birch D. O'Neal, who had been CIA liaison to the Warren Commission and had previously been CIA station chief in Guatemala.[4] O'Neal's group was custodian of the agency's file on Lee Harvey Oswald, the alleged Kennedy assassin, and Nosenko claimed to have been the Soviet intelligence officer in charge of keeping a watch on Oswald while he lived in Russia. According to Helms, Jim Angleton's advice, given early on and repeated, was to release Nosenko, then follow him to see what he might do.[5] Peter Deriabin, a KGB defector from the early 1950s, also furnished leads, picking holes in the Russian's fanciful tales. Pete Bagley remained convinced Nosenko was a plant.[6]

It was Bagley who managed the day-to-day operation. Angleton kept a finger on the pulse of the interrogation. The counterspy undoubtedly perceived Nosenko as a threat. Richard Helms's professed motive in ordering the inquisition was to determine once and for all the veracity of Nosenko's claims that the KGB had had nothing to do with Kennedy's assassin Oswald. No doubt Helms wanted any CIA mole found too, and Angleton must have assured him the inquisitors were nearing their goal. In November 1964 Helms ordered the case wound up. Faced with persistent contradictions, the Soviet Division could not make up its mind. Helms canceled his instructions. Nosenko's questioning stopped for a month or two, but it resumed in early 1965.

Langley's security experts worried that neighbors would become suspicious of the parade of automobiles trailing into the Maryland house where Yuri Nosenko was being held in captivity. So an actual black prison was built at the CIA's Camp Peary training facility outside Williamsburg, Virginia. The agency moved the Russian there in the summer of 1965. Nosenko was blindfolded and handcuffed, bundled into a car, then put on a plane for the flight to Camp Peary. Senior CIA officer John L. Hart, reviewing the Nosenko case more than a decade later, found that the prisoner was permitted "fewer amenities than he would have received in most jails or prisons within the United States."[7] That was correct. Nosenko was given nothing to read, no access to radio or television, was not even allowed outside to exercise until much later—and then for no more than a half hour a day. Food was porridge.

Interrogators stopped just short of physical torture, but employed many of the coercive techniques that proved so controversial in the war on terrorism. Agency officers asked to use truth drugs but were denied permission, although whether or not such drugs were in fact administered is disputed. The Hart review concluded that four kinds of drugs had been used on Nosenko. Langley's scientists and security experts had experimented with drugs, including LSD, in the 1950s, and the effort had notoriously led to the death of a participant. It seems reasonable to suppose CIA officials would be loath to permit the use of drugs a decade later. Pete Bagley takes umbrage at charges Nosenko had been put in a "dungeon" or subjected to a "torture vault." Bagley later wrote the critics "must have been aware that Nosenko had regular (as I remember, weekly) visits by a doctor to ascertain his health and the adequacy of his diet."[8]

In August 1966 Dick Helms, now CIA director, renewed his demand that the case be closed. Helms set a two-month deadline. The director felt the agency would not be able to withstand the congressional and media scrutiny when it emerged that "we had held him in these circumstances and in what would be interpreted as outright defiance of law and custom."[9] Nosenko's treatment included a false arrest (the CIA has no arrest powers—and his "crime" was simply lying to debriefers), false imprisonment, the operation of a CIA prison facility, solitary confinement during the entire period of incarceration, extended (twenty-four-plus-hour) interrogations, and the inducement of psychological stress plus sensory deprivation. Agency officers speculated about discrediting Nosenko, putting him in a psychiatric hospital, even eliminating him.

Soviet Division chief David Murphy persuaded Director Helms to extend his deadline through the end of the year. Nosenko was given another polygraph exam purely to rattle him, with bells and lights controlled from outside the room and sounded or lit to startle the detainee. The inquisitors followed up with a marathon interrogation session. But then questioning largely stopped. CIA focused on interpreting the data it already had. In all, between Nosenko's incarceration and release he was confined for 1,277 days and interrogated on 292 of them. Pete Bagley compiled a massive analysis designed to document Nosenko's perfidy, concluding he was a deception agent. Within weeks of its filing, a reports officer in the Soviet Division filed a rejoinder out of channels to Helms that took apart Bagley's study. It was only now that handlers began allowing Nosenko to walk outside his prison.

Eventually Helms asked his deputy, Vice Admiral Rufus Taylor, to look into the whole affair. Taylor started wheels rolling that ultimately freed Nosenko. James Angleton opposed the move, but Helms overruled him—one of the few times those two ever disagreed. In October 1967 the Soviet Division was taken off the case. Nosenko was transferred to custody of the CIA Office of Security, which abandoned hostile interrogations in favor of friendly debriefings. Osborn's unit moved Nosenko out of the black prison. He passed a polygraph held under better-controlled conditions in 1968. The Office of Security did its own review and decided the

Russian was a legitimate defector. The CIA Office of Security actually looks good, in contrast to its showing on some other Family Jewels, professing itself increasingly concerned with the illegality of CIA's holding a defector under these conditions. Meanwhile, the CIA Inspector General issued a survey of the Soviet Division in May 1968 that confirmed the unit was being ripped apart by the controversy over Nosenko. On October 4, 1968, Vice Admiral Taylor concluded that there was no reason to believe "that Nosenko is other than what he claimed to be."[10] Taylor's memorandum shows the FBI used Nosenko's information to open or develop nine different espionage cases.

Helms assembled the constellation of officials concerned with this matter later that month and again in January 1969, finally ruling that Nosenko should be released and even given a contract as a CIA consultant. Freed in March 1969, Nosenko was eventually given a $150,000 settlement ($953,000 in 2012 dollars) by the CIA, and he became a consultant both to Langley and the FBI. But Helms told the House Select Committee on Assassinations in 1978 that he had never reached *any* final conclusion on Nosenko's bona fides or signed a document containing such a judgment.[11] Indeed, in 1975 James Angleton, by then in retirement, gave the Rockefeller Commission a paper baldly asserting that the question of Nosenko's bona fides "has been permitted to fester without any authoritative conclusion because it is an interagency problem affecting other Soviet Bloc cases which are controlled elsewhere in the community."[12]

This is not the place for a detailed recitation of the mole hunt of which the Nosenko case formed a part. The hunt generated mountains of paper at Langley, both within Angleton's staff and the Soviet Division. Interested readers may follow the affair in the substantial literature that has developed around it.[13] Director of Central Intelligence Stansfield Turner comments, "After reading the Hart study of

Nosenko and thoroughly studying the CIA's involvement in drug testing, I realized how far dedicated but unsupervised people could go wrong in the name of doing good intelligence work."[14] In 1978 Nosenko himself, John Hart, and Helms testified on the matter before the House assassinations committee. Nosenko also gave his views on the KGB and Lee Harvey Oswald—an angle about which CIA had been remarkably reticent when the Warren Commission conducted its original investigation.

In an April 1978 order, CIA Director Stansfield Turner overruled his Directorate of Administration (what is today the Directorate of Support) to order inclusion of the Nosenko case in training top CIA managers. Admiral Turner instructed, "If you and I don't take every precaution to ensure that [something like Nosenko] doesn't happen again, we could be endangering the Agency's future."[15]

In the heat of today's controversies, there are no doubt CIA people who wish they had had a management attitude like this. One lesson of the Nosenko Family Jewel is that activities that involve abuse are not merely disturbing to the public. Intelligence officers are conscientious people and have their own feelings on morals and appropriate behavior. Contentious operations create disputes within the agency, not just outside it. Both winners and losers in these power struggles may become sources of leaks that breach secrecy and reveal Family Jewels. The *character* of an intelligence operation bears its own consequences.

The lesson the denizens of Langley chose to learn from Nosenko was different: that if hard measures are to be used, best to do so beyond the reach of U.S. law. Thus in the war on terror the CIA secret prisons were created *outside* the United States in part to avoid the legal complications that bedeviled Langley in the Nosenko affair. But the spooks missed another point: the KU/Bark Manual actually did not go far enough— it is the *use* of coercion, not whether it is authorized, that creates jeopardy, and that jeopardy extends beyond the CIA to implicate the entire United States government, indeed the nation itself. The war on terror would make that abundantly clear.

A nother lesson came during Bill Clinton's presidency. This time the scene moved to Guatemala, and the precept was that vulnerability could result even from the acts of others, allies in the CIA enterprise. Guatemala had long been the locale for armed conflict. The covert operation the CIA had sponsored there in 1954 to overthrow the elected government had not introduced stability. The CIA-backed leader would be assassinated in 1957, followed by decades of coups or attempted coups, disputed elections, or other ones coupled with right-wing violence. In the late 1960s the "White Hand," a shadowy network of rightist militants, began to disappear liberal and populist figures. When conservative governments held sway, the militant network morphed into government death squads. A succession of leftist or peasant guerrilla organizations emerged to oppose the Guatemalan regime. The troubles were not exactly a civil war; they amounted more nearly to a government effort to suppress indigenous Indians. The peasantry defended itself with what arms it could. There was never any possibility the resistance might defeat the oligarchs. But there also seemed no chance the government could overcome the rebellion. Settlement talks were underway by the early 1990s. Factions across the political spectrum attempted to influence the process through violence, with the clear advantage in the hands of right-wing elements allied with the military. Ever on the lookout for communist insurgencies, the Central Intelligence Agency wondered about the Guatemalan rebellion. Drug trafficking had also become a CIA interest and Guatemala a waypoint on the cocaine road into the United States. The agency forged close links with Guatemalan security forces. Those links led to the CIA's problem.

As the warriors fought themselves to exhaustion, there were dangers for those on the sidelines, foreigners included. United States citizens living in Guatemala were not exempt. Nine disappeared during the 1980s. In June 1990 another, Michael DeVine, was brutally murdered and his corpse found. DeVine was an eighteen-year resident of Guatemala who had developed local ties. He and his wife ran a small hotel near the town of Poptun. DeVine was returning there with beer and other supplies when he was taken by an army patrol, interrogated, and killed. Then there was Efrain Bamaca Velasquez, a rebel *comandante* with one of the resistance groups. Bamaca was captured and interrogated after a firefight with government forces in March 1992. His body was never found. Both men were kidnapped in a combat zone where one of CIA's sources was assigned. That man, Colonel Julio Roberto Alpirez, was important to the agency because he had been the chief of the Presidential Security Department, a military-dominated secret police unit under the direct control of Guatemala's leader. The CIA had been in official contact with Alpirez since 1987, when he was still with the secret police, and at some point he became a paid agent. At the time of the DeVine killing, Alpirez commanded a Guatemalan Special Forces school near Poptun. It happened that Bamaca was married to an American lawyer, Jennifer Harbury, who sought to uncover the truth about the kidnappings and killings.

The killings became problematic for Langley before Harbury started her crusade—and the CIA's problem hinged on what had not been done when the Guatemala City station, searching for information about the DeVine murder, was covering up after receiving intelligence the military had been involved. The data became the basis for United States diplomatic démarches and a partial block on aid. Guatemala responded by arresting and convicting some enlisted men and one officer for the DeVine killing. Then the agency received intelligence contradicting the official version, plus other information alleging that Colonel Alpirez had been present at DeVine's interrogation. The station passed the reports to Langley in October 1991. At headquarters this data led to referral of the case to the Department of Justice by the CIA's Office of General Counsel on November 19, 1991.

These dates were important because of CIA's responsibilities to inform others of its intelligence. Under oversight rules written into a 1980 law and solidified during and after the Iran-Contra affair (see Chapter 9), the agency was supposed to notify the Senate Select Committee on Intelligence and the House Permanent Select Committee on Intelligence fully and currently on all significant activities and findings. The CIA station in each country also had a duty to inform the United States ambassador there. Neither of these things was done in connection with Alpirez. Insofar as congressional oversight was concerned, Langley officials had actually prepared notes for a presentation to Congress on the affair but never used them. This failure to notify continued over four years despite repeated contacts with the congressional committees, including some on U.S. programs in Guatemala—where the CIA funded Guatemalan security services—and one specifically on CIA's knowledge of Guatemala's human rights record.[16]

The Bamaca disappearance took this problem to a new level. Jennifer Harbury began to shuttle to Guatemala, and she asked the United States embassy for help. The spooks at the embassy were not forthcoming. A September 1993 Defense Intelligence Agency report on Bamaca was withheld from Harbury for fourteen months. By January 1994 Harbury had nevertheless established to her satisfaction—and this was in embassy cables—that Alpirez was one of two Guatemalan officers who had tortured Bamaca. Beginning that May the CIA station received several additional reports indicating Colonel Alpirez's direct involvement. The last of these asserted that Alpirez actually killed Bamaca. The colonel had a reputation among the Guatemalan military as a loose cannon—some held this was why he had been reassigned out of the Presidential Security Department—so a January 1995 report that he had done the killing, though secondhand, was considered credible.

Agency Inspector General Frederick Hitz was brought into this matter on January 17, 1995, when acting CIA director Admiral William Studeman discovered the Guatemala station had sat on the last Alpirez report for days before forwarding it to headquarters. Jennifer Harbury's public crusade was making this a high-profile issue, Studeman knew, and the station's inaction automatically raised questions. Studeman relieved station chief Fred Brugger and ordered up the IG investigation. He sent the intelligence to Congress immediately. Fred Hitz, reviewing the substantive material, ultimately decided other evidence called the report into question.[17]

But that did not excuse the CIA station's delays in reporting to headquarters, its failure to keep the U.S. ambassador in the picture, or Langley's tardiness in informing Congress. Hitz may have questioned the association of a CIA agent with Bamaca's torture, but he also confirmed the systematic failure at both station and headquarters. Latin America Division chief Terry Ward accepted the responsibility. The investigation was ongoing in late March when Senator Robert G. Torricelli (D-NJ) publicly charged a cover-up. After that the pressures on CIA became immense. The Senate oversight committee raked Admiral Studeman over the coals in public session. The press quickly discovered information about the various failures in CIA reporting.

President William J. Clinton reacted almost immediately. On March 24 the White House announced the removal of station chief Brugger and added that President Clinton would order the dismissal of anyone at the CIA found to have deliberately withheld information. A week later Clinton ordered his Intelligence Oversight Board (IOB), the highest-level presidential monitoring mechanism for secret activities, to conduct its own review. The CIA's internal investigation lasted through the summer of 1995, the IOB inquiry through June 1996. The Board found that the CIA had paid little attention to allegations of abuse when vetting its agents, and had given Congress a lopsided impression of progress on human rights by submitting semiannual reports that emphasized positive developments while maintaining silence on abuses. Jennifer Harbury continued her crusade, and her road led to the Supreme Court, where she was finally unable to enforce accountability.

Meanwhile, in September 1995, a new CIA director, John M. Deutch, took action on the basis of the Hitz report. Deutch made the trek to Capitol Hill to declare, "I have made it clear to all levels that I shall insist that the CIA and other elements of the Intelligence Community keep Congress 'fully and currently informed.'" Director Deutch issued fresh orders on vetting prospective agents and fresh provisions for "ambassadorial notification," plus he created new mechanisms for timely notice to Congress. Deutch disciplined a dozen CIA officers—Fred Brugger and Terry Ward were sent into retirement.[18] The following year a directive systematized arrangements for congressional information. Under these, each agency division periodically reviewed its operational activities and prepared materials to forward to the spy chieftain. The CIA director made final determinations on which items to send Congress.

The Guatemala affair was a Family Jewel of the Clinton years. The abuses of CIA allies had been abetted by agency officers' attempts to keep the lid on the matter. Langley's response—new regulations for agents plus stringent rules for informing Congress—was not popular. CIA insiders groused that strictures on recruiting agents crippled collection, since bad guys were the best sources. The contradictions between upholding human rights versus aggressive spying remained largely unexplored—a dilemma that carried over into the war on terror and contributed to the making of another Family Jewel. In 2000 Terry Ward, whose sterling reputation among spooks had not suffered from falling on his sword over Guatemala, was quietly summoned to CIA and awarded a medal. In the wake of the September 11 attacks, Ward would be recalled for active service. As for the rules on informing Congress, following 9/11 they were thrown overboard.

After 9/11 it was more than regulations that were thrown overboard. Indeed, the Central Intelligence Agency seems to have forgotten—or purposefully ignored—the lessons it had learned. All the elements that had made Yuri Nosenko's treatment so damaging to the CIA of the 1960s were replicated. The black prisons, the planes shuttling detainees among secret sites, the hostile interrogations (now under the euphemism "enhanced interrogation techniques"), and the degrading physical treatment of individuals added up to a pile of Family Jewels. The agency heaped them up with its "rendering" of prisoners to third countries and its intrusive operations in cooperating nations. Suspected enemies were not merely arrested in sweeps with the assistance of friendly police and security services, people were kidnapped right off the street in foreign lands. Nosenko had been a single individual subjected to inhumane treatment. Now the outrageous methods were applied a hundredfold.

The September 11 attacks were quite properly viewed as a major challenge to American national security. The entire government apparatus went into high gear to prevent additional attacks and apprehend terrorists of the group Al

Qaeda, quickly identified as the perpetrators. For the CIA, that meant pushing its spies to produce new leads, and activating all its alliances with intelligence services in other countries to arrest or neutralize terrorists of every stripe. According to George J. Tenet, the Director of Central Intelligence at the time, within six months of 9/11 roughly 2,500 real or suspected terrorists were taken into custody across the globe, most by foreign security services, but many by local authorities cooperating with CIA.

Terrorism was not a new problem. Langley had been increasing its capacity in this area for many years. Already in the early 1990s, the agency had created what it called the Counter-Terrorist Center (CTC), a unit designed to bring together both analysts and operators, creating a focal point for intelligence collection on terrorism, reporting to understand it, and an action arm to combat this enemy. The neutralization campaign begun after 9/11 relied on CTC's data, and the most important endeavors utilized its operators.

The initial mass street sweeping mostly amounted to a security exercise. It did not meet the need to track down the perpetrators of 9/11 and other horrific terrorist attacks that had already taken place, whom the CIA soon called "high value detainees" (HVDs), or to produce what Langley saw as "actionable intelligence" on particular terrorists and groups. Al Qaeda was known to reside in Afghanistan. The United States invaded Afghanistan in October 2001, but it did not succeed in wrapping up the Al Qaeda network. At the battle of Tora Bora that December, Afghan partisans fighting alongside the U.S. pulled their punches, the U.S. military command refused to commit regular troops, and Pakistani soldiers did not block their side of the border, leading to the escape of the most dangerous terrorists into Pakistan.

Led by its Counter-Terrorist Center, the CIA then began an intensive operation to locate and capture the leaders. Within days of 9/11, the redoubtable Dick Cheney, now vice president of the United States, set the tone, telling a television interviewer, "We've got to spend time in the shadows in the intelligence world. A lot of what needs to be done here will have to be done quietly, without any discussion, using sources and methods that are available to our intelligence agencies." It would, he said, be a walk on "the dark side."[19]

How dark was illustrated a couple of months later. A Gulfstream V executive jet landed at Bromma, Stockholm's international airport, on the evening of December 19. The plane had already been to Cairo, where it picked up a couple of Egyptian officials, and when it landed at Bromma it disgorged a CIA team. They took custody of a pair of Egyptian nationals from Swedish security police. The Egyptians were put in prison coveralls, chained, hooded, sedated, and hustled aboard the Gulfstream, which took off just over an hour later. This was the first recorded incidence of something that became ubiquitous in the "war on terror"—ghost planes in the night, CIA teams to snatch suspects or take over detainees, long flights carrying HVDs to destinations they never knew. In this case the Gulfstream headed back to Cairo, where the prisoners disappeared into the maws of the Egyptian secret police.

The first known operation of this kind had occurred in 1985, when the United States had transferred the hijackers of the cruise ship *Achille Lauro* from Egypt to Italy. A couple of years later another terrorist hijacker had been brought from Cyprus to the United States. Relying on new law and court decisions, from the early 1990s the U.S. acted as a kind of international posse, usually in conjunction with foreign allies, to apprehend wanted fugitives, delivering them to countries where they would be incarcerated or tried. The capture of the terrorist Carlos Ramirez Sanchez ("the Jackal") in the Sudan in 1994 was an example. Another, taken in 1997, was Mir Amal Kansi, the CIA murderer who had shot up agency employees during morning rush hour outside

Langley headquarters. The act came to be known as "rendition." During the Clinton administration there were some rules. Suspects would not be "rendered" to lands where they might be tortured, or worse, and the actions were kept secret only during the active phase of the operations. Seventy persons were rendered this way, twenty of them to trial in the United States. State Department annual reports on global terrorism trends listed renditions—by name and where captives were sent—for the previous year. After 9/11 rendition disappeared into the shadows of a secret compartment. The act would be called "extraordinary rendition" by the Bush administration even if not at CIA. The rules were abolished. Renditions were not acknowledged, much less announced. Langley acted in concert with others sometimes, but unilaterally where it preferred to control interrogations directly.

The first notorious rendition took place in Pakistan. With Counter-Terrorist Center intelligence and FBI eavesdropping, by March 2002 the CIA had identified a wide array of suspected Al Qaeda safe houses. Here there was local cooperation. A Pakistani security officer actually provided the crucial information, tracing a telephone wire to a nearby house that proved to be the real enemy hideout. On March 27, 2002, late in the afternoon (Washington date and time; 1 a.m. on the 28th in Pakistan), Pakistani authorities simultaneously raided sixteen places that on the basis of the U.S. surveillance information could have been Al Qaeda safe houses. Islamabad station chief Robert Grenier supervised the operation. FBI special agents accompanied some field units, CIA officers others. At the Shahbaz Cottage, a gaudily painted building in Faisalabad, the Americans struck gold. Circumstances are disputed between John Kiriakou, a CIA team leader with one of the Pakistani takedown units, and Jose Rodriguez, chief of operations for the Counter-Terrorist Center.[20] Kiriakou reports leading the CIA team with the Faisalabad assault unit. Rodriguez insists Kiriakou accompanied a different team.

There was a shootout in the terrorists' second-floor apartment, in the stairwell, and on the roof. Among those captured was Abu Zubaydah, whose name, CIA Director George Tenet relates, "had been all over our threat reporting" even before 9/11.[21] Zubaydah was hit in the leg, stomach, and groin. Rodriguez insists Zubaydah's injuries were inflicted by a single bullet ricocheting through his body. Pakistani special forces wanted to kill Zubaydah in revenge for the loss of one of their men in the gun battle. Kiriakou convinced the Pakistani commander to take the terrorist to the hospital instead. Rodriguez gives him no credit for that. Zubaydah would have died except that Kiriakou stanched the bleeding long enough for doctors to stabilize him. Here was an enemy who seemed worth the effort. After Grenier's appeals, Pakistani authorities handed over the wounded man. Alvin B. Krongard, Langley's executive director, happened to be on the board of Johns Hopkins University Hospital, which lent the CIA a top surgeon to treat Zubaydah. The—classified—place where Zubaydah was taken was in, shall we say, Thailand.

Abu Zubaydah's capture crystallized an American dilemma. What to do with HVDs had been a sore point all along. The Pakistanis had captured another man, Ibn al-Shaykh al-Libi, in the borderlands during December, and that fellow had been taken to the U.S. military prison at Bagram air base in Afghanistan. But al-Libi, erstwhile chief of an Al Qaeda training camp, had been an unknown when taken, his identity discovered only when his particulars were fed through intelligence databases. Holding him at a regular military facility was okay until the CIA knew who he was. After that it endangered security—too many would see al-Libi, note he was treated differently, and wonder why. So he was handed over to the Egyptians, who tortured him. That cast doubt on al-Libi's information, and the detainee later recanted his confession. That could not happen again. Zubaydah had been targeted. For CIA, Bagram was out of the question.

Another factor consumed Washington. In previous high-profile terrorist cases, like that of the truck bombing of a United States barracks in Saudi Arabia in 1995, or the boat bombing of a U.S. warship at Aden in 2000, CIA and FBI investigators had been frustrated because Saudi and Yemeni local authorities restricted their access to terrorist suspects. The Americans were desperate to conduct unilateral interrogations. That could only be done at a U.S.-controlled facility. This was the origin of the notorious CIA "black prisons." The first was merely a safe house, the place where the agency took Abu Zubaydah as soon as it was okay to get him out of Pakistan. Jose Rodriguez of the Counter-Terrorist Center cleared the project with the Thais, arranged for construction of a prison facility within the same house, and traveled to Thailand to check on the arrangements personally.

The point of unilateral interrogations was to manage all aspects of the approach to the detainee, as well as focus the questioning precisely as American inquisitors wished. It also permitted unlimited follow-up and re-interrogation. Two elements were keys to success: the state of knowledge of the background and particulars of an HVD—the intelligence—and the methods of interrogation. Prior knowledge was not a trivial matter. Consider the Nosenko case: in working against the KGB, the CIA had acquired extensive operational experience plus the benefit of long years of data collection with attendant opportunity to accumulate files. One reason for doubts about Nosenko was that so many of his assertions could be checked against this knowledge base and found wanting.

By contrast, U.S. intelligence against Al Qaeda was in its infancy. For a long time in the 1990s, the CIA could not even agree whether Osama bin Laden functioned as a commander or merely a financier. The situation with Abu

Zubaydah was similar. Some thought him the Al Qaeda field commander who had taken over after the November 2001 death of Mohammed Atef (see Chapter 6); others saw Zubaydah as the group's logistics chief. Many agreed that he was a senior leader. One view was that the man was a mastermind who had not only trained operatives but authored the Al Qaeda textbook on resisting interrogation. Others viewed Abu Zubaydah as not even an Al Qaeda member, but more a hanger-on and facilitator, who functioned as travel agent and arranged the movements of the 9/11 plotters, among others. Jose Rodriguez insists that Zubaydah's actual status was a meaningless distinction—and it was—*except* that Americans might harbor much greater enmity for someone they thought Al Qaeda versus another who was not.

Reactions to the Zubaydah capture reflect the uncertainties. Operatives of the Counter-Terrorist Center showed a photo of the wounded man to a source who told them the detainee was not Abu Zubaydah after all. As a result, according to FBI inquisitor Ali Soufan, the CTC literally missed the plane—they failed to put an interrogation team on the Gulfstream sent to retrieve Zubaydah from Pakistan. The FBI did not repeat that error. Soufan made the CIA flight along with the Johns Hopkins doctor and other Bureau specialists. As a result it was the FBI, not the agency, that got the first crack at the captive.[22]

Understanding who Zubaydah was had consequences for CIA's expectations for what he would know. A basic problem in the entire terrorism interrogation mess is that hopes for what the detainee must know, should know, might know, ought to be expected to know, too often substituted for questioning built from a solid knowledge base. No doubt this factor diminished later on, but in 2002 it was rampant. When the detainee did not answer as anticipated, the response was to think he was lying. Then the inquisitors would want to force out the "truth"—and they thought they had an instrument for that. On the assumption that all detainees would lie, in December 2001 a pair of psychologist consultants to the CIA had proposed a design for interrogations that would break down the captive, make him dependent on the inquisitors, and supposedly elicit what the agency wanted. Proposed measures included stripping the HVDs naked; depriving them of sleep; putting them in discomfiting "stress positions" for prolonged periods; subjecting them to heat and cold, loud music, intense questioning in very lengthy sessions, grabbing by the neck, pushing against the wall, facial slaps, belly slaps, confinement in a box; and even pretending to drown them in a technique called "waterboarding."

Many of these same methods had been used against Yuri Nosenko without affecting his story. Such techniques had long been rejected in the CIA's own "KU/Bark Manual." Several of these, in particular waterboarding, are torture. American military men had been court-martialed for waterboarding in the Philippine insurrection of 1899–1902. Japanese were sent up for war crimes on the same basis after World War II. The method had been popular during the Spanish Inquisition and plainly understood as torture then. Psychological manipulations can be tantamount to torture as well. Torture is illegal under United States law, international treaty, and the Geneva Conventions, which prohibit any action that has the purpose or effect of dehumanizing a person. In the CIA's terror war program, these things were sanitized by the euphemism "enhanced interrogation techniques." By definition, strong-arm methods meant flirting with Family Jewels.

Meanwhile, the FBI interrogation team of Ali Soufan and Steven Gaudin were actually questioning Abu Zubaydah. According to Soufan, they achieved good results: the captive gave up the name and *nom de guerre* of Al Qaeda commander Khalid Sheik Mohammed, the real mastermind of the 9/11 plot; the name of American citizen and terrorist wannabe

Jose Padilla, soon arrested on his return to Chicago; and leads to a terror plot that could be broken up. Rodriguez disputes Soufan's account of the questioning, alleging not only that it was CIA, not FBI, which elicited information from Zubaydah, but even that the detainee objected to Soufan's methods, not those of the agency. For good measure Rodriguez accuses his FBI counterparts of an obsession with obtaining trial evidence, not intelligence.[23] These disputes cannot be resolved on the basis of the public record to this point, but eventually data should emerge that will provide greater precision.

Back at the Counter-Terrorist Center, operations chief Rodriguez called in one of the agency's psychologist consultants and gave him a contract to advise CIA's own team, sent to question Zubaydah once the inquisition was underway.

In Washington the high command of the secret war huddled on its instructions to the field. George J. Tenet writes, "It took until August to get clear guidance on what Agency officers could legally do."[24] That statement cloaks a darker reality. It is logical—and apparent from the account by national security advisor Condoleezza Rice—that an initial meeting on methods took place immediately upon Abu Zubaydah's capture. She recounts that President Bush asked whether the proposed interrogation program was necessary and if it would be legal. The president ordered senior officials to discuss the matter with CIA. Vice President Cheney, Attorney General John Ashcroft, Rice, and her deputy saw Tenet that same afternoon. An investigation by the Senate Armed Services Committee confirms that the agency sought this approval in the spring of 2002.[25] Dick Cheney affirms the process consumed several months and resulted in legal opinions. "George said that he would argue to the President that the program was necessary," Rice notes. "He explained in general what techniques he would recommend, including waterboarding, and the safeguards that would be employed, including the presence of medical personnel."[26] Ashcroft promised the Justice Department would review the techniques for legality.

In May there was another high-level meeting, at which the CIA reported it believed Abu Zubaydah was withholding information. The agency listed specific coercive countermeasures. Jose Rodriguez recounts taking a team from his shop to an NSC Principals meeting with those officials, plus Alberto Gonzales, where the CTC described its aggressive methods in detail. "I got the sense from no one," Rodriguez writes, "that our menu of techniques had gone too far."[27] In June the CTC operations chief commissioned his consultants to convert their interrogation design into an actual program. The prisoner would be checked by doctors as questioning proceeded. Much like Pete Bagley with Yuri Nosenko, the CIA considered that medical observation somehow excused inquisitors' behavior. In any case, the policy moved forward. NSC lawyer John Bellinger raised objections but did not press them.

Legal advice fell to John Yoo, the one lawyer at DOJ's Office of Legal Counsel with Top Secret clearance. Work on a preliminary version of his study began in April with minimal help from others. On July 13 CIA lawyers met with Gonzales and Bellinger of the White House plus FBI and Justice officials to study the plan. Four days later Director Tenet saw Condoleezza Rice. She delivered the word: the CIA could proceed, provided the Justice Department agreed. That was fine with Tenet, anxious to protect officers from criminal jeopardy. On July 24 John Yoo called the CIA attorney's office to report that Ashcroft would approve the proposed methods.

At Justice, John Yoo produced a pair of new drafts. These went to his superior, Jay S. Bybee, for final review. The memos eventually bore his name. Bybee later maintained he had had minimal time to examine them because Langley insisted it needed to start the coercive interrogation at the beginning of August. The Justice Department met that deadline. Its approval took the form of one paper sent to CIA lawyer John Rizzo, making legal arguments to support a specific set of techniques the agency had proposed, plus a letter to White House lawyer Alberto R. Gonzales summarizing this material, finding bases for legal defenses against war crimes charges, and covering a copy of the longer opinion.

A detailed critique of the Yoo memos, their arguments, or the fashion in which they were compiled is beyond our scope here. They have been extensively picked apart by experts.[28] The papers built on Yoo's expansive vision of presidential power. They constructed novel definitions of pain and suffering to argue that various forms of injury inflicted on a person would not fall into prohibited categories, and approved the CIA's list of aggressive measures. All this was disgraceful—the Yoo memos would be rescinded by the Justice Department later, Attorney General Michael B. Mukasey would publicly label them a "mistake," and the lawyers involved remain under a cloud. More important for present purposes are three points: First is the flaw in a system that could construe a Justice Department opinion as tantamount to a Supreme Court decision legalizing torture. Second, the CIA not only took the Justice paper as a hunting license against detainees, it either misrepresented the severity of the interrogation methods it intended to employ, or else it exceeded in practice what had been proposed in theory. Third—and also essential—reading between the lines suggests *the CIA did not wait for the Justice Department go-ahead* to begin strong-arming detainees.

A s with other aspects of the war on terror, there are questions as to how well the Bush administration met its obligation to keep the congressional oversight committees fully and currently informed. Langley later produced several different documents detailing when the agency reckoned that Congress had been told of various developments.[29] In one, CIA described George Bush's marching orders, his presidential finding on October 3, 2001; and mentions notifying Congress of Abu Zubaydah's capture on April 15, 2002. There was no mention of interrogation methods. A second CIA list, explicitly titled "Interrogation Briefings to the Hill," records meetings with both the House and Senate committees on April 24, including "references to techniques." This document confirms the questioning of Abu Zubaydah had already begun, and it notes the presence of Nancy Pelosi, the ranking minority member on the House side.

Much later, in 2009, amid bitter controversy over who in Congress had been told of CIA torture, and when, and how much they knew, Langley made public a supposedly definitive list captioned "Member Briefings on Enhanced Interrogation Techniques." Langley's 2009 document dropped any reference to the April 24, 2002, congressional briefings. The controversy of that moment revolved around Representative Pelosi, by then speaker of the House, whom the CIA listed as attending a September 4, 2002, meeting where torture methods were described. Jose Rodriguez specifically claims that he led the agency team at the briefing, that by this point Abu Zubaydah was a compliant detainee, that CTC officers detailed all the interrogation methods employed on him, and that Nancy Pelosi attended.[30] Pelosi insists she did not learn of waterboarding until February 2003, and even then was given the impression the methods were legally approved but not necessarily in use against detainees. Porter J. Goss, the House committee chairman in 2002, who would follow George Tenet at the head of the CIA, weighed in with his recollection that techniques had been thoroughly aired that September and both Republican and Democratic leaders had supported them.[31] Criticism of Pelosi raged. Senator Jay Rockefeller IV, of the Senate's oversight panel, questioned the accuracy of CIA's record, pointing out a different error: he had received the torture talk on September 4, 2003, though

Langley's document had him in an earlier entry, marked as receiving a "later individual briefing."[32]

It appears that Nancy Pelosi was right. The CIA document "Interrogation Briefings," only declassified in 2010, has Representative Jane Harman, not Pelosi, attending the September 2002 briefing. Moreover, the contents of the agency's record of a February 2003 meeting indicates it was only *then* that Congress was told of the Yoo memos, hence waterboarding. Pelosi *could not* have learned of waterboarding at the House committee meeting that she attended in April 2002. The Porter Goss commentary cited above actually makes no specific assertion of Pelosi's presence, glossing over the matter by referring only to the minority political party. In the context of the dispute over Representative Pelosi, in addition, the juxtaposition of CIA's two lists raises other questions, as does the Rodriguez memoir. The agency operative dates the inception of the harsh methods to June 2002, but confirms that Abu Zubaydah was under interrogation using several different techniques from shortly after his capture.

Amid the controversy over Pelosi, another key point has gone unnoticed. The April 24 CIA briefing sessions were open to the full oversight committees on both the House and Senate sides and did include mention of interrogations. The documents make clear—and Porter Goss's article confirms—that subsequent briefings, beginning in September 2002, were restricted to the Gang of Four. Thus a subject that had been within bounds for intelligence oversight was suddenly restricted. The committees would not be "fully and currently informed" of CIA torture until late 2006. To its use of illegal techniques, papered over with dubious legal opinions, the CIA added minimization of intelligence oversight. The cutting of this Family Jewel was complete within a year of the 9/11 attacks.

By far the worst aspect of all this is that it evaded proper legislative superintendence. The notification rules put in place after the painful Guatemalan affair were honored in form but robbed of content. What Congress was told consistently ran behind what CIA was doing—except where it was a matter of claiming credit. Langley briefed quickly on the capture of Abu Zubaydah, but waited months until broaching how he was being treated. By restricting *that* information to the Gang of Four, the CIA pulled a curtain of secrecy over its actions. As with the NSA's eavesdropping, it was impossible for the Four to conduct meaningful oversight. The Bush administration approach was quite deliberate. Its point was to retain freedom of action. With Family Jewels, manipulations of the record always serve a purpose.

M eanwhile, back in March 2002, the questioning of terrorist Abu Zubaydah began before he left the hospital and continued throughout his time in Thailand. Thus, the interrogation was in progress *for four months* before John Yoo's legal opinion even existed. At first the inquisitors were the FBI team. Ali Soufan recounts getting important early information from Zubaydah, adding that Director Tenet was amazed this intel began flowing without the aggressive methods.[33] Dick Cheney admits this was the case.[34] Asking that congratulations be sent to the CIA interrogation team, Tenet was dismayed to learn the Counter-Terrorist Center (CTC) had yet to put any inquisitors in place and it was the FBI that was securing the intelligence. A CTC team was on the next plane to Bangkok. The group included a questioner, a polygrapher, an agency psychologist, and one of the private contractors who had proposed the strong-arm methods. When CIA began to use them, Abu Zubaydah clammed up. A cable exchanged between Langley and the field in late April shows the CIA was already taping interrogation sessions.[35] In an "EYES ONLY" cable on May 6, headquarters issued explicit instructions for handling the videotapes, noting, "though we recognize that the tapes might be cumbersome to store, they offer evidence of Abu Zubaydah's condition/treatment . . . that may be of value in the future (apart from actionable intelligence)."[36]

The CIA interrogations stalled. The private contractor tried nudity, loud music, then sleep deprivation. The contractor, who had never actually interrogated anyone before, applied increasingly harsh methods with no effect. In frustration, agency officers gave way to the FBI team, which again succeeded in getting information from Zubaydah. But CIA analysts questioned their product, while Langley pressed to implement its strong-arm program. In June the FBI interrogators, not willing to be part of this any longer, returned to the United States. Then the agency started in with its euphemistically termed "enhanced interrogation techniques." Before the CIA was done with Abu Zubaydah, he would be waterboarded eighty-three times.

Clandestine service officers, Jose A. Rodriguez felt, needed to be defended forcefully. Once, at a retreat called for senior agency officers to clear the air, Rodriguez darkly warned critics to get out of the way of those at the "pointy" end of the spear. That is certainly where he put himself. By 2002 Rodriguez had spent a quarter of a century with the agency's spooky arm. In Washington without an assignment on September 11, 2001, Rodriguez had rushed to Langley and pitched in to help at CTC. He made himself indispensable to Cofer Black, then the unit's boss, and was soon the effective operations chief for the Center. Born in Mayaguez, Puerto Rico, Rodriguez also considered himself the top *puertorriqueño* at the CIA, though there he had competition from Carmen Medina, a rising star in Langley's intelligence directorate. Rodriguez was an operations officer, a spy. He had spent his entire career in the Latin America

Division. Counterterrorism was what he fell into after 9/11, but he threw himself at the problem without skipping a beat. The Counter-Terrorist Center was moving quickly on rendition, and the function of an operations chief, the third man in a CIA unit, was to exert direct control over field teams and serve as conduit for the boss's messages to station chiefs. With Cofer Black preoccupied managing alliances with foreign security services, the fifty-four-year-old Rodriguez inevitably became the major player supervising day-to-day operations.

The Counter-Terrorist Center was riding high. According to human rights reports and international flight records, Abu Zubaydah's capture was just one of thirty-nine renditions carried out between 9/11 and mid-2002, and CTC could also take credit for the elimination of an Al Qaeda commander killed by drone in Afghanistan, and another terrorist leader dispatched the same way in Yemen. It was a time of change at the Center, with a huge influx of personnel, expanded missions, and a plethora of fresh responsibilities. The CTC conference room morphed into an operations center and then into an Al Qaeda task force office. The Center's rank and file mushroomed from 300 to 1,500, both analysts and operators. There were desks in the hallway of its first-floor office suite. Cofer Black, nearing the end of his tour, was set to retire, and soon pulled away to prepare for the inevitable public investigation of agency failures before September 11. Henry Crumpton, the erstwhile CTC deputy director, had been drafted away to lead the CIA's field operation in Afghanistan, then went to the State Department as government-wide counterterror coordinator. Ben Bonk, his replacement, was an analyst. Given the need for an experienced hand at the helm of CTC, and the high prestige the Center had gained, George Tenet promoted Jose Rodriguez to head CTC in May 2002.

No question but that Rodriguez loved the work. Emulating Cofer Black, he spanned the globe, touching base with CIA units, leaving many day-to-day tasks in the hands of his deputy or chief of operations. There were new agency operations centers distributed around the world to be established under Black's program for cooperation with key allies. The CTC had a big piece of that action. The black prisons had to be fashioned from whole cloth. In due course the Thai government tired of hosting a CIA prison and demanded changes. There Rodriguez had an assist from Kyle D. ("Dusty") Foggo, chief of the agency's logistics base in Frankfurt. Foggo, approached in the spring of 2003, helped with the next set of prisons, set up in Morocco, Romania, and Lithuania. Some prisoners were returned to Bagram after all. Later facilities were established in Poland and perhaps Egypt. The air support infrastructure had to be regularized for ghost planes to be routinely available. And, of course, CIA officers long trained using the KU/Bark Manual needed convincing that "enhanced interrogation techniques" were necessary. Rodriguez was the ringmaster, proselytizing, commanding, demanding, and imploring everywhere he went. He pulled CTC into the new era.

Under Jose Rodriguez, CTC activity accelerated to blazing speed. The 9/11 plotters Khalid Sheik Mohammed and Ramzi bin al-Shibh were apprehended on the basis of information from Abu Zubaydah, as was Binyam Mohamed. The Indonesian terrorist leader Hambali was taken in the summer of 2003. There were fifty renditions in all on Rodriguez's CTC watch, in addition to all the garden variety arrests by various countries' security services acting alongside the Central Intelligence Agency.

As for CIA torture, the water was boiling on that within months. The interrogation of Abu Zubaydah was ongoing. He was actually judged compliant prior to his final waterboarding session, but was subjected to the procedure anyway. Another terrorist, Abd el-Rahim al-Nashiri, became the audience for a mock execution. Guards fired a gun outside his cell and al-Nashiri was conducted down the hall past a CIA man, shackled and hooded, lying on the floor pretending to be dead. He was also threatened with an electric drill. Dismayed officers complained up the line. The agency's director of operations, James L. Pavitt, informed the Inspector General John Helgerson and asked for an IG inquiry. And yet Jose Rodriguez believes the cruelest thing done to al-Nashiri was when two of his CIA inquisitors blew cigar smoke in his face.[37]

Langley now put the interrogation program on a more formal basis. Jim Pavitt sent a team to Thailand for a firsthand look at procedures. The agency instituted a training course for prospective inquisitors in November 2002. Meanwhile, CIA's top lawyers audited the interrogation tapes.[38] The goal was to check them against logbooks and the daily cables updating headquarters, ensuring the written record corresponded to what the tapes showed. The tapes themselves could then be destroyed. Lawyer John McPherson of the Office of General Counsel (OGC) did the work. There were ninety-two tapes, thirty-one of Zubaydah, the rest of Nashiri. A CIA record of Helgerson's interview with an OGC lawyer— his name deleted but presumably McPherson—reveals that the tape review was uneven. McPherson found the labeling spotty, some tapes undated, others with nothing but start times. He had to put them in some kind of order. Some tapes contained just a half hour or so of content, some were blank, on some the audio or video was poor. Others had clearly been repeatedly started and stopped. The lawyer maintained he had watched the whole set, either in real time or at fast forward.[39] On January 9, 2003, McPherson wrote a memo that concluded the written records accurately reflected the tapes. The Helgerson investigation, by contrast, established that nearly a dozen tapes were blank, two had only a couple of minutes recorded, and another pair were broken. No tapes documented a twenty-one-hour period featuring two waterboarding sessions.[40] Inspector General John Helgerson issued one report specifically on the Nashiri case and another on the interrogations overall. He began to meet with Rodriguez on a routine basis, once a month.

This tape review was preliminary to new moves to legitimate the High Value Detainee (HVD) Program. Director Tenet gathered the key players on January 10. Agency General Counsel Scott Muller described recent meetings with White House, NSC, and Justice Department officials, including presidential counsel Alberto Gonzales. Muller also reported McPherson's conclusions from the videotapes. Tenet decided to have them destroyed. In preparation for that, on January 28 he issued directives governing both black prisons and interrogations. Counterterror chief Rodriguez was to be responsible for crafting a plan to destroy the tapes while keeping the congressional oversight committees and White House on board.

On February 4 and 5 James Pavitt led the CIA delegation briefing the Gang of Four. Both Jose Rodriguez and Scott Muller went with him. The meeting record indicates this was the first time Congress was told that aggressive interrogation had been "approved by a bevy of lawyers," making more of the John Yoo papers than they deserved. For the first time also, Pavitt and Rodriguez admitted CIA had videotapes of detainee interrogations. The agency also notified Congress of the inquisitors' excesses during the interrogation of HVD Nashiri. Rodriguez sat mute as Pavitt spoke disparagingly of the mock execution incident and added he had asked the Inspector General to look into it. (Rodriguez says nothing of this episode in his memoir.) Stanley Moskowitz, CIA's congressional liaison, rejected a bid by the Senate oversight committee to conduct an independent assessment of the HVD Program. Both Zubaydah and Nashiri were described as fonts of useful information. Muller mentioned his comparison of the tapes with records and reported the correspondence was "perfect." He went on to portray CIA officers as concerned that the tapes might endanger themselves and their families.

Then Muller disclosed that the agency wished to destroy them. Senator Pat Roberts is reported as agreeing with that proposition. On the House side the record is yet to be declassified. Vice-Chairwoman Jane Harman opposed any attempt to get rid of the tapes. Nancy Pelosi, her successor, has said she did the same. Press reports suggest that Porter Goss opposed the move while he was still in Congress, but Jose Rodriguez insists Goss supported the destruction.[41]

Faced with objections, the CIA dropped its plans for the moment. Counter-Terrorist Center operations continued apace. Early in March the Pakistanis captured the true architect of 9/11, Khalid Sheik Mohammed, and handed him over. Nothing prevented the torture of Mohammed. "Muktar," as he was known to Al Qaeda, was waterboarded 183 times, exceeding Zubaydah's record.[42] All these prisoners were of intense interest to the 9/11 Commission, the blue ribbon panel that Congress demanded and the White House finally accepted, which would make a detailed inquiry into the September 11 attacks. The Commission asked for records of CIA's questioning of the prisoners. Following the marching orders of a White House striving to thwart the inquiry, the agency assured the panel on May 9 that it had handed over everything in its files. Langley made no mention of tapes. In June the Commission came back, asking specifically for any records pertaining to 118 named individuals. Again, no tapes.

Besides the 9/11 Commission there were the agency's own officers to worry about. Some would maintain this was all about tapes, but the true divide was over interrogation methods. Just as the FBI had walked out on Zubaydah over the techniques used by CIA inquisitors—and would do the same at Guantanamo over U.S. military methods—the agency's own officers were restive. In the case of HVD "Captus," for example, CTC officer Glenn L. Carle, the team leader, was aghast at what headquarters proposed. Carle had done fine utilizing the KU/Bark approach, but CTC wanted the detainee questioned with strong-arm techniques. Carle cabled Langley to protest. He was given no alternative.[43] Torture was illegal. Officers knew it. The tapes were a problem not because some terrorist was going to lay hands on them and chase a CIA family; the real dilemma was that they documented war crimes.

The agency's front office confronted the problem at the director's staff meetings. Tenet determined to seek fresh guarantees. At the White House one day, he asked Condoleezza Rice for a written approval. In mid-June the CIA sent the Justice Department a revised legal approval paper, one drafted at the agency. This was recycled to Langley without change as an opinion of the department's Office of Legal Counsel. The later DOJ investigation of its torture papers found that no one at Justice had originated any part of this "opinion."[44]

Langley's new push led to a full-dress White House meeting on July 29. Tenet was worried because his agency and the Bush White House had just clashed over who was responsible for a manipulation of Iraq intelligence that had led to the notorious "16 Words" inserted in the president's 2003 state of the union address that helped justify President Bush's invasion of that country. Now Tenet detailed progress and revisited the aggressive interrogation methods. The agency had set up a new training course for interrogators interviewing HVDs who were compliant. The CTC wanted freedom to mix techniques and less necessity for seeking higher approval. Attorney General Ashcroft confirmed his Justice Department had issued a revised legal memorandum. Vice President Cheney had no objections. Condi Rice saw the interrogations as a CIA show. She was encouraged at the capture of Khalid Sheik Mohammed and Ramzi bin al-Shibh: "It was a bit like having Field Marshal Erwin Rommel, the brilliant and notorious Nazi general, under lock and key in World War II."[45] A few days later CIA dispatched fresh instructions on the tapes. In early September, for the first time, Director Tenet personally led the agency briefing team that put on a slide show for the Gang of Four defending "enhanced interrogation." Ten days after that Tenet met with Colin Powell and Don Rumsfeld to coordinate their departments' support for CIA activities.

T
he agency likes to talk about "operational tempo." Jose Rodriguez achieved high tempo, and recalls the time after 9/11 as his proudest, officers working flat out, harder than ever, the best cooperation with foreign intelligence services ever, the finest technical support in his experience. Rodriguez felt his hard measures succeeded. But it was also on his watch that the CIA program spiraled out of control. European Community authorities investigated the ghost planes used for renditions; human rights organizations began to track disappearances. Along with rendering real terrorists, the CIA swept up innocents and subjected them to horrors. Even real terrorists were treated in ways that stacked up the flap potential. An Afghan detainee was beaten to death by CIA contract officer David Passaro, who would be tried for it and found guilty.

The Canadian Maher Arar, arrested while transiting Kennedy Airport, was rendered to Syria, where he was tortured without benefit of any of CIA's legal niceties. The Arar case led to deep embarrassment for the Canadian authorities working with the agency, a big cash settlement, the resignation of the head of the Royal Canadian Mounted Police, and a government commission of inquiry that found extensive abuses. Only fancy legal footwork evaded the Canadian's lawsuit directed at CIA. The case of Ibn al-Shaykh al-Libi, tortured by the Egyptians, ended in recantation, forcing an embarrassing CIA retraction of all reporting based on his information. Langley handed al-Libi over to Libya, where

Muammar Gaddafi's intelligence service, a newfound ally that cooperated for a time, kept the man under detention. Al-Libi's mysterious death in a Libyan prison followed.

In February 2003 Jose Rodriguez sent a snatch team into northern Italy to grab a Muslim cleric nicknamed Abu Omar. Egypt was the recipient of the rendition. Omar was tortured. His case led to Italian criminal prosecution of the chief of its own intelligence service along with several subordinates, plus the indictment and trial of CIA's Milan base chief, Robert S. Lady, and two dozen other agency officers or special operations assignees, among them the Rome station chief. This marked the first time in its history that CIA personnel on mission in a friendly country had been subjected to criminal prosecution. They were judged guilty and given sentences of seven to nine years in prison. The verdicts were appealed to Italy's highest court, which heard the case in July 2012. That September the court confirmed the trial verdicts. The operatives are long gone from Italy, but at least one officer's usefulness for clandestine activity has been destroyed, and the Italian legal proceedings embarrassed the CIA at each stage of the process. The headaches from this fiasco multiplied when one of the team, Sabrina DeSousa, sued the United States for not defending her before the Italian courts; in effect, this was CIA throwing its officers to the wolves. That aspect of the Abu Omar affair is also not yet resolved.

Then there was Khaled el-Masri, a German national sequestered by Macedonian security on CIA orders in January 2004. El-Masri's case was pure mistaken identity. Rendered and tortured, he was eventually freed, and the scandal led to a German parliamentary investigation and the near-filing of criminal charges against German intelligence officers who had collaborated with CIA. In the case of Binyam Mohamed, taken in Pakistan soon after Zubaydah, the scandal would blow up in the face of British intelligence. An Ethiopian granted asylum in the United Kingdom, Mohamed was tortured at Bagram air base and later at Guantanamo. His release was ultimately ordered by British courts specifically on the grounds of mistreatment. The affair led to charges of MI-6 and MI-5 complicity in torture, an official inquiry in the United Kingdom, the judicially compelled release of CIA documents, false statements by the British government in Parliament, and the apparent destruction of British records of rendition flights through Diego Garcia. Equally upsetting for the spooks, Langley was obliged to make an official admission that ghost planes had used Diego twice. Then a lawsuit against a CIA proprietary had to be suppressed by resort to the dubious "state secrets" legal doctrine. At this writing the investigation of British secret service complicity in torture continues, with further embarrassment likely to ensue.

In Poland, where one of the CIA's black prisons had been located near Szymany airport so prisoners could be flown there, the chief of the Polish intelligence service at the time, Zbigniew Siemiatkowski, was indicted in January 2012 for violations of international law by the public prosecutor's office in Krakow. Lescek Miller, then the prime minister, has also been warned he is subject to prosecution by the Polish State Tribunal on related charges. In addition, there have been Lithuanian investigations of officials who cooperated with the CIA on black prisons. European Union inquiries may be reignited as a consequence of developments in these or other cases. From the standpoint of CIA flaps, all these are booby traps waiting to explode. It is probably not surprising that in his memoir of the war on terror, Jose Rodriguez fails even to mention any of these cases. As for cooperation from foreign services, these concrete instances of legal jeopardy as a result of working with American spooks pose a far greater threat to the CIA enterprise—and U.S. national security— than many of the alleged terrorists caught up in the CIA net.

Another flap took place over the 2004 Athens Olympics. The CTC led the American contribution to Olympic security there. Jose Rodriguez was in and out of Athens before the event. His comment here is "The experience of advising the government of Greece convinced me that I might have a productive and lucrative second career ahead as a consultant."[46] Less than a year later, in what has come to be known as the "Vodaphone scandal," the Greek press reported that electronic eavesdropping, traced to receivers near the United States embassy, had been employed in Athens. The Greek government not only confirmed this, it revealed the taps had targeted cell phones of the prime minister, other senior government officials, military officers, Arab journalists, antiglobalization activists, businessmen, and even the U.S. embassy itself. Beginning just prior to the Olympics, the eavesdropping continued for six months.

The charges acquired greater precision in 2006. The pot boiled with a parliamentary inquiry. Here there was an investigation by a public prosecutor too, and a secret review by the Greek intelligence agency. By the spring of 2008 the situation had become serious enough to require the intervention of the State Department's top lawyer, John Bellinger, whom Condoleezza Rice had recruited from the NSC when President Bush appointed her secretary of state.[47] There is some irony in this: Bush loyalists privately lambasted Bellinger as a softy because he kept open channels to people who were not conservatives, most notably lunching periodically with Lloyd Cutler, former White House counsel under President Jimmy Carter. Now Bellinger's cooperation became necessary to pull the neocons' chestnuts out of the fire. His April 2008 visit was successful. The Greek government graciously excused the United States in the Vodaphone scandal, but the particulars remain highly suspicious.

For Jose Rodriguez's operatives, high operational tempo came with a huge price tag. From early 2003 through mid-2004 there was the constant worry of the Helgerson IG investigation. The inside stories of all the other scandals remain hidden, but the Abu Omar affair, with its indictments of CIA officers, obviously triggered a flap. Concerns grew about the continued cooperation of foreign intelligence services. By then Porter J. Goss had become CIA director and Rodriguez chief spy, the head of the National Clandestine Service, as the agency's espionage arm has been restyled. Director Goss wanted John Helgerson to look into the Abu Omar episode. Rodriguez convinced Goss to drop any IG inquiry.

The elephant in the room remained the existence of videotapes documenting interrogation sessions. The 9/11 Commission still pressed for information, which George Tenet specifically denied them at a lunch on December 23, 2003. A month later Tenet rejected the Commission's request for direct access to the HVDs. In April 2004 sensitivity attained even higher levels with the revelation of the military's use of torture at Abu Ghraib in Iraq. Jose Rodriguez calls this "an explosive event that added to our conviction that getting rid of the tapes was vitally necessary."[48] That observation puts the lie to CIA claims that its interest in destroying the tapes was purely for the purpose of protecting agency personnel from terrorist counterattacks. The military personnel involved in Abu Ghraib were all court-martialed and imprisoned. The CIA tapes showed identical—and worse—behavior by interrogators. But after Abu Ghraib, "getting rid of the tapes" meant destruction of evidence.

On May 11, 2004, CIA attorney Scott Muller received explicit instructions from White House lawyers David Addington and Alberto Gonzales that Langley should preserve the tapes. In July, Rodriguez and James Pavitt, the new and outgoing chiefs of the clandestine service, presented the results of the Inspector General's torture investigation to the Gang of Four. The IG's report included extensive discussion of the tapes. Scott Muller and John Helgerson disputed whether CIA techniques violated provisions of the Geneva Conventions. Muller left the CIA not long afterwards. Here was a concrete instance in which restricting presentations to Congress avoided accountability for an abuse by preventing oversight.

But the ground was shifting. When the CIA presented new requests for approvals that fall, the NSC sent back word it no longer wanted to be involved. In January 2005, nominated as attorney general in his own right, Alberto Gonzales was confronted at length about the interrogations at his Senate hearings. The Bush operative proved uninformative before Congress, but within the Justice Department he made sure the John Yoo legal opinions were replaced by a new set of papers that argued the arcana more thoroughly.

In March 2005, with Senator Pat Roberts wavering in his support for the HVD Program, Vice President Cheney took the extraordinary step of presiding at a CIA congressional briefing. Roberts dutifully subsided. In the meantime, Dusty Foggo, having now become the agency's executive director, and John A. Rizzo, its acting General Counsel, toured the black prisons to assure CIA people their actions were lawful. Really this assurance ought to have been conveyed by Porter Goss, but he had little stock with the rank and file after indulging in a bloody purge upon his arrival at Langley. Jose Rodriguez still pushed for operational tempo.

Senator John A. McCain, who had been a prisoner tortured by Hanoi during the Vietnam war, moved in the fall to craft legislation that would outlaw torture all over again. McCain aimed at the U.S. military, and built his project around the strictures in the military's field manual on interrogations—similar to the CIA's "KU/Bark" document—but agency officers were naturally concerned the statute would be broadened to include them. Director Goss, pressured both to accept additional restrictions and to continue the interrogations, let the congressional debate take its course. But

Vice President Cheney intervened, even leading one discussion when the Senate Armed Services Committee was considering the McCain bill. The McCain legislation passed the Senate on October 5, by an overwhelming vote of 90 to 9. At a luncheon meeting of Republican senators on Halloween, Cheney had the room cleared of staff and launched into a talk extolling the virtues of "enhanced interrogation." Just before Christmas, Porter Goss sent President Bush a memorandum asserting that the Detainee Treatment Act exposed CIA officers to legal jeopardy for actions they had been told were lawful. Goss suspended further hostile interrogations.

As Cheney already knew but the legislators did not, *Washington Post* reporter Dana Priest now had the story of the CIA's black prisons. The Bush administration made a serious effort to spike it. At Porter Goss's request, Jose Rodriguez became the first line of defense. The leaves were piling up around CIA headquarters at Langley when Rodriguez invited Priest to meet. By his account this was a rare encounter with a journalist.[49] The session took place in his office on a November day. Sitting on his colonial-style sofa, Rodriguez argued without irony that the story would cause difficulties for U.S. allies, as if it were the press reporting and not the CIA's own operations that lay at the root of the problem. Dana Priest was not impressed.[50] Next, *Post* editor Leonard Downie found himself summoned to 1600 Pennsylvania Avenue. There he found President Bush, Vice President Cheney, and John Negroponte, the Director of National Intelligence, all gathered to greet him. They mounted a full-court press to convince Downie to kill the story on national security grounds. The *Washington Post* editor, who had kept Priest's story under continuous review as she reported it, had had many discussions with his editors on the national security issues involved. Downie informed President Bush and his cohorts that the *Post* would go ahead with publication but agreed to withhold the names of countries where black prisons had been located.

Clandestine service chief Rodriguez had told colleagues that he was not going to let his people get nailed for what they had been ordered to do. More than a decade earlier he had earned a CIA reprimand for poor judgment in intervening with authorities in the Dominican Republic to secure the release of a friend caught holding drugs. During Iran-Contra, from El Salvador, Rodriguez had seen his agency mentors Jim Adkins and Jack McCavitt cashiered for following what they thought were legal orders. In the Guatemala affair he witnessed the crucifixion of Terry Ward and Fred Brugger from a perch with the CIA station in Buenos Aires. Now, not trusting that locations would stay secret, Rodriguez immediately issued orders to shut down the black prison in Thailand within ninety-six hours. He feared a new purge. Priest's story would win a Pulitzer Prize. It appeared in the *Post* on November 2.[51]

With revelation of the black prisons, Rodriguez moved to ensure the destruction of the agency's torture tapes. By November 2005 Langley was under standing orders from the president's counsel, Harriet Miers, to refer to the White House before doing anything with the tapes. Jose Rodriguez insists no one ever told him, though John Rizzo in the counsel's office was acutely aware of White House sensitivity. John Negroponte, the Director of National Intelligence and Porter Goss's boss, also resisted destroying the tapes. They had become evidence in a court case when CIA materials were subpoenaed by the federal judge trying terrorist Zacarias Moussaoui. And destruction of the tapes had been opposed by a galaxy of officials, even in Dick Cheney's office. Jose Rodriguez dismissed all of that.

The CIA's operations chief began by consulting lawyers Robert Eatinger and Stephen Hermes, not attorneys from Rizzo's office but with CTC. The best alternative would be to appear to be responding to a request from the agency's station chief in Thailand. Rodriguez instructed CTC chief

Robert Grenier to draft language for the cable, which would be sent to the Bangkok station by back channel. The station chief could then paste the text into a cable to Langley. Robert Grenier did as requested on November 4, though he took the precaution of also sending his text for approval to Rizzo's office. The latter somehow missed this action.

The back-channel message went to Bangkok. In due course, at 9:04 a.m., Washington time, on November 8, Bangkok originated an "EYES ONLY" cable to Director Goss requesting permission to destroy the tapes based on the fact they were no longer material to the Inspector General's investigation, plus the General Counsel's determination that written materials "accurately" recorded the interrogations.[52] Jose Rodriguez stumbles on this point: he retails *two* versions of what happened to the tapes. One follows the outline given here, but in another place the spy chieftain writes, "Some midlevel person in CTC, whose name I do not know, correctly believing we weren't getting any useful intelligence from the tapes, recommended that they be thrown onto a bonfire that was being lit nearby."[53] The tapes were about to be turned into useless molten plastic when a Langley cable ordered them preserved. There is no declassified record of such an eleventh-hour action to save the torture tapes, only one of the effort to destroy them.

Late that Saturday night Rodriguez replied with a message instructing Bangkok to destroy the tapes "as proposed . . . for the reasons cited."[54] He did this personally, in an exception to his usual procedures. By his own account Rodriguez thought, "I was just getting rid of some ugly visuals that could put the lives of my people at risk. I took a deep breath of weary satisfaction and hit Send."[55] The CIA station reported the next day that the tapes had been dealt with as ordered. Their elimination had consumed a little over three hours. Agency officials informed Porter Goss. John Rizzo was furious, though he never confronted Jose Rodriguez. At Goss's afternoon staff meeting Rodriguez told the director, according to another officer present, "if there was any heat he would take it." Goss laughed and shot back, "Actually it would be [me] . . . who would take the heat." Goss had opposed destroying the tapes when he headed the House intelligence committee. Now he approved. "If the tapes ever got into [the] public domain . . . they would make us look terrible; it would be devastating to us."[56] So are Family Jewels born.

Revelation of the black sites triggered a storm of controversy. This came at a moment when Condoleezza Rice, now secretary of state, was in Europe. The European press, even less enamored of the war on terror than the American, handled Rice with some savagery. The McCain bill was guaranteed approval. President Bush signed it into law at the end of December. Not long afterwards Jose Rodriguez engineered the dismissal of his successor at the Counter-Terrorist Center, Robert Grenier. If heads had to roll they could be someone else's.

But the pressure was on CIA and mounted steadily. Amid fierce public debate over the reality of torture and the meaning of "enhanced interrogation techniques," Langley failed to rise to the level of its alleged convictions. Florida Senator Bill Nelson, a former astronaut, decided to undergo waterboarding himself so as to form a personal opinion of its severity. In spite of the fact that the agency could have controlled this experiment far more tightly than it did with its prisoners, and that it would have had medical staff right there to intervene, the CIA director refused to permit Senator Nelson to be waterboarded. The agency could not have withstood the heat had anything gone wrong.

By the fall of 2006 the HVD Program could no longer be sustained. That September President Bush publicly acknowledged its existence, as well as that of the black prisons, ordering them closed and the remaining detainees transferred to Guantanamo Bay. General Michael V. Hayden, a new CIA chief, brought the full congressional oversight committees into the picture for the first time. The administration would soon be circling the wagons to protect itself. That is the way with Family Jewels.

But the directives that enabled the CIA to engage in renditions and operate clandestine detention facilities remained on the books. In January 2009, on the second day of his presidency, Barack Obama signed an executive order banning torture and ordering the closure of the detainee facility at Guantanamo Bay, as well as prohibiting black prisons. The directive Obama signed had been modified: when the CIA saw it in draft, Langley's top lawyer complained to the new president's chief counsel. John Rizzo told the White House lawyer that the language in the executive order would preclude CIA from holding detainees even for the short length of time necessary to arrange their rendition. The text of the Obama executive order was changed to permit the agency to do that. The move to close Guantanamo also failed, though over a longer period of time. That, too, is the way with Family Jewels.

6

≡ ASSASSINATION ≡

One of the most notorious Family Jewels appears in the original documents primarily in the form of successive versions of a denial Bill Colby wrote for public consumption, a brief note on a plot against an African leader, and a short report on the Central Intelligence Agency's contacts with the Mafia. The degree to which the CIA had been involved in assassination plots long remained a mystery wrapped in an enigma. Kennedy assassination buffs speculate on whether Langley's schemes aimed at Fidel Castro had led to some Cuban role in the murder of the president, or alternatively whether the CIA itself had somehow been involved. The murder of Ngo Dinh Diem in South Vietnam was often laid at the CIA's doorstep. Newspaper columnist Drew Pearson had published a series of pieces in 1967 on CIA-Mafia associations and their role in plots against Castro, leading President Lyndon Baines Johnson to fuss that the agency must think it could run some kind of "Murder Incorporated" assassination unit. That led Dick Helms to order up an Inspector General's report on the Castro plots. But little of this found its way into the Family Jewels documents, because they focused on domestic activities, not foreign ones.

Nor did assassinations form part of President Ford's marching orders for the Rockefeller Commission. After his exchanges with Director Richard Helms and Henry Kissinger (see Chapter 2), and his own experience on the Warren Commission, Ford was careful to try and keep the subject off the docket. Ironically, after the White House's strenuous efforts at damage control, it was Gerald R. Ford himself who put this Family Jewel on the agenda.

Jerry Ford injected assassination into the Year of Intelligence by mistake. It began innocently enough. During Ford's time as vice president under Richard Nixon, the *New York Times* had him to lunch at its Washington Bureau. As president, in January 1975 Ford returned the favor, arranging an intimate lunch in the family quarters dining room on the second floor of the East Wing. Those around the table engaged in some amiable ruminations. *Times* executives and editors posed questions on the issues of the day. Late in the conversation, Abe Rosenthal, the newspaper's executive editor, asked Ford how he thought the Rockefeller Commission could have much credibility, given that its members were largely defense-oriented and could be expected to protect the CIA. The president repeated what he had told Dick Helms on January 4: that he had selected the commissioners carefully and drawn their terms of reference narrowly to ensure they stayed on domestic issues and did not intrude into foreign matters that were "a cesspool." America's image was important.

Abe Rosenthal wondered what could be so embarrassing. Jerry Ford blurted out the first thing that came into his head. Barely two weeks before, Henry Kissinger, William E. Colby, and Lawrence Silberman—the latter referring to "unique questions"—had all warned the president on the assassinations matter, and Ford had discussed the subject privately with Richard Helms. Ford, of course, had been a member of the Warren Commission, which investigated the Kennedy assassination, and he could not help but know of the charges of plots that had swirled around the tragedy for years. Gerald Ford had himself written a book about the Kennedy assassination. So he was especially attuned to the assassinations issue. At lunch, answering Rosenthal, the president replied, "Assassinations!" Later Ford asked to keep this—plus remarks he'd made about Dick Helms—off the record.

The *New York Times* officials debated what to do. Typically news is placed "off the record" by prior understanding, not subsequent appeal. The journalists decided to honor the president's request anyway. But, Washington gossip being what it is, rumors soon spread about Ford's remark.[1] Sy Hersh learned about the conversation, but *Times* editors prevailed on him to keep quiet. Another who heard was Columbia Broadcasting System (CBS) reporter Daniel Schorr. He thought the rumor concerned domestic assassinations and spent weeks in a fruitless search for possible cases. Schorr even sought evidence on a New York traffic accident in which Soviet diplomats had died. But he could find nothing. Then, late in February, the CIA accepted Schorr's long-standing request for an interview with Director Colby. The encounter took place on February 27 and mostly concerned Watergate (Chapter 9). Toward the end of their conversation the journalist sought to draw Colby out, venturing that he heard Ford had a problem with the CIA on assassinations. Schorr asked if the agency had ever killed anyone in the United States.

"Not in this country," Bill Colby answered.

The next day Daniel Schorr recorded an item for Walter Cronkite's *CBS Evening News* that reported, "President Ford has reportedly warned associates that if current investigations go too far they could uncover several assassinations of foreign officials involving CIA."[2] According to historian Kathryn Olmstead, this news transformed the Year of Intelligence.[3] Bill Colby began a fight to prevent, then marginalize, inquiries into Langley's role in assassinations. President

Ford may have disagreed with Colby's approach to other aspects of the investigations, but on this they were as one. Officially the president was responsive. But Ford counted on his staffers Jack Marsh and Roderick Hills to carry the torch for a minimization strategy inside the White House, and on Nelson Rockefeller to hold the line within his commission.

Rockefeller did not succeed. His key opponent became David W. Belin, the inquiry's executive director, handpicked by the president. Belin had served the Warren Commission as assistant counsel, so he had Ford's confidence. Bringing the Iowa lawyer into the Rockefeller group had seemed a safe choice. But the Kennedy investigation and Warren Commission had sensitized Belin to all manner of assassination issues, and instead he made the CIA plots a special concern. Later, in mid-March, the vice president ran into Daniel Schorr at the National Airport and disclosed that conversations with Ford had convinced him to look at assassinations, but under a formula that amounted to examining only those that had included major activity or training inside the United States.

The Rockefeller Commission staff sent Langley a general requirement for a listing of possible unlawful activities. Belin drew on the Colby Report to request data on many specific items, things like Projects Chaos or Merrimac. One thing they got back was the Family Jewels documents, but with blank pages. Belin asked his CIA liaison, Deputy Director E. H. ("Hank") Knoche, what material was missing, and the latter replied that the deleted items concerned things that fell outside the commission charter. Belin was incensed. Like any good investigator, he was not about to let someone else decide what was germane to his inquiry. The lawyer used the commission's authority to go out to Langley and read the full text. Mentions of the CIA and the Mafia leaped out at him. Belin began a battle for jurisdiction to put the agency's assassination plots under the microscope.

Parsing the language of Rockefeller's charter, David Belin argued strenuously to include this matter. That debate was underway when Daniel Schorr revealed the assassination story he had gotten from Colby. The dam broke. President Ford was obliged to widen the commission's scope and extend its deadline by two months specifically to cover assassinations. Vice President Rockefeller then imposed his convoluted formula, and his executive director countered by lobbying the commission members. Governor Ronald Reagan became a strong supporter. Alert to the political ramifications of assassination plotting, Reagan insisted they be examined. Agency historian Nicolas Dujmovic finds that Governor Reagan's view persuaded most of his colleagues, who voted down Rockefeller when the commissioners considered whether to put this on their agenda, and they rejected the vice president's narrow formula.[4]

With jurisdiction settled, Belin pitched in. Buried in CIA's responses to various requests were snippets of data, including an admission that plans had been made to assassinate foreign leaders. The Family Jewels had a bit more. David Belin collected key documents, including the Inspector General report of 1967, and sent his assistant, R. Mason Cargill, to fish through agency files. Henry Kissinger played his usual game, dragging his feet until the commission's deadline neared, then furnishing a few National Security Council papers. Those of the "special group" managing covert operations were denied. That grudging bit of cooperation was secured only after Vice President Rockefeller interceded with Kissinger's deputy, Brent Scowcroft.

Rockefeller's investigators did talk to national security advisors Gordon Gray, McGeorge Bundy, and Walt Rostow. Belin interviewed a range of CIA officials, including the security chief who had supervised early plots against Castro, the head of the clandestine service at the time, the field officer who had led the first "executive action" unit, the case officer responsible for one of the more advanced schemes, and former CIA director John McCone. Belin extended his analysis to include plots against leaders of the Congo, Dominican Republic, and Indonesia. He tried to assemble case studies.

By mid-April 1975, Belin expected to have a draft report ready at the end of the month. On the 15th he met with White House aide James A. Wilderotter to discuss the commission's status. Meanwhile, on Capitol Hill, the Church Committee had filed requests for a wide array of documents, some of them now held by the Rockefeller Commission. Belin had no problem with passing the materials along once the commission had completed its work. In the course of the conversation he mentioned his "special preliminary report" on assassinations.[5] Wilderotter passed that information up the line. On May 12 commissioner Douglas Dillon told the press that the Rockefeller report would include discussion of assassinations. Belin labored on his paper, intended as a chapter in the final report, into late May, delayed by the sluggish responses to his requests. Dillon's affirmation, however, would be retracted two weeks later.

White House intervention made the difference. When the commission met to review the assassinations draft, Rockefeller objected that the State Department—headed by his friend Henry Kissinger—felt this discussion of assassinations would not be appropriate in the commission's report. According to David Belin, Rockefeller learned of Kissinger's concern directly from Gerald Ford. This time the commission backed Rockefeller. Belin then planned a news conference where he would disclose the assassination findings. The day before this event, upon seeing Belin's intended release, Dick Cheney and Phil Buchen both intervened. They conceded Belin's appearance was up to him, but given Kissinger's position that disclosure "was not in the best interests of the country," and that Belin would be taken as a spokesman for the Rockefeller Commission, the event could be very damaging. Belin reluctantly desisted. In retrospect he felt he had made a major mistake.[6]

On June 9 President Ford presided over a public commemoration of the Rockefeller Commission's achievement, noting its records would be passed to the Church Committee, and that the Rockefeller report was being prepared for publication. That "preparation" amounted to an extensive rewrite. One thing that ended up on the cutting room floor was assassination plots. The only discussion to appear in the Rockefeller Commission report was its treatment of John F. Kennedy's murder. Presidential lawyer Roderick Hills worked hard on this. Gerald Ford appointed Hills to head the Securities and Exchange Commission shortly afterwards. David Belin returned to Des Moines to resume his law practice. There he filed a Freedom of Information Act request for many records he had seen during the Rockefeller investigation.

David Belin's suppressed report ran to eighty-six pages of densely packed detail. It found CIA discussion of, but no action in, the death of Congolese leader Patrice Lumumba; discussion of, but only a preliminary search for an assassin in, the plot against Indonesian leader Achmed Sukarno; action, including the provision of weapons, in the death of Dominican dictator Rafael Trujillo; and an extensive record of activities aimed at Fidel Castro. Investigators found no record of presidential approval for any of this. McGeorge Bundy vaguely recalled talk of plots against Castro but did not remember any recommendation to okay one, and added that he would be surprised if the CIA had moved without coming to him first. Gordon Gray and Walt Rostow insisted they had never discussed assassinations with anyone. In his conclusion Belin wrote, "It is against the constitutional and moral principles for which this Republic stands for there to be any direct or indirect participation of any agency of the

United States Government in any plans involving the assassination of any person in peacetime."[7]

This document was retrieved from Dick Cheney's Ford-era White House files.

The Belin report, his notes and interviews, and other records held by the Rockefeller Commission, went to the Church Committee a few weeks later—not without some more fighting for custody, but that is less important. "For the committee," staffer Loch Johnson notes, "access to these documents was equivalent to finding the Rosetta stone."[8] Fortified by this evidence, the Senate investigators at once advanced their inquiries. With fresh leads, documents, and the power of the subpoena, the Church Committee interviewed seventy-five witnesses and compiled eight thousand pages of sworn testimony. It sought to get to the bottom of the United States government's complicity—and that of the CIA—in murder. The subject was an obvious Family Jewel.

When it came to "dirty tricks," it is remarkable how many threads led back to Colonel Sheffield Edwards. The Church Committee never could discover them all, for the colonel passed away just a few weeks after it received the Rockefeller documents. Investigators were left only with the interview Edwards had given David Belin and the committee's own preliminary talk with the colonel, one that took place days before Rockefeller's people closed up shop and before the senators knew what to ask. Already quite ill, Sheffield Edwards died on July 12, having dropped the bombshell that CIA Director Allen W. Dulles and his deputy for operations, Richard M. Bissell, had ordered him to assassinate Cuban leader Fidel Castro.

Formally responsible for security at the Central Intelligence Agency until 1963, Edwards seems to have functioned as a sort of Mr. Odd Jobs for dark work. Nothing in his background obviously equipped the colonel for this. Filled with patriotism at the height of the Great War, Edwards had obtained an appointment to West Point. "Shef," as he was known, compensated for his stutter with finesse. He had been an artillery officer, a staff marvel, and chief of staff for air units. In World War II he had earned the Bronze Star, risen to full colonel, and ended up as a section leader on Omar Bradley's Twelfth Army Group intelligence staff. After the war Edwards joined the Central Intelligence Group, the progenitor of CIA, where he worked well with its brilliant boss, General Hoyt Vandenberg. He continued as chief of security while the CIA grew and matured. Colonel Edwards managed the buildup as the Office of Security expanded from a tiny appendage of thirty-five officers to an apparatus of seven hundred persons.

This was the story of a conscientious man, a successful military officer and agency official with a sterling record. Yet there was another side to Sheffield Edwards. The FBI viewed CIA with suspicion from the beginning, when the agency took over its operations in Latin America and poached its G-men. Bureau people had difficulty talking to agency officers. Shef Edwards stepped into the breach, becoming the contact for Bureau liaison Cartha DeLoach, to the degree that some agency officers saw him as J. Edgar Hoover's spy inside the CIA. In his security role Edwards participated in the persecution of Carmel Offie, hounded out of the agency as a homosexual—a security risk—in 1950. That might have been in keeping with the times, but in 1953 "Wild Bill" Donovan, the founder of the Office of Strategic Services and a major mover in the CIA's creation, discovered he was being followed around Bangkok, where Donovan was by then the United States ambassador to Thailand. He traced the action to Shef's CIA office. Yet Colonel Edwards had been the agency's emissary to Wild Bill for several years. Unknown to Donovan, Edwards had been communicating with the FBI about the spy chieftain's "loyalty" for some time.

Near the end of his career Edwards had a piece in another bit of skullduggery, the witch hunt that unfairly marked Peter Karlow, CIA's first station chief in Moscow, as a Soviet agent. It was the dawn of the spy war that sucked in Yuri Nosenko and crippled CIA espionage.

With U.S. intelligence preoccupied with Russia's supposed capability to "brainwash" people, during 1950 Colonel Edwards had participated in the CIA's decision to launch Project Bluebird, the use of drugs on detainees under interrogation. A few years later, with the agency tampering with the U.S. mail, Colonel Edwards agreed to have his Office of Security do the actual illegal letter opening. In 1958, when the CIA's Far East Division wanted to smear Indonesian leader Achmed Sukarno by making him appear to be the male actor in a pornographic film, Edwards prevailed on the police commissioner of Los Angeles to procure a supply of porn movies from which to select a template. The following year the colonel's operatives illegally wiretapped an American journalist (see Chapter 7). The Office of Security had had a hand in polishing several Family Jewels.

Perhaps it is not surprising, then, that when the idea of assassinating Fidel Castro came up, spooks thought of Shef Edwards. When the CIA Inspector General reviewed this history in 1967, he concluded the idea came from J. C. King, chief of the agency's Western Hemisphere Division, who took it to clandestine service chief Richard Bissell. The concept was to act through the Mafia, whose gambling interests in Cuba were being dismantled by the Castro regime. Bissell summoned Colonel Edwards in late September 1960. Edwards told Rockefeller and Church interviewers that both Bissell and CIA Director Allen W. Dulles knew of the plan, and that it had high-level approval, though no written evidence of the latter has ever been found. Based on his understanding, the colonel asked his chief of support to identify a suitable intermediary with Mafia links who could be the go-between. That person, Robert A. Maheu, a private detective and former FBI operative, had done several previous jobs for the security office. Maheu connected with Mafia don Johnny Rosselli and other mafiosi the latter recruited. Office of Security deputy James O'Connell became the case officer, though Shef Edwards once met with Rosselli himself.

The details of the sordid plots to kill Fidel Castro are intricate. The core point is that this was a real initiative, carried out over a period of years, involving identifiable agency officers and acknowledged by the CIA. Events are documented by David Belin's report, an agency IG investigation, the Church Committee's assassination inquiry, the House Select Committee on Assassinations (1979), and a mass of documents declassified by the John F. Kennedy Assassination Records Review Board in the 1990s. There were at least six major plots. The Mafia plot failed in this initial phase, but was revived after the disastrous botch of the CIA's Bay of Pigs invasion. Another scheme aimed to kill Castro with poisoned skin-diving gear. There were multiple plans for a sniper to assassinate the Cuban leader and one to engineer a military coup to overthrow him. Execution was taken away from Edwards and handed to a task force conducting operations against Cuba, then its successor. The agency's Office of Technical Services developed poison pills for the Mafia plot. As John F. Kennedy traveled to Dallas for his own fateful encounter with an assassin, a senior CIA officer was in Paris to meet one of the Cuban operatives recruited to kill Castro. Every scheme to get Castro miscarried.

Church investigators examined other CIA initiatives also. While delving into covert operations, the committee discovered that in Chile—a natural target of the inquiry since claims of CIA involvement there were already swarming in public—there had been two tracks to the policy ordered by Richard Nixon. As Tom Karamessines told his interlocutors, from his perspective as Langley's director of operations, the supersecret "Track II" had never ended. That facet had involved assassinations, and the CIA had latched onto a plot by certain Chilean officers to murder the general who barred the way to a military coup against elected president Salvador Allende. The agency supplied money and guns to the plotters, though the general had been eliminated by another cabal instead. His demise cleared the way for the coup that overthrew Allende. Rumors of CIA participation in that September 1973 coup, during which Allende died by his own hand, could not be resolved based on the evidence the committee was able to elicit.

Another extensive record of CIA activity the Church Committee established was of CIA's role in the November 1963 coup against South Vietnamese leader Ngo Dinh Diem, during the course of which Diem was assassinated. There was explicit evidence of CIA participation over a period of months right up to and during the day of the coup, but none of agency complicity in or even advance awareness of the murder itself. The Diem case was also unique in demonstrating close participation by top levels of the United States government—President Kennedy and his top advisors—who met repeatedly to consider coup prospects and U.S. backing.

In the cases of Castro, Chile, Diem, and the Congo, the Church Committee could talk to CIA officers who had actually carried out the actions. The CIA's record in the Congo was clear: when headquarters ordered officers to eliminate Congolese Prime Minister Patrice Lumumba, some had refused. Others traveled from Washington to the Congo to further the plot, recruited agents to do the deed, and moved snake venom and rifles for purposes of the assassination. But the trail of authority—the directive from on high—remained obscure. Agency instructions to its station in the Congo coincided in one case with talk at the "Special Group" that managed covert operations, and in another with a discussion at the National Security Council, but White House staff could not recall—or refused to affirm—President Dwight D. Eisenhower issuing such an order. And the CIA did not actually kill Lumumba. As in the Chilean case, a different set of plotters, now established to have been led by Belgians, murdered him. Yet CIA's conspiracy had been a real one, and the agency was not excused.

One more case explored was the assassination of Dominican dictator Rafael Trujillo on May 30, 1961. Church investigators found that the Special Group had considered a covert operation in the Dominican Republic in February 1960 and that a couple of months later President Eisenhower had approved a plan to move against Trujillo if conditions deteriorated any further. In May 1960 Dominican dissidents asked for weapons, and the CIA supplied them. Many other requests followed at various times, and CIA headquarters contributed plans of its own for shipments, with more weapons actually shipped to Santo Domingo but never delivered. The Special Group approved certain weapons shipments on the very eve of Eisenhower's leaving office. The incoming Kennedy administration had doubts and took some measures to discourage the Dominican plotters, who nevertheless moved ahead and killed Trujillo.

Investigators also discovered that the agency had had a management unit in the 1950s nicknamed the "Health Alteration Committee," that this had endorsed at least one plan, to incapacitate an Iraqi army officer, and that in 1961 the CIA had moved to create a standing unit for "executive action" using the cryptonym ZR/Rifle. Project Rifle was not known to have carried out any actual assassinations. The agency apparently succeeded in hiding the fact—now revealed in declassified documents—that during the covert operation that overthrew the Guatemalan government in 1954, the

CIA had created and maintained lists of Guatemalans who were to be killed or neutralized once the agency-backed rebel forces had triumphed. Evidence confirmed the CIA had provided weapons to potential assassins of Sukarno in Indonesia plus opponents of "Papa Doc" Duvalier in Haiti, but those things were not mentioned in the Church report. The Committee did not examine certain allegations, such as that CIA had considered the feasibility of killing China's Zhou Enlai and Egypt's Nasser.

Having asked the Church Committee to pursue this inquiry, President Ford attempted to suppress its result. Phil Buchen of the White House arranged for officials at CIA, the Pentagon, and State Department to read Church's draft report. All of them viewed the prospect of publication as a disaster. Scott D. Breckinridge produced the CIA audit of the draft. Breckinridge portrayed the Church product as confusing, listed names to be protected, objected to the disclosure of sources and methods, plus cryptonyms, and found the paper anything but crisp. Director Colby forwarded this review to President Ford, emphasizing (as did both of the other agencies) "grievous damage to our country." CIA opposed release.[9] On Halloween Ford duly sent the committee a letter demanding its report be kept secret. Not trusting Frank Church to deal straightforwardly, Ford sent identical copies to every committee member. Vigorous debate ensued. Senator Church nearly resigned. The committee decided to send its assassinations report to the full Senate for a decision, with a recommendation it be released to the public. On television, reporters interviewing Church confronted him with the administration's expressed claim that publication would harm United States foreign relations.

"What are we talking about, here? Agencies of the government that are licensed to undertake murder," Senator Church shot back. "Is the president of the United States going to be a glorified godfather?"[10]

Behind the scenes the Central Intelligence Agency demanded that thirty names be deleted from the report, including those of some of its Chilean agents who had not only been exposed but convicted in a Chilean military court. The Church Committee agreed on most, substituting pseudonyms, but kept the rest. The agency went to court. Federal district judge Gerhard Gesell ruled that government officials whose personal conduct was being reviewed by Congress had no right of privacy. Bill Colby called a press conference—only the second in CIA history—to denounce the committee for naming names. Meanwhile, Langley appealed Gesell's decision over the identity of one senior scientist involved in the Lumumba plot. To avoid further delay, the committee agreed to redact the man's identity. On November 20 the matter of approval went before the full Senate. The chamber debated for hours, but could not bring itself to take a vote. That left the initiative to the committee itself. As the session ended, Church Committee staff began handing out copies of the assassinations report.

The republic was not destroyed by revelation of the Central Intelligence Agency's role as executioner. Rather, the deep crevasse of controversy immediately squelched debate. President Ford himself, in announcing that he was passing the assassination investigation along to the Senate committee, declared: "I am opposed to political assassinations. This administration has not and will not use such means as instruments of national policy."[11] Ford was actually building on existing CIA directives. Both Richard Helms, in March 1972, and William E. Colby, in August 1973, had ordered that no assassinations should be conducted, induced, or even suggested. Both Helms and Colby expressed themselves to the Church Committee as unalterably opposed to CIA participation in assassination plots.

The Church Committee took the same line as had David Belin. In fact, the senators went further, recommending that a prohibition on assassination be written into law. "Administrations change, CIA directors change, and some day in the future what was tried in the past may once again become a temptation." The committee even supplied proposed language, making clear that the "foreign officials" who were to be off limits included even members of "an insurgent force, an unrecognized government, or a political party."[12]

Gerald Ford had no desire for a statute forbidding assassinations—thus tying his hands—or for that matter a law establishing a formal charter for intelligence agencies. Ford sought to obviate congressional action by means of presidential directive. The White House steering group dealing with the Year of Intelligence was already finishing work on an instrument of this kind. The text reached final form in January 1976 and appeared on February 18 as Executive Order 11905. Here President Ford codified his own proscription. Among its restrictions on intelligence agencies, the executive order provided that "No employee of the United States Government shall engage in, or conspire to engage in, political assassination."[13]

Debate on intelligence reforms that had been ignited by the 1975 investigations extended into the presidency of Jimmy Carter. A statutory charter was actually debated, though it did not pass Congress. But the draft indeed outlawed assassinations. President Carter issued his own executive order on intelligence in May 1977. That directive left the Ford assassination prohibition in place verbatim. On January 24, 1978, Carter promulgated an extensively reworked replacement. With a few changes to wording, the Carter executive order *widened* the prohibition, extending it to persons working "in behalf" of the United States government, and getting rid of the qualifier "political" in describing the act of murder. Thus, President Carter's Executive Order 12036 prohibited anyone working for or in behalf of the United States from engaging or conspiring in *any* act of assassination whatever.[14]

Ronald Reagan defeated Carter in the 1980 election and took office in January 1981. He too revised the presidential directive on intelligence activities. In the matter of assassinations, however, the Reagan executive order merely renumbered the Carter injunction, repeating it precisely.[15] President Reagan's executive order remains in place today. No person working for or in behalf of the United States may conspire or engage in assassination. In summary, there is an unbroken chain of regulation, though not in statute. The presidential commission and Senate committee that investigated CIA plots in 1975 both condemned assassination as a policy. President Ford repudiated it and then, by executive order, banned political murder. President Carter widened the prohibition to all such acts and every person working for or on behalf of the nation. *Five* presidents since Carter's time have continued that provision. But as the Church Committee said long ago, presidents and CIA directors change—and the senators ought to have added circumstances as well. In the war on terror, temptation proved to be too much.

The Year of Intelligence certainly impressed John A. Rizzo. With service as a Treasury Department lawyer under his belt, Mr. Rizzo decided the Central Intelligence Agency was going to need more attorneys. Later he cited the Church Committee and Rockefeller Commission as specific factors in his decision to join CIA. John Rizzo came on board just two months after George Herbert Walker Bush replaced Bill Colby at the head of the agency. The wounds of the Year of Intelligence were fresh and the system of congressional oversight about to be born. Rizzo began as a lawyer in the Office of General Counsel. A lot of eye-opening stuff happened during that formative era. The clandestine service got in trouble over its handling of Soviet defector Nicolas Shadrin, grabbed right out of its hands during a trip to Vienna, and there came the final resolution of the Nosenko case. The CIA was in the hot seat during the Iran Hostage Crisis, and it began covert operations in Nicaragua and Afghanistan. Rizzo moved up to OGC's front office soon after Bill Casey took the helm at Langley.

Born in Worcester of Irish-Italian parents, John Rizzo had grown up in Boston, where his father was a department store executive. He went to Brown University, joined a fraternity, and acquired a taste for flashy clothes. Rhone wine and French cooking were his style too. John Rizzo loved Washington. His law degree came with honors from George Washington University. He lived in a Virginia suburb. Rizzo worked customs enforcement and narcotics issues for three and a half years at the Treasury Department. He spent his entire working life in Washington. At CIA, the legal bloodhound was highly regarded in the Directorate of Operations. One subordinate described Rizzo to a journalist as a classic DO lawyer, admiring the case officers: "They trust him to work out tough issues in the gray with them."[16]

The Iran-Contra affair (Chapter 9) became another of John Rizzo's indelible experiences. Tremendous scandal broke out in the summer of 1984 over the CIA's mining of ports in Nicaragua, and shortly afterwards the thirty-seven-year-old lawyer moved over to the agency's Inspector General office. In that capacity he investigated alleged wrongdoing at a couple of CIA stations and participated in several of the IG's periodic reviews of agency components. In February 1986, Rizzo was assigned to the congressional liaison office as deputy chief. That fall the Iran-Contra affair broke into the open with revelations about U.S. actions in both Nicaragua and Iran. Rizzo was in the thick of the action. Director Casey appeared before the Senate Intelligence Committee in November 1986, presenting misleading testimony. Then came reports a White House aide who had acted in close concert with Casey had been destroying records related to the affair, followed by news the CIA had failed to inform Congress of covert action approvals. Summoned to another hearing to explain himself, Casey called on John Rizzo to help prepare him. Rizzo stood in the hallway outside Casey's door, waiting to enter and brief the director, when Casey suffered a seizure and collapsed on December 15, trapped by the intolerable tensions of a web of fabricated chronologies and misleading testimony. The classic CIA lawyer would tell a Minnesota law school audience his greatest regret had been his failure to press harder, be tougher with the operations people, to avoid the agency being swept up in Iran-Contra. By his own account, the ordeal left Rizzo with an abiding sense that reporting fully to the congressional committees was not only the law, it was politically savvy and good for the Central Intelligence Agency.[17]

But working out problems for CIA operatives could also mean cutting corners. As deputy general counsel for operations, in 1990 attorney Rizzo would have had a role in issuing the order for the CIA to destroy the records of its mail-opening project HT/Lingual. One source described him as a "legal enabler," a fixer, searching for ways to make possible what the operators wanted to do. In Rizzo's construction, an agent working for the CIA—"in behalf of the United States" in the meaning of the assassination prohibitions—could legally participate in a death squad so long as he made sure to miss when he fired.[18] That was Rizzo's stance in the Guatemala fiasco. His approach landed the dedicated lawyer in hot water when it came to the war on terror. It was Mr. Rizzo, by then acting General Counsel, who stood at ground zero in the entire matter of the Justice Department opinions authorizing CIA torture. That involved the question of how accurately the agency—in the person of John Rizzo—had described its interrogation techniques. Even beyond that, however, Rizzo's participation in the agency's drone war placed him athwart the line of three decades of presidential prohibitions on CIA assassinations.

Had it not been for CIA ingenuity, the lawyer might never have faced this quandary. The "unmanned aerial vehicle," now familiar as the "drone," had been an important aviation technology program through the 1990s. The air force and CIA collaborated on one version of this craft called the Predator, first used over the Balkans in 1995, which became fully operational soon afterwards. The drone was guided remotely by a "pilot" monitoring its sensors, at first from a van at the airfield, but with improved communications after 2000, from facilities in the continental United States. Reconnaissance was Predator's mission. Its cameras could scan the ground in great detail from ten thousand feet in altitude and broadcast the imagery to controllers and troops on the ground. The air force, anxious to preserve the combat role of manned aircraft, resisted arming the Predator. Langley, on the other hand, proved much more enthusiastic. The CIA had been frustrated several times in the 1990s when it made sightings of terrorist Osama bin Laden, but was powerless to act on the information. "Armed reconnaissance," with a drone that could see the target, then attack immediately, could be an ideal solution. When he headed the Counter-Terrorist Center through and past the Afghanistan invasion, Cofer Black pushed hard on the development of an armed Predator.

Director George Tenet paid attention. The effort against Al Qaeda had become CIA's most important operational mission. The agency deployed a Predator scout unit to Pakistan in the fall of 2000, using air force crews and an air force–CIA support and analysis team. Fifteen reconnaissance flights were carried out before December, when the Afghan winter forced curtailment of the program. On two of those flights, the operators had seen bin Laden. Once this had been an after-the-fact judgment based on imagery analysis, but the other time the crew was sure they had bin Laden in their sights: a tall, white-robed man surrounded by a coterie of supporters, in a place where other CIA intelligence indicated bin Laden would be that day. Because the Predator was not armed, nothing could be done. Tenet convinced the air force to experiment with a version of the drone modified to carry a pair of Hellfire missiles. The Hellfire, developed as a supersonic, air-launched antitank missile, was extremely powerful and had precision guidance. Tests of the armed drone took place between May 22 and June 7, 2001. The weapon proved excellent against structures and stationary individuals, but less effective when aimed at vehicles. With Hellfire's laser-pointed guidance, moving objects posed a greater challenge, and cloud, rain, or even water vapor could disrupt the system. Work began to adapt a radar-guided version of the missile for Predator.

Beyond the diplomatic task of arranging with foreign countries to host Predator detachments lay the aspect that concerned John Rizzo—in George Tenet's words, "a command and control arrangement that could respond to fleeting opportunities while ensuring the right level of leadership control."[19] Within days of the September 11 attacks, President George W. Bush had signed a presidential finding, the memorandum of notification that authorizes a covert operation. This was a "lethal" finding—one that permits operators to kill. One contradiction in the basis for CIA activities lies in the idea that a president, having promulgated an executive order with the status of law that prohibits assassination, then waives his own regulation with a simple finding. An argument that the United States is engaged in war fails, because the prohibition in the executive order is absolute, not dependent on belligerent status, and in any case it is legally disputable that the congressional resolution passed after 9/11 is tantamount to a declaration of war. The question of the preeminence of executive order versus memorandum of notification has never been resolved. Operational requirements have been permitted to trump the legal underpinnings for U.S. intelligence activities.

Equally important, lethal operations are approved at a high level, yet for armed reconnaissance to work, it was necessary to make instantaneous decisions to kill during Predator attack missions. In conjunction with White House and other government lawyers, John Rizzo and Scott Muller evolved a system to maintain an approved target list. Call this an assassination list, a hit list, a kill list, or what you will, the mechanism was for CTC to work up a paper on a selected individual, describing why that person had to be neutralized. The recommendation was then considered by senior officials, and approved targets were added to the list. Those individuals could be attacked on sight by Predator crews. If others were killed as the targets were taken out, that was just collateral damage.

Early in September 2001, Director Tenet deployed the weapons-capable drone unit. The CIA Predators were in place on September 16. The first Predator flew over Kabul and Kandahar two days later. It was strictly a scouting mission. Tenet did not send the missiles right away, because the host country had yet to approve flying armed missions from its soil and because the Hellfire's technical shortcomings were still being resolved. But with 9/11 the stops were pulled out. Missiles soon reached Pakistan, which approved attack sorties on October 7. An initial armed mission took place the next day. About half the early drones carried missiles. Henry A. Crumpton was the overall commander of this aerial sniping venture. "The attorneys were always involved, but they were very good—very aggressive and helpful, in fact," Crumpton would recall. "They would help us understand international law and cross-border issues, and they would interpret specific language of the presidential directive."[20]

There were, of course, operational problems. Communications links to the drones could be lost, and the planes would go out of control and simply fly on until they crashed. Thirty percent of the initial air force buy of Predators were destroyed in their first five years in service. The drones might fade in and out of control, or lose their optical feed, or at the critical moment of attack the missile release mechanisms might not work.

Target discrimination is a perennial problem, only somewhat alleviated by other intelligence available to operators. With a platform flying at speed and altitude plus a list of potential targets, any one of whom might be on the viewscreen—no matter how good the optics—certainty could not be guaranteed unless the target was fixed or his identity validated by an outside source. A typical example took place early in the Afghan war, about a week after the first CIA team was inserted. Agency team leader Gary C. Schroen got a call from Washington—a Predator was circling a new, supposed Al Qaeda airstrip where a bunch of men were visible. They looked like terrorists, and headquarters wanted a strike. As Schroen considered the location, he realized the operators were talking about his own CIA teammates. This problem has not disappeared. Most recently, in April 2011, marine Staff Sergeant Jeremy Smith and navy corpsman Benjamin D. Rast were killed when analysts working a Predator mission, though not certain, decided to regard them as Taliban.

Nevertheless, the Predator quickly proved itself. On the night of November 15–16, 2001, a Predator blew up an Al Qaeda safe house south of Kabul. Killed in the attack was Mohammed Atef, the terrorist group's military commander, along with seven other persons. That result solidified support for the Predator program. Since then there has been a steady stream of Predator attacks and a parade of Al Qaeda number 3s eliminated. The main operational theaters for CIA aircraft have shifted from Afghanistan to Pakistan, Yemen, and

Somalia. And collateral damage continues as well. Observers are now debating whether Pakistani civilians killed by drones number in the hundreds or the thousands.

This program began with an air campaign in tandem with the U.S. invasion of Afghanistan. Once the shift to Pakistan began, flights were made only in small increments. Initially there was time for careful approvals. But as Predator operations became routinized that changed. President Bush and his advisors turned their eyes to Iraq and other issues. At Langley the targeting memos stopped on the desks of Scott Muller, the top lawyer, and John Rizzo. Memos shrank from five pages to two, with a supporting file to crack open if one had the time and inclination. Rizzo would send a poorly argued recommendation back to the CTC, where a team of nearly a dozen lawyers would rework it. After the first burst, a dump of the Center's intelligence on Al Qaeda, the requests came at a rate of about one a month. At any given time, Rizzo recalls, there were about thirty approved targets. "They were very picky," recalls Michael Scheuer, who headed CTC's bin Laden unit until 2003. "Very often this caused a missed opportunity. The whole idea that people got shot because someone got a hunch—I only wish that was true. If it were, there would be a lot more bad guys dead."[21] Picky or not, the Predator program reached the point where people were being marked for death by an agency lawyer without further reference.

Fresh complications entered the picture in November 2002. A year into the attack program, by now the drones had begun to fly over Yemen. The CIA laid on a mission out of Djibouti to eliminate Al Qaeda organizer Qaed Salim Sinan al-Harethi, believed to have organized the explosive boat attack against the U.S. destroyer *Cole* in Yemen's port Aden in 2000. Al-Harethi was crossing the desert in a truck on his way to a meeting with a CIA operative, who confirmed the target for the Predator. A Hellfire demolished the truck.

Also eliminated were five others, including American citizen Kamal Derwish. Agency officials' certainty the man had been in the truck indicates his presence was known in advance. The Derwish killing injected a new issue, since, as an American, the man was entitled to constitutional protections and trial by jury. It did not matter that Derwish was a known member of a group of American Muslims, the so-called "Lackawana 6," who had been convicted under new antiterrorist laws. Derwish was killed in cold blood without any legal proceeding. Now the CIA—at the level of staff lawyers—was acting as judge, jury, and executioner.

John Rizzo and the Bush administration said little about the Derwish affair. Rizzo continued to plug away at his many tasks. When Scott Muller left, Rizzo became acting General Counsel. Transformed into the program's sole legal guardian, Rizzo kept the target list current. As with many other awkward subjects, National Clandestine Service chief Jose Rodriguez, who had the primary operational interest in this, has nothing to say about Predators. Rizzo, meanwhile, nursed the ambition of formal promotion to General Counsel. President Bush finally tapped Rizzo for the job in 2005. Then his nomination languished, with a Senate confirmation hearing not even scheduled for more than a year, and postponed repeatedly after that. John Rizzo finally faced the senators on June 16, 2007. All the public's attention focused on the fixer's role in the CIA torture memos, and the senators were quite exercised as well about the Bush administration substituting narrow briefings of the Gang of Four for full and current notification.

The Predator program, if it was addressed, was discussed only in closed session. The closest the participants came to taking up the issues of Derwish and the drones was when Oregon Senator Ron Wyden asked Rizzo whether a president had the authority to order the CIA to capture and detain an American citizen in a foreign country. "It would be extraordinarily difficult," Mr. Rizzo replied, "given the rights that attach to a U.S. citizen in terms of due process, for the President to direct the CIA to capture a U.S. citizen overseas."[22]

John Rizzo never got his prize. Senators who were infuriated at the Bush White House's shabby treatment of the intelligence committee put a hold on the nomination. In September 2007 he withdrew his name from consideration. But, survivor that he was, John Rizzo hung on at Langley for two more years. He retired in 2009.

By then the Obama administration had taken office. Barack Obama came to the White House determined to energize the Afghan war, which to his mind was being lost because Washington had stopped paying attention, and because leaders were not taking a regional view of the conflict. Conceptualizing the combat theater as Afghanistan and Pakistan together, or "AfPak," President Obama ordered a surge to the Afghan front. For Pakistan there was the Predator. The Washington policy review that led to these decisions included specific consideration of escalating the drone war in AfPak. Within Afghanistan the military, primarily the air force, would be responsible. Over Pakistan the drones belonged to the CIA.

These choices were problematic. Drone strikes had never been popular in Pakistan, with which America's alliance was already shaky. Frustration that the Pakistani military resisted action led Obama to order the CIA to do more. In effect, the Obama administration converted the drone operation from a program of selective, precision strikes into an aerial interdiction campaign. One positive development has been that President Obama has brought the procedure for putting enemies on the target list back into the White House. A strike in Pakistan soon after he assumed office killed a number of civilians. Obama not only demanded explanations, he arranged that Pentagon target nominations be discussed by a wide array of officials in regular teleconferences, and that the CIA have a more closely held, but similar, process. Interagency approvals go to the White House, where the president personally has the last word. Driven by the logic of his escalation, however, President Obama later diluted that procedure by sanctioning "signature" strikes—targets in certain locations, in certain kinds of facilities or vehicles, even associated with certain telephone numbers, could be attacked under standing orders.

But there was no possibility the CIA could mount a sufficient number of Predator strikes to exert true military weight, particularly once the agency reduced the explosive charges in the weapons carried by its drones in an effort to reduce collateral damage. Ratcheting up the offensive effort also increased the already-significant problem of the militarization of the agency. In the rugged mountains of Pakistan's northwest frontier provinces, air strikes had marginal effectiveness. At the same time, more numerous Predator attacks meant more Pakistani civilian casualties, further inflaming bilateral relations. Military experience in Korea, Vietnam, and even World War II—all with astronomically greater U.S. force applied—showed that aerial interdiction could not stop a determined adversary.

Meanwhile, all of this was supposed to be about Al Qaeda—and CIA data showed that organization down to a few dozen adherents. The drone attacks had some success in killing senior operatives. But the biggest fish of all would be netted by old-fashioned methods. A raid by Navy SEALs inside Pakistan eliminated Osama bin Laden in May 2011. One consequence would be to throw together the issues of assassination and torture. There were claims that only torture had enabled American operators to obtain the intelligence that identified the house in which bin Laden lived. This dispute came to a head in late 2012 with release of the Kathryn Bigelow film *Zero Dark Thirty*, a dramatization of the covert operation that could be seen as backing the torture argument. Informed opinion held that bin Laden's hideout had been found by conventional methods: a Pakistani tipoff identified the enemy's courier, monitoring the courier's movements and cell-phone calls enabled operatives to localize the place, satellite and ground observation led to increasing confidence in the intelligence. President Obama did not have complete certainty when he approved the SEAL mission, but he had enough to give the okay. In the wake of *Zero Dark Thirty* three senators, including intelligence committee chairwoman Dianne Feinstein and John McCain, issued a joint statement denying that information from torture had informed the raid. They were followed by the acting director of the CIA, then Michael J. Morell, who told agency employees in an official statement that the facts were otherwise. The director rejected the strong sense the movie conveyed that torture had been the key to finding bin Laden. "That impression is false," Morell noted.[23]

After bin Laden the agency approached the end of its Al Qaeda thread. Washington now switched enemies for CIA's operation, from Al Qaeda to the Taliban partisans fighting the Afghan war, and it added Pakistani extremists, framing them as Al Qaeda appendages. The net effect was to rob Langley's drone campaign of any remaining connection to retaliation against the terrorists of 9/11. The CIA's drones became an appendage too—of the conventional military campaign inside Afghanistan.

The one real advantage of the drone war was that it could be *controlled*. Rather than depending on indifferent local allies, Washington could plan and conduct its activities and switch emphasis at will. That, too, Obama did, moving to expand the network of Predator bases throughout the Near East and Horn of Africa. Yemen and Somalia became major foci of Predator strikes. The escalation cast President Obama in the role of war manager. At this writing, CIA drone attacks carried out on Obama's watch exceed the number conducted through the entire eight years of George W. Bush's presidency. If the trend continues, Obama's drone war will exceed Bush's by a considerable margin before this book reaches print.

It was inevitable that a CIA campaign of such ferocity would lead to the recrudescence of the assassination issue. Targeting foreign nationals was already delicate. Deliberately targeting Americans crossed the line—and it brought repetition of the highly questionable practice of crafting Top Secret opinions to justify illegality. In a still-secret exercise over a period of months in 2010, the Obama administration created arguments to nullify the constitutional rights of citizens. It should have known better. Barack Obama was a professor of constitutional law before he became a politician. The responsible official at the Justice Department, Harold Koh, is an expert on war powers and belligerent rights during hostilities. They have not dared expose the product of their labor to public scrutiny. Instead, the legal paper was used to authorize the CIA targeting of American citizen Anwar al-Awlaki.

A Muslim cleric who left northern Virginia for Yemen, Awlaki was credited with influencing others to make terrorist attacks. These included a fellow Muslim cleric, an army chaplain who went on a shooting rampage at Fort Hood, a Nigerian who attempted to blow up an airliner, and a Saudi who crafted bombs embedded in copier machines to destroy cargo planes over the United States. The conspiracies were real enough, but the threat of Awlaki's activities was deemed to override everything. Rather than attempt to capture Awlaki and bring him to trial, the intent was to blow him up. The CIA succeeded in that in September 2011. Another American, Samir Kahn, was killed with him. Kahn's offense was to be an Al Qaeda propagandist. Awlaki's sixteen-year-old son, Abdulrahman al-Awlaki went to Yemen to search for his father, and a month later the Predators took him too. "It was a very good strike," Richard Cheney said on television, interviewed on Cable News Network. "The president ought to have that kind of authority to order that kind of strike, even when it involves an American citizen, when there's clear evidence that he's part of Al Qaeda."[24]

In contrast to the ideal of the covert operation that has "plausible deniability," the drone war has acquired the trappings of a military operation. The effort is divided between the CIA and the Pentagon's Joint Special Operations Command. A typology of missions has evolved. "Signature strikes," aimed at generic categories of targets, can be carried out without specific approval. Attacks aimed at specified individuals are still subject to high-level sanction. Senior officials at the Pentagon have weekly videoconferences to consider the menu options. The CIA has a similar but highly classified routine. The approved target lists go to the White House for review. President Obama approves the most sensitive missions personally. It is reported that during the runup to Obama's reelection in 2012, his administration moved to standardize this decision model and the associated legal justifications in order to have a permanent structure in place for a possible successor. Obama's electoral victory renders the standardization effort unnecessary, but the mere fact this effort took place indicates the United States government now considers targeted aerial killings a legitimate type of activity. As this goes to press the United Nations is on the verge of creating a panel to examine drone killings and their legal justification. War crimes charges are one possible result.

While all this moved steadily forward in the field, it turns out the Central Intelligence Agency also replicated the apparatus for Langley's classic assassination plots. According to press reports, this was another project whose existence was withheld from Congress on the orders of Vice President Cheney.[25] Soon after 9/11, George Tenet approved the formation of a standing unit, essentially a commando team, that could carry out assassinations. This was another Counter-Terrorist Center brainchild, one more of Jose Rodriguez's booby traps. Tenet put the scheme on hold before he left, but planning continued. Known as Project Cannonball, the activity apparently reached a decision point in 2004 and briefly attained some operational capability the following year. Several high-level meetings were held about Cannonball and more than a million dollars spent on it. The unit never conducted any operational missions. Agency deputy director Stephen Kappes, as well as Rodriguez's successor at the head of the clandestine service, Michael J. Sulick, both determined to hold back Cannonball. It came to Director Panetta's attention in mid-2009, when CIA officials contemplated reviving the enterprise, taking it to a level requiring congressional notification. Panetta shut it down instead, and on June 24, 2009, informed Congress of its existence.

Details remain obscure at this writing. For example, the extent of CIA legal review is not known, though it would be highly unusual for the General Counsel not to have put its seal on the project. Personnel were selected, apparently including individuals employed by the private military unit Blackwater (later Xe Corporation, now Academi Corporation) under a 2004 contract, and planning took place over several years. By one account the CIA never could contrive a practical formula. The logistics of moving a team on short notice for a lethal mission while keeping the target under observation were daunting, and the arrangements to extract the hit squad could never be settled. Accounts agree that the program was revamped several times—which is to say the agency kept at it. Although what we know about this venture is entirely based upon press reporting, Director Panetta's notification to Congress is a matter of record, and the hit team also became the subject of an official statement issued by the Central Intelligence Agency. Its creation exactly replicated the special unit formed at the CIA under William

K. Harvey in the early 1960s. As several agency veterans commented in this instance, one of the most difficult aspects of the scheme was to keep it secret. Another Family Jewel on the pile.

During the Year of Intelligence, the revelation of CIA plots for assassinations inflamed the public. The Ford administration tried its hardest to finesse inquiries and then suppress the resulting reports. The plots, the attempts against Fidel Castro, the murders actually carried out by CIA allies, and the agency's creation of an assassination unit were universally deemed reprehensible, a Family Jewel. President Gerald Ford outlawed assassinations by executive fiat. Every successor has followed in his footsteps. Yet now the procedure is to maintain the official prohibition while secretly canceling it by means of presidents' operational directives. To this hypocrisy is added a massive covert campaign that aims to kill people rather than capture and bring them to trial, the extrajudicial targeting of American citizens, a formal hit list, and even the replication of the CIA hit team as a mission unit. Some of this is legal, but most of it is not—and all of it is a Family Jewel. Americans would be appalled to discover the true extent of these covert operations. But over the years Langley has worked very hard to cloak its daggers.

≡ CLOAKING THE DAGGER ≡

The standard Central Intelligence Agency response to all its problems is to try and keep them from the public, partly through secrecy, partly by means of manipulation. Attempts to influence opinion belong legitimately in an examination of the Family Jewels because only public concern induces the spooks and their overseers to scrub down and legitimate operations. The subject here is not so much "spin doctoring" per se or public relations—though these undoubtedly begin with the fear that a negative impression will inhibit CIA freedom of action—as it is active measures to shape the CIA's image. The spooks minimize flap potential by currying favor with journalists or other well-known figures, giving them privileged access and selectively releasing material favorable to itself while suppressing more disquieting knowledge. These are efforts to forestall the emergence of data the spy mavens consider damaging to their interests. Americans are the target. Citizens can debate whether these are charter violations, but taken together the record is chilling even where it is not illegal.

Agency interactions with the media, broadly conceived to include not only newspaper reporters, magazine writers, authors, broadcast journalists, and so on, are a huge and thorny subject. In the past it has been almost entirely viewed in one of two ways: as a question of how the intelligence agency produced propaganda for the Cold War—which often had repercussions on domestic opinion—or as one of the CIA's use of media outlets as cover for its officers on mission. Yes, there was an operational side in how the CIA used media to cloak the identities of its operatives. This has received nearly all the attention given to the subject and will not be rehashed here. There was also an operational effort to plant books, articles, films, and other items to further CIA propaganda aims. Simply circulating the artifacts of Western culture behind the Iron Curtain—by no means limited to CIA's own doctored or inspired products—did weaken the hold of communist ideology.[1]

But much more sinister is the issue of what the CIA did to influence the ways in which it, itself, is portrayed. As will be seen, this has been a direct, constant effort that reached far beyond press releases or spin doctoring and has been a domestic activity from the start. It has included attempts to shape what is known about international events, to secure the dismissal of journalists or discredit commentators considered unfriendly; the active surveillance of American citizens; the suppression of works by the CIA's own employees (see Chapter 8); meddling in authors' research to limit what can be discovered about the intelligence services; manipulation of the Freedom of Information Act and other declassification regulations; lawsuits; and even intervention in the marketplace. These things have been done in the name of protecting intelligence "sources and methods," which the CIA has a responsibility to do under a 1949 law. But that authority has been used to justify a host of actions that have nothing to do with protecting the technical secrets of intelligence, but everything to do with flap potential. Just to put this record in one place is stunning. Preventing disclosure has meant near-malevolent actions. This discussion will adopt the term "suppressive maneuvers" to describe the whole gamut of these activities.

From the perspective of Family Jewels, our concern is not the wider CIA cultural Cold War, but the interactions where CIA operations had or intended to have an effect on American public discourse. This is distinct in another way also. In this area the CIA played defense. With the exception of the agency role in Watergate, many of the Family Jewels documents described programs or projects, activities of clear or potential criminality as perceived by the agency's own officers, dubious suppressive maneuvers, or plain violations of a charter prohibiting domestic activities. Those were the products of CIA units pursuing projects they were instructed to carry out. But in the public arena Langley sought to shape, moderate, or ameliorate what Americans thought and said about the Central Intelligence Agency.

Over the longer arc of CIA history, this is the persistent struggle of an assortment of CIA components to influence what Americans said or did about the agency, and in some instances public opinion about United States government policy. Only a small part of this was public relations. More often it amounted to strong-arming media moguls or U.S. corporations, or the employment of methods that, had they been directed against a foreign country, would fairly be seen as part of a psychological warfare campaign. In certain instances suppressive maneuvers involved wiretapping persons who wrote stories the CIA considered threatening, in others the muzzling of former agency officers. One became the object of an active covert operation. With a magazine, the agency grasped every straw in its effort to silence a critical voice. Multiple episodes show CIA sensitivity regarding the Kennedy assassination. Here, the agency planned actions with respect to books on that tragedy, as it did with at least one book on the war in Southeast Asia.

Suppressive maneuvers began very early in the CIA's history. Allen Dulles, the agency's director from 1953 to 1961, famously manipulated the *New York Times* during the 1954 paramilitary operation in Guatemala. Having decided that *Times* reporter Sydney Gruson's presence would be inconvenient—both headquarters and the CIA station leading the effort compiled analyses of Gruson's articles that claimed he was friendly to the government the CIA intended to overthrow—the spooks tried to neutralize him. Capitalizing on the Guatemalans canceling Gruson's visa after a story they disliked, forcing the reporter to move to Mexico, Director Dulles went to *Times* publisher Arthur Hays Sulzberger and the paper's general manager to claim that Gruson could not report objectively and should be kept in Mexico. Of course, what the agency meant by "objective" was journalism shaded to present the Guatemalan government as somehow illegitimate. The *Times* actually acceded to Dulles's demand, though Sulzberger's suspicions grew and a few months later he confronted the CIA director. Gruson himself broke with instructions and got back to Guatemala. But by then the agency had done its work, and the CIA stood on the verge of paramilitary success.[2]

Some CIA actions in this back-alley struggle, illegal because they were domestic activities, would have been subject to criminal penalties had they been carried out later. In 1959 Shef Edwards's security mavens tapped the phones of Charles J. V. Murphy after the journalist published articles on the "Missile Gap" intelligence dispute. Warrantless wiretapping next took place with Project Mockingbird, which CIA Director John A. McCone, Dulles's successor, ordered on the telephones of Washington reporters Paul J. Scott and Robert S. Allen in March 1963. McCone's executive assistant Walter S. Elder recounts that initiative came at the instigation of Attorney General Robert F. Kennedy. The CIA Office of Security records that both journalists, a team who wrote the "Allen-Scott Report" published by the Hall Syndicate, had published columns that at times quoted Top Secret documents and even communications intercepts. Scott's son believes that stories they wrote about the Cuban Missile Crisis were the catalyst. With the telephone company's help (shades of recent controversy over giving the companies legal immunity for this kind of intrusion), taps were installed at the reporters' offices at the National Press Building and both their homes.

Scott and Allen quickly learned they were being wiretapped—Paul Scott's son James was at home playing with a friend when the phone rang. When he picked it up he could hear voices in an undertone talking about changing the audiotape. His father immediately told James to be careful and that someone was listening in on their telephones.[3] No doubt Scott drew the appropriate conclusion. The CIA overheard a number of sources and identified many of them, including a plethora of people on Capitol Hill, an assistant to Bobby Kennedy, a White House staffer, and an aide to Vice President Lyndon B. Johnson, but no one from the intelligence community. CIA maintained the wiretaps for three months. Paul Scott felt chilled enough to leave the United States. He took his journalism to Mexico.

"Journalist" was given the widest possible definition for suppressive maneuvers. Bernard B. Fall was an academic expert on Vietnam, one of the best in the United States, teaching at Howard University. Fall produced a wide variety of both scholarly and journalistic writing. When he published a piece on the war in South Vietnam in the *Christian Science Monitor* in early 1962, it raised eyebrows at the Kennedy White House. President Kennedy made inquiries about Fall, to which John McCone responded with a memo crafted by his analysts. The heavily redacted version of this paper currently available appears to show the CIA had a high opinion of Fall's work, but it also notes that "Fall now holds the view that the only real solution to the problems facing the United States in South Vietnam is a negotiated settlement."[4] Shortly thereafter, Fall and his wife Dorothy noticed they were being followed, and their phones tapped. Bernard Fall became a casualty of the Vietnam war, killed by a mine in 1967 while accompanying a U.S. Marine patrol. Years later, using the Freedom of Information Act, Dorothy Fall applied to see Bernard's FBI file. After repeated requests and two decades of pushing, Dorothy got the file. It revealed the surveillance had gone into high gear with wiretaps in July 1963, around the time of Kennedy's inquiry to the CIA. The excuse was that U.S. authorities were trying to establish whether Fall was a *French* spy.[5]

The records of CIA Director John McCone's interactions with President Lyndon B. Johnson are eye-opening in terms of the agency's sense of vulnerability to the media. This vein opens as early as November 29, 1963, a week after LBJ succeeded the dead Kennedy. Bringing Johnson that morning's President's Daily Brief (PDB),[6] in commenting on one of its items McCone noted press "distortions," very likely on Vietnam, and accepted the president's instructions to see the chairman of the *New York Times* and complain that its supposedly skewed reporting damaged U.S. interests.[7] McCone reported back on December 3 that the *Times* had tempered its coverage. This was a sequel to efforts Kennedy had made previously with *Times* editors to silence their reporters Neil Sheehan and David Halberstam. Six days later, waiting to enter the Oval Office for another PDB presentation, national security advisor McGeorge Bundy asked McCone whether the CIA was doing damage assessment on an article regarding reconnaissance satellites that had appeared in the *Washington Post*. McCone answered "yes," then immediately ordered an investigation when he returned to Langley.[8]

McCone blamed the well-known aviation writer, Charles J. V. Murphy, now a repeat offender. The agency considered his piece objectionable—so McCone invited him over to give Murphy chapter and verse on why he was wrong. Note that, in the furor that erupted after the Bay of Pigs, Murphy had been considered reliable enough that CIA leaked information to him for an account favorable to the agency that he published in *Fortune* magazine.

In January 1964 Senator Eugene McCarthy wrote an article critical of the CIA in the magazine *Saturday Evening Post*. President Johnson saw the piece and mentioned it to Director McCone, who agreed "to see McCarthy to discuss the article . . . and try to put an end to this type of criticism that he has been directing toward the agency."[9] Senator McCarthy's transgression was simply that he advocated a joint congressional committee to oversee U.S. intelligence. When the Soviet Union tried and failed at a space shot toward the planet Venus, both the *Times* and *Post* reported in terms very similar to those used in U.S. intelligence reports. Director McCone brought this to the president to ask if he would accept the intelligence community doing an investigation of the leak. LBJ had no problem with that.[10]

A striking episode in this intricate dance took place over 1965–1966, when the *New York Times* prepared a five-part series on U.S. intelligence generally, and the Central Intelligence Agency in particular. In the fall of 1965, *Times* managing editor Turner Catledge, mystified at the shady schemes of America's spooks, had exclaimed, "For God's sake let's find out what they are doing."[11] That led to a months-long project worthy of the agency itself—the *Times* queried its correspondents in far-flung corners of the world and put a team together to compile the results. It was, says Harrison Salisbury, "the first big venture by the *Times* into the journalism of the late sixties." Reporter Tom Wicker took charge of the investigative team.

Agency counterintelligence guru James Angleton discovered the *Times*'s inquiry in short order from CIA officers under cover at the newspaper, no doubt from the interview that Timesman John Finney did with McCone, and from field reporting as well. By October 1 CIA media monitor Stanley Grogan was addressing Richard Helms about a *Times* "threat to the safety of the nation." The proposed solution?— have both Helms and recently appointed Director William F. Raborn intercede with the publishers. The buck went as high as Secretary of State Dean Rusk, who spoke to Catledge and Arthur Ochs Sulzberger. The *Times* finally agreed to let John McCone (now retired) review the article drafts before its series went to press. That happened in February 1966. McCone raised issues the newspaper dealt with one way or another. But like Rusk, McCone opposed any publication at all. The *Times* went ahead anyway.

When the stories began to appear on April 25, 1966, CIA headquarters dispatched a global alert to its stations instructing them to report back which specific items in the *Times* articles got the most attention in their countries. Langley also furnished talking points for station personnel to rebut the stories. Both McCone and Rusk remained angry at the *Times* for the newspaper's simple exercise of its Fourth Estate role. Meanwhile, quite apart from CIA's efforts to counter the series within the United States, it crafted a campaign to neutralize the reporting in the lands affected by the *Times* revelations. The agency succeeded on at least one front—after publication of the articles, Richard Helms and Tracy Barnes met with top *Times* officials and convinced them to drop plans for a book expanding on the series.

It was now that CIA effectively went to war against *Ramparts*, a San Francisco–based journal of political commentary. *Ramparts* opposed the Vietnam war and the CIA's foreign adventures and commissioned articles that struck at agency operations. One, in June 1966, exposed the Vietnam activities of a group of Michigan State University consultants, as well as their work in tandem with the CIA and role providing cover employment for agency personnel. Written by a disaffected former project coordinator and one of the magazine's editors, the exposé was authoritative. Langley obtained advance knowledge of this *Ramparts* article. Admiral William F. Raborn, in his last months as director, demanded a briefing on the magazine and authors from his Office of Security.[12] With a couple of days of name checks the spooks pulled together scraps of information from agency files on as many as 40 percent of *Ramparts* writers and staff. Howard Osborn could tell Raborn that the journal had morphed from a religious magazine to one of political commentary, and maintained offices in New York, Paris, and Munich. It had more than fifty staff, among them two members of the Communist Party of the United States. But all that digging yielded no gold, and in May 1966 the CIA was obliged to tell Walt W. Rostow that *Ramparts* had no identifiable foreign communist ties.

A couple of *Ramparts* editors, including one of the article's authors, Robert Scheer, planned to run for Congress opposing the Vietnam war. Richard Helms, shortly to be elevated to CIA director, immediately passed this to the Johnson White House and bent more effort to burrowing into the journal's universe. By then Langley had developed dossiers on the editors and had begun probing its freelance writers. On June 16 Admiral Raborn asked Osborn to advise the FBI that *Ramparts* ought to be investigated as a subversive threat. The security chief complied, telling the Bureau that CIA would be interested in any "derogatory material" it turned up. The FBI investigation of Robert Scheer undoubtedly had a negative impact on his campaign. He indeed lost the election. The CIA's role in this has not been established.

Not long afterwards Mr. Helms succeeded Admiral Raborn at the head of the agency. The focus of the *Ramparts* operation shifted from Osborn's office to CIA's Counterintelligence (CI) Staff. Agency officer Richard Ober, assigned to CI upon completing the course at the National War College, took charge of the files. The CI Staff put nine professionals, later a dozen, to work on this project. Eventually they accumulated files on 127 freelance writers, staff, and editors and almost 200 others associated in some way with *Ramparts*. Another agency unit, the Domestic Contact Service, supplied data on *Ramparts* writers and employees through its San Francisco field office. These files later formed the nucleus of the CIA's entire operation to monitor domestic political dissent (Chapter 3).

Meanwhile, Edmund Applewhite coordinated operational activity against *Ramparts*. Applewhite recalled, "I had all sorts of dirty tricks to hurt their circulation and financing.... We were not in the least inhibited by the fact that the CIA had no internal role in the United States."[13] There were efforts to dissuade advertisers and weaken the magazine's subscriber base, but the agency could do little about the most important source of *Ramparts*'s funding—investments by the publisher Edward Keating. Langley tried to persuade the Internal Revenue Service (IRS) to audit Keating's tax returns only to learn the tax enforcers had already done that—for both funder and the magazine itself, and for Robert Scheer—over several years running. The enforcers' actions had had no impact on *Ramparts* people.

In January 1967 the CIA learned—again in advance—that *Ramparts* was on the verge of revealing that the agency secretly funded the National Student Association, an explosive charge that explicitly showed Langley engaged in illegal domestic activity. (At the time, membership dues accounted for as little as $18,000 of the association's $800,000 annual budget—about $5.2 million in 2010 dollars.) The news electrified Applewhite's unit. CIA redoubled efforts to get at *Ramparts* through the IRS. The key meeting between agency officials and Thomas Terry, special assistant to the IRS commissioner, took place on February 1, 1967—before *Ramparts* even blew the whistle. The CI Staff supplied tax investigators with inside information on the magazine's backers. By midmonth Langley had a copy of Keating's tax return. Almost simultaneously, on February 14, *Ramparts* disclosed its findings in full-page ads in both the *New York Times* and *Washington Post,* with front-page articles in both newspapers discussing the facts.[14]

Foreknowledge—and the desire to learn about the money that fed *Ramparts*—led the CIA to reach out to the IRS anew. The agency now asked to see *Ramparts*'s corporate tax returns and asked for an IRS briefing on its taxes, illegal under U.S. law. Langley planted articles elsewhere to discredit *Ramparts.* Its operations against the magazine included recruiting a source who reported on staff meetings and advertising accounts, attempting to recruit former employees, priming a CIA asset with answers to feed *Ramparts* reporters who were to interview him, and using the feedback to plan further suppressive maneuvers. Completed on April 5, 1967, more than forty years ago, this plan aimed at Americans, not a foreign enemy, and it remains secret today. It is said to have included recommendations to induce funders to desist, pressure on advertisers to drop *Ramparts* as a venue, and smearing the magazine with phony stories planted in other media. Articles of this ilk actually did appear in the *Washington Star* and in the weekly *Human Events.*[15] Domestic activity, including this kind of propaganda placement, is prohibited to the agency. Edmund Applewhite would be promoted to CIA Deputy Inspector General.

Yet *Ramparts*'s revelation of agency funding of the student association triggered a wave of public concern that overwhelmed such attacks. Further disclosures quickly

followed—Langley's money flowing through private founda-
tions, secret subsidies to Radio Free Europe/Radio Liberty.
Then came President Johnson's order to halt CIA funding to
any and all youth or student groups, followed by a presidential commission review of agency relationships with private
and voluntary organizations. The atmosphere became too
charged, further suppressive maneuvers against *Ramparts*
too sensitive. After the first wave of CIA countermeasures,
the plan would be filed away, though the Ober unit went on to
more intrusive work against American political groups and
private persons (Chapter 3).

During the Watergate era the CIA would be extraordinarily touchy about all manner of allegations. Notes of
the director's staff meetings are replete with entries regarding the leak of the Pentagon Papers, agency involvement in
Watergate itself, and other charges against the CIA. These
were often put on the list for debunking. A typical example is
legislative liaison John Maury's July 1972 paper on the CIA
and drug trafficking, which surveys charges made by various journalists and authors over the period from April 1970
to July 1972. In the face of elaborately detailed charges, the
CIA's entire defense was the summary assertion in one sen-
tence that "Intensive investigation has revealed that each of
the above, and similar, allegations which have come to our
attention are unfounded."[16] There had in fact been an Inspector General (IG) survey made on the drug accusations, but
that IG report is not mentioned nor are its detailed findings
relayed, possibly because they *confirmed* the charges in at
least one aspect—that employees of the CIA proprietary Air
America had carried drugs on their planes during agency
flights (the IG disputed whether this was witting and argued
the pilots had no control over what people brought on board
the aircraft). Executive Director William E. Colby made

similar denials in a letter to the editor published in *Atlantic* magazine. But by the summer of 1972 the atmosphere in the United States had passed the point where summary denials were going to get the Central Intelligence Agency off the hook. Its own leadership was to blame for not, in the phrase of CIA baron and Helms intimate Cord Meyer, Jr., facing reality.

D ebunking was pretty much standard fare for government agencies stung by media reporting, but, as with *Ramparts*, CIA suppressive maneuvers repeatedly went further. See what happened in 1964 when authors David Wise and Thomas B. Ross published their book *The Invisible Government.*[17] The Wise and Ross work would be considered pretty tame fare today. But, inspired by the spectacular failure at the Bay of Pigs and the authors' sense that behind the scenes certain agencies operated far differently than their official images suggested, they sought to penetrate the façade of U.S. intelligence. Their book discussed the Defense Intelligence Agency and NSA as well as the CIA and included a discussion of agency efforts to use the Peace Corps for cover. Wise and Ross were the first to go beyond the heroic image of CIA covert operations in Iran and Guatemala—or the opposite in Cuba—to present such cases as Burma, Indonesia, and Laos, pairing tales of derring-do with a discussion of the struggle to control the agency.

Langley's operatives had managed to obtain—"covertly," Wise recalls—a copy of the galleys for the book. Desperate to quash it, CIA officials went to the Department of Justice, where they saw Deputy Attorney General Nicolas deB. Katzenbach. More than two decades later a select committee of the U.S. House of Representatives, investigating the assassination of John F. Kennedy, questioned Katzenbach on the treatment of Russian defector Yuri Nosenko (Chapter 5), on which the agency also consulted him. Katzenbach could not recall the Nosenko matter, but what he did remember was the CIA effort to suppress publication: "Whenever they wanted a book suppressed they came to me and I told them not to do it."[18] The works concerned were *The Invisible Government* and Haynes Johnson's history that would be titled *The Bay of Pigs*.

The authors learned the CIA had their manuscript when John McCone invited them to lunch. They found McCone to be a "wonderfully polite man." But once the plates were cleared, the CIA boss took out a paper that listed ten "national security breaches," which he demanded they remove from their text. Tom Ross noticed the paper was stamped "Top Secret" at the top and bottom—something that leaped out in those days, since classification markings were applied by rubber stamp using bright red ink. "Mr. McCone," Ross replied, "we don't deal in classified documents." They could not possibly take the CIA's list with them. Suddenly agency Inspector General Lyman Kirkpatrick appeared from a side door and, with scissors, snipped off the offending markings. But the CIA's exercise in instant declassification proved futile—Wise and Ross did not change a thing.[19]

Director McCone then discussed the book with President Johnson at some length when they met privately on May 20, 1964. Aside from warning the president that *The Invisible Government* might damage agencies beyond the CIA, McCone confirmed to Johnson that he had asked Wise and Ross for changes. More than that, he told the president, McCone had intervened with their editor at Random House, Robert Loomis, even threatening him with espionage charges. When Loomis persevered, the CIA chief approached corporate executives, and he also complained to the publisher of *Look* magazine, which was about to run an excerpt. McCone judged he had failed, and pressed LBJ to enter the fray with a public condemnation at a news conference.

Lyndon Baines Johnson, ever attuned to personal image, refrained from doing so.[20]

Langley then offered to buy every copy of the book. Random House countered that it would see the book to print no matter what the agency did.

The president might have been careful, but the Central Intelligence Agency was in panic mode. An ad hoc group formed to deal with the fallout. It recommended mobilizing agency assets to ensure that *The Invisible Government* received poor reviews. An all-stations cable went out over McCone's signature ordering additional counteraction. Propaganda staff at headquarters crafted a phony "book review" to be planted in the foreign press. What seemed so sensitive to Langley was Wise and Ross's affirmation in the book that all covert operations were approved by a White House Special Group, revealing that all such ventures were, in effect, approved by the president. The CIA propaganda mavens concocted a counterargument that, according to agency veteran Joseph B. Smith, "contained a view of the president's office which would have forced James Madison to rewrite the *Federalist Papers*."[21] Smith would have known. His duty post prior to assignment in Argentina had been with the propaganda staff. A decade later, with the CIA under fire as a "rogue elephant" beyond presidential control, the data in *The Invisible Government* would have helped the spy barons. All hands ignored the lesson that national security "damage" was in the eye of the beholder.

This was not the first time, nor the last, Langley would act to neutralize works considered inimical to its interests. During McCone's tenure similar action surrounded publication of the Haynes Johnson book on the Bay of Pigs.[22] Illustrations of the CIA's war on books are powerfully reinforced by evidence of its sensitivity to works regarding the murder of John F. Kennedy. Whether due to its assassination attempts against Fidel Castro, its other Cuban operations, its information on Lee Harvey Oswald, the Nosenko affair, or for some other reason, throughout the Helms period the agency remained extraordinarily sensitive about Kennedy assassination books. Soon after the 1964 release of the Warren Commission's report, member Gerald R. Ford came out with his own account of the investigation. A staffer analyzed this for Dick Helms. "In general," he concluded, "my feeling is that the less we touch in this manuscript the better." In fact, CIA was relieved that then-representative Ford had little to say about it.

Mark Lane's Kennedy assassination book *Rush to Judgment*[23] received a full treatment in August 1966, with a summary memorandum to Helms along with appendices dissecting Lane's claims and offering rationales to discredit them. The CIA director received another, separate analysis as well, one focused on the agency's appearances in Lane's book. Langley was so desperate to see the William Manchester account of Kennedy's murder[24] that it became the subject of a November 9, 1966, *operational* cable—almost two months prior to publication—in which a spook reported on efforts to obtain a copy of the manuscript.

This material, other published works, and the Warren Commission Report became the grist for a lengthy analysis of the then-existing literature on the Kennedy assassination as part of a CIA psychological warfare study, "Countering Criticism of the Warren Report," issued on January 4, 1967. Included were observations on the negative impact of conspiracy theories on public opinion, the assertion that no significant new evidence had emerged on the Kennedy assassination—even though the agency's own reporting on Oswald was already being questioned—an analysis of books published so far, and guidelines for countering criticism of the CIA. This lengthy cable, the work of William V. Broe, at that time chief of the Western Hemisphere Division, went to all stations, to be given to CIA assets to use making arguments about the assassination. Though nine attachments to this guidance were never secret (in fact, rated "unclassified"), when forced to release these documents the CIA kept back most of them.

These suppressive maneuvers are ironic, given the CIA's own history as the "Mighty Wurlitzer," the propaganda machine combining entities like Radio Free Europe with subsidies to publications created during its early years. The agency is credited with commissioning, subsidizing, or encouraging a mountain of books. Yet in the suppression campaigns we see the agency leaning over backwards to neutralize, minimize, or even neuter books it considered less favorable. But the secret warriors did not stop to consider that psywar plays both ways. When the truth emerged about CIA's maneuvers, where its raison d'être was to defend a nation that prizes free speech, there would be a cost to weigh against any gains from publication manipulations.

On Dick Helms's watch more books antagonized the agency. One was by a young graduate student, Alfred McCoy, assisted by others, called *The Politics of Heroin in Southeast Asia*, which condemned both the CIA and the U.S. war in Vietnam.[25] It too contained extensive detail on drug trafficking by the agency's Laotian and South Vietnamese allies, as well as their links to Air America. McCoy's book was scheduled by Harper & Row. The CIA learned of it, but failed to obtain the details it wanted. Then Cord Meyer, who happened to be a friend of Harper board member Cass Canfield, cadged a copy of the manuscript from him. In July 1972 OGC attorney Lawrence Houston wrote Harper & Row, demanding not only a front-channel copy, but the right to review the book's content, claiming publication could endanger the lives of agency officers. Terrified Harper lawyers induced management to permit this infringement. (While CIA officers sign contracts promising to protect secrets, American publishers have no such obligation.) The agency hit the publisher with a twenty-page list of changes it demanded. According to McCoy, the review actually improved his book—he insisted the CIA fully document every change it wanted. He used that material to extend his analysis. The agency overreached, and both McCoy and Harper lawyers rejected its overblown demands.[26] The controversy also drew attention from the *New York Times*, where Sy Hersh published a big piece on the manipulation.

Central Intelligence Agency officials, led by William Colby, then tried to counter the McCoy book's charges with letters to the editor in magazines and newspapers where the author placed articles, including the one in *Atlantic* mentioned earlier. The CIA's campaign to discredit McCoy backfired. The major news coverage from Hersh drew attention to *The Politics of Heroin*. The book garnered even more interest. After that Langley reprised its ploy on *The Invisible Government* and made plans to buy out the entire print run of the book. Harper & Row merely increased the size of its printing. This CIA suppressive maneuver backfired.[27]

Even friends of the agency could be swept up in CIA's enthusiasm to police the public domain. At a July 1971 staff meeting, the agency's Vietnam director, George Carver, told Deputy Director of Central Intelligence Robert Cushman that air force General Edward Lansdale, who had been intimately involved in agency operations in the Philippines and Vietnam as well as Cuba, had completed a memoir he'd been writing for almost two years. It was in the hands of the publisher, again Harper & Row. Carver hoped the agency could get a look at that manuscript too. While CIA actions in regard to Lansdale's book cannot be ascertained, when *In the Midst of Wars* appeared a year later, the work proved remarkably uninformative about the CIA.[28] The memoir of a major figure in the secret wars sank without a trace.

A 1960 memorandum in which General Lansdale surveyed U.S. clandestine warfare assets in Southeast Asia surfaced as part of the Pentagon Papers, a major Department of Defense review of the Vietnam war's history that leaked in June 1971. This Lansdale paper also figured among the specific items discussed at agency staff meetings. Indeed, the Pentagon Papers as a whole were a staple of conversation among Helms's barons. As early as September 1970, months before Daniel Ellsberg actually leaked the papers, CIA considered suspending his security clearances. When the Pentagon Papers finally emerged, the agency was all over them. George Carver headed the team performing the damage assessment, identifying secrets that were compromised. Helms's minutes make clear that despite sworn affidavits the United States government filed in various courts to affirm the Papers were full of intelligence secrets, the CIA review *had not even been completed* when the Supreme Court issued its *final* ruling crushing Nixon administration efforts to quash publication. Langley later considered a lawsuit to prevent Boston's Beacon Press from issuing the Senator Gravel edition of the Papers, contemplated reprimanding officer Sam Adams, who appeared as a witness for defendants Daniel Ellsberg and Anthony Russo at their subsequent criminal trial, and maneuvered to evade subpoenas for other agency personnel or documents.

Erroneously or deliberately, George Carver, who could tack to the wind better than almost anyone, told the CIA barons *after* his study that the Gravel edition's four volumes could be the so-called "negotiating volumes" of the Pentagon Papers. This is incomprehensible, since, presumably, Carver had been looking at what had actually appeared in public. The diplomatic volumes tracked Johnson administration efforts to engage North Vietnam in talks that might end the war. They were materials that Dan Ellsberg had protected, refusing to leak them precisely in order to protect their secrecy. The Helms notes also disclose that the CIA knew of the creation and activities of the White House "Plumbers" unit, which formed at this time with the intended purpose of plugging leaks like that of the Pentagon Papers.

L ike the Nixon White House, with its notorious "Plumbers," the CIA ran its own ops. Journalists became targets. One of the first was *Washington Post* reporter Michael Getler, whose articles on intelligence bothered the agency, while his pieces on U.S. arms control talks with the Soviets irritated the White House, which also prodded Langley. A December 1970 Getler article describing intelligence disputes over the Soviet missile buildup annoyed defense secretary Melvin Laird, who approached national security advisor Henry Kissinger. Another on CIA patrols into China raised CIA eyebrows in August 1971. Wiretaps were placed on Getler for four days in early October under Project Celotex I, for the entire period from October 27 until December 10, and on January 3, 1972. The CIA used an observation post at the Statler Hilton Hotel, created to surveil Jack Anderson, to watch Getler's comings and goings from across the street. His name or work figured at several of Helms's meetings. Undeterred, Getler came up with a new scoop. On February 8, 1972, he published "New Spy Satellites Planned for Clearer, Instant Pictures." The article described the general features of the next-generation U.S. reconnaissance satellite, KH-11, or "Big Bird." At Director Helms's morning confab, the CIA barons denounced Getler. Furious, Helms ordered more investigation. The spooks never uncovered Getler's sources.

But the *Post* discovered the investigation, and the domestic intrusion came back to bite. The newspaper provided Getler a top-flight lawyer. The journalist chose to go easy, met with CIA counsel, and obtained a cease-and-desist agreement under threat of open legal action.[29] The surveillance of Michael Getler suggests the CIA's sensitivity had hardly changed since John McCone's day. It still made for operational assignments—aimed at Americans.

Columnist Jack Anderson also aroused the CIA's ire—and even before the Getler affair. Anderson had published columns regarding secret U.S. intelligence knowledge of the Tonkin Gulf incident in the Vietnam war. The National Security Agency conducted an internal review and reported to Director Helms that it had been able to identify several NSA items that might have been a basis for the journalist's columns. But there were also inaccuracies in the articles, *and* statements made on the floor of the United States Senate had referred obliquely to the same information. The NSA concluded it would be too difficult to prove that the journalist had been culling from its secret documents.

Helms was pushed further by Nixon, who dreaded what would be in the book *The Anderson Papers*.[30] Already alarmed by Anderson's newspaper columns detailing Nixon administration decisions on Cambodia in 1970, the India-Pakistan war of 1971, NSA interception of the radio-telephone conversations of Soviet leaders, and agency mind control experiments, Helms wrestled with what to do. He came down hard. The National Photographic Interpretation Center tried to photograph the screen during Anderson's television show to capture images of documents on his desk. Enhancing the pictures might reveal what papers were there. But television broadcast with low screen resolution in those days, while primitive enhancement made the effort futile. There was a straight leak investigation too. By Anderson's count the agency questioned no fewer than 1,566 persons in its effort to uncover his sources. Nixon officials settled on a young sailor as culprit. The yeoman shuttled documents between the Joint Chiefs of Staff and the National Security Council. But *after* he was reassigned to Alaska, Anderson came up with more revelations, this time about U.S. policy on talks for a new treaty on bases in Japan. Nixon demanded action.

Some of the Japanese bases, in Okinawa, the CIA used to support its operations in Vietnam, while others in the home islands were the mainstay for National Security Agency monitoring of Soviet and Chinese radio transmissions in the Far East. The FBI dissuaded the White House from initiating an illegal telephone wiretap, fearing Anderson would stumble on its surveillance and reveal it. Langley was leery too. As early as 1967 the CIA had analyzed Anderson's reporting as opinionated and self-righteous. It assembled a fresh analysis now. The CIA's Office of Security mounted Project Celotex II, full physical surveillance of Anderson and his colleagues Britt Hume, Les Whitten, and Joseph Spears. According to Anderson, the physical surveillance was called Project Mudhen. Anderson was given the cryptonym "Brandy." The surveillance was ordered in January 1972, shortly after the columnist's Japan articles. Beginning on February 15, Anderson and his colleagues were followed 24/7, and the Statler Hilton Hotel observation post was busier than ever. Sixteen officers were on the mobile teams, two to a vehicle, and there were four to staff the stakeout. At one point they followed and photographed as Anderson was being filmed by a crew for the CBS television series *Sixty Minutes*. On March 17 they surveilled him at lunch with Richard Helms, recording the CIA's own director as Anderson complained of the surveillance, which he then believed was an FBI initiative. Visits to art museums, sorties to take the kids to school—Celotex II generated mountains of records but no substance at all.

The watch went smoothly for a month, but late in March Anderson realized he was being followed—a friend who lived nearby noticed cars in the parking lot of a church across the road, and men with binoculars and cameras. The lot was a perfect vantage point from which to watch Anderson's home, his friend warned. Anderson visited the place and saw for himself. Driving around, the journalist soon spotted the CIA tails. He suspected Justice Department official Robert Mardian as author of the plot, but discovered it was the CIA by tracing the license plates of the trailing vehicles. On March 27 the journalist's teenage kids pulled up in the parking lot, blocked the CIA cars where they were, and photographed the watchers. It became a game. The reporter's nine children and their friends once piled into cars and sped off in different directions to stymie the minders. Or they would flash their headlights as if giving some secret signal. Or they would drive past the CIA people and wave. The spooks decided to halt the surveillance of Anderson's home, but keep it up at his office. The reporter countered by filing a lawsuit alleging breach of privacy. Discovery forced the CIA to yield surveillance files and subjected Director Helms to deposition. Helms called off the hunt. The agency gave up Celotex II in embarrassment on April 12. The Mudhen files filled a suitcase when they came to Anderson. He quotes the order terminating the surveillance as admitting its search had been "'rather unproductive.'"[31]

Jack Anderson had had some reason to suspect the Federal Bureau of Investigation as his persecutor. Most surveillance of reporters during the Nixon years was in fact carried out by the FBI—its White House–ordered wiretaps became infamous during Watergate—but one more CIA case needs mention because it figured in the original Family Jewels documents. By this time, wiretaps had been illegal for four years, and CIA physical surveillance of American citizens a borderline case (potentially justified almost exclusively in the case of an agency employee spying for a foreign power).

Most often the spy barons merely ruminated on how to counter stories. Talk of specific journalists and their articles was a recurrent topic at the director's staff meetings. Among those whom Helms and his top managers discussed, in addition to Anderson and Getler, were William Beecher, Tad Szulc, John Crewdson, David Burnham, James Reston, Robert A. Wright, and Seymour Hersh of the *New York Times*; David Kraslow of the *Los Angeles Times*; Stanley Karnow and Sanford Unger of the *Washington Post*; Thomas B. Ross of the *Washington Star* (who had earlier been in the CIA's crosshairs for *The Invisible Government*); Nicholas Horrock of *Newsweek*; Hugh Sidey of *Time*; plus syndicated columnists Joseph Alsop, Rowland Evans, and Robert Novak. Among the subjects that exercised agency officials were real intelligence matters, but more often such things as the Pentagon Papers case, the White House Plumbers (before Watergate), Watergate itself as it related to the agency, revelations of CIA cooperation with local police across the nation, allegations of CIA surveillance of the Democratic Party (inaccurate, given our information at this writing), and the agency's role in the Chile covert operation and such associated matters as the International Telephone and Telegraph Corporation affair, or a break-in at the Chilean embassy in Washington.

Langley knew that Seymour Hersh was working the CIA domestic abuse angle long before the story hit the paper. In fact, Helms and his colleagues discussed Hersh's inquiries on January 18, 1973, *before the Family Jewels documents were even created*. And Hersh knew the CIA was witting. Expecting his story would come under attack, the reporter approached Senator Edmund S. Muskie. Hersh wanted to prep someone to defend the *New York Times* revelations and offered to show Muskie his evidence. Not wanting to be drawn in, the senator refused. The story appeared and the furor was instantaneous—numerous officials attacked the *Times* for using the word "massive" in connection with the government domestic spying. But the same night Hersh learned he was all right—his friend David Wise called with the message. "Sammy the Fish Man says you're okay," Wise reported, alluding to his best CIA source.[32]

The Year of Intelligence and the Family Jewels marked only a waypoint in a continuing conflict between journalists—and their sources—and the CIA, other intelligence agencies, and the White House. Because of the interests of government, the First Amendment of the United States Constitution, and the mission of the Fourth Estate to report and illuminate public policy, a staple of the government-press dynamic has been a kind of love-hate relationship. The press is important to the CIA in more ways than one—it can be used to promote the agency's message and its mission, provide a vehicle for information the government *wants* to put before the public, and serve as a mechanism to be employed in the war of leaks that forms part of the environment in which policy is hammered out. At the same time, the press follows its own drummer in seeking out stories and reporting them— and those stories often prove embarrassing, especially to the Central Intelligence Agency. The result is a natural tension between spooks and gumshoe reporters. When officials are not congratulating themselves on the coup of placing certain information in the media, they are often denouncing the press for covering stories the spy mavens would prefer not to see in print or on broadcasts. Even though the United States lacks a shield law at the national level to protect reporters, the First Amendment guarantees their freedom of speech, and effectively suppressing unwanted reporting has proven supremely difficult.

This does not mean government—and the intelligence agencies—have given up the fight. The surveillance operations just recounted show the use of one tool in the battle. Surveillance and investigation inevitably have a chilling effect on reporters' activities. Another tool—legal proceedings—has proven much more difficult to employ. The CIA did not go after Seymour Hersh for the Family Jewels. But it did consider moving against him for another CIA story he publicized, the agency's Project Azorian, the attempt to use a specially designed deep-sea mining ship, the *Glomar Explorer*, to raise a sunken Russian submarine from the bottom of the sea. The Ford administration Justice Department, Ford's NSC, and the CIA circulated papers, but could find no viable legal strategy for a prosecution.

Another journalist, Daniel Schorr of the Columbia Broadcasting System (CBS), also wriggled in the crosshairs. Schorr had earned official enmity as the man who revealed President Ford's admission the CIA had planned assassinations, deepening the intelligence crisis of 1975. When the Ford White House succeeded in suppressing the report of the congressional Pike Committee, it leaked anyway. Schorr was widely viewed as the culprit who had scaled the wall of official secrecy. In the superheated atmosphere, CBS executives backed away from him as the White House encouraged its allies in Congress to take aim at the reporter. A New York congressman proposed a special inquiry into the leak to be carried out by the House Ethics Committee in an unusual move approved by the full House of Representatives. The Ethics Committee subpoenaed Schorr, who refused to divulge his sources and risked a contempt of Congress citation. The inquiry faded, but Schorr nevertheless lost his CBS job.

Sy Hersh's neck was on the chopping block again after Gerald Ford handed the presidency over to Jimmy Carter. Hersh had continued to follow the CIA's secret war in Angola and had several stories in the *New York Times* revealing serious discrepancies in official disavowals of any CIA role, such as how the agency had recruited mercenaries in the face of its own denials of doing so. In the summer of 1978 Hersh wrote of a Carter administration decision to counter the growing

Cuban role in Africa by renewed covert operations on a wider scale. The CIA project began with propaganda efforts, and the journalist crafted a fairly accurate account. Heads hit the roof at Langley. Admiral Stansfield Turner, by then head of the agency, made Hersh's reporting a special target of denunciation in his secret briefings to the intelligence committees on Capitol Hill. But again the CIA had no legal recourse against the journalist.

In the spring of 1979, the Carter administration initiated a CIA covert operation aimed at Afghanistan and the Soviet forces helping their communist ally there. In December 1979 a meeting of an NSC subcommittee determined to broaden the Afghan effort by increasing U.S. propaganda programs aimed at Muslim citizens of the Soviet Union. Within days, journalist David Binder had a detailed account of the decision in the *Times*, complete with the names of the officials who had been at the White House with NSC intelligence staffer Paul Henze.

Furious at the leak, national security advisor Zbigniew Brzezinski at first focused on Henze, who assured his boss that his sole contact with Binder had been the latter's phone call soon after the meeting, in which Henze had refused comment. This flap continued for over two months, during which Henze was obliged to provide further assurances, polygraphs were used to question those involved, and officials considered putting Binder under surveillance. The investigation proved inconclusive.

The interesting point is that when the journalist first telephoned Paul Henze, he already had most of his story. It also happens that, in 1978, when Carter rebooted U.S. radio propaganda policy by fashioning a new department to coordinate better among the former CIA entities Radio Free Europe/Radio Liberty and the Voice of America, officials had used David Binder as a conduit for the administration to trumpet its accomplishments. Government helps create the links between journalists and sources that, when it is a matter of a different story, lead to embarrassing disclosures.

Over the years the process has acquired much of the formalism of Japanese theater. The agency and White House nearly always know that a story is coming. President Lyndon Johnson knew enough about the *Times* CIA series of 1966 to try and shut it down. He heard of the CIA/National Student Association revelation in *Ramparts* sufficiently early to recall Richard Helms from a trip to the Nevada nuclear test site. The Carter White House knew of the Afghan radio story at least four days in advance. George W. Bush's people tried to spike the black prisons story at the CIA level, then, with all guns blazing, right at the White House—and with enough warning for the CIA to close up the black prison in Thailand and destroy the torture tapes. At a minimum, the government learns when the reporter calls to seek official reaction to his story. The Kabuki goes like this: journalists discover key information; government tries to squelch the story; media executives are pressured and respond, quite often by delaying the story or ensuring it avoids certain areas or some data; the revelation appears; government denounces the media regardless of the degree of cooperation it has received; then the CIA, FBI, or whatever department is involved investigates journalists' sources.

Other times the leaks are quite deliberate. A few weeks after the Afghan propaganda project flap began, the Soviet Union upped its stake in Afghanistan, intervening with major ground forces. Amid the flurry of Carter administration efforts to elaborate its response, Secretary of Defense Harold Brown suggested, in all seriousness, that the administration scrub some of its intelligence information and put it out to the public. The Reagan administration made an art of this kind of approach, cherry-picking the most alarming intelligence on Soviet military forces for a series of annual pamphlets and for special reports on the supposed threat from Nicaragua, a variety of Cuban issues (most especially its links with Grenada), Afghanistan, and Soviet research on ballistic missile defense. In addition to these major projects were innumerable "tactical" leaks. For example, on May 11, 1983, President Reagan's CIA director, William J. Casey, shot a memo to his deputy for intelligence analysis, then Robert Gates, with an attached secret paper intended to provide a rationale for covert operations in Central America. Casey wanted his deputy's ideas on beefing up and improving the paper. The rationale, the CIA director noted, was that "I have been requested to give something like the attached to *Time* magazine."[33] The mother of all leak programs, of course, has been the second Bush administration's orchestration of leaks through 2002 designed to build public support for starting a war against Iraq. So much has been said and written on that subject that no comment here is required.

Thus, aside from being targets, journalists and authors could be subjects for cultivation—or denial. This mechanism served both to unveil stories the agency wanted out for policy or propaganda purposes and to shape those the agency found unfavorable. As the other side of the coin for anticipated negative coverage, this practice began very early. Columnist Joseph Alsop, quite close to the CIA, did favors for the agency, even a Far East trip on behalf of then-operations chief Frank Wisner in the early 1950s. Allen Dulles feared what the *New York Times* might reveal about Project PB/Success, the CIA's covert operation in Guatemala, so he turned around and leaked to journalists Richard and Gladys Harkness, providing them a rosy view of the agency they incorporated into a three-part series published in the *Saturday Evening Post*. Cued by Dulles, Dwight D. Eisenhower beamed at the coverage and satisfied himself as to CIA management. When the president commissioned a review of CIA operations, carried out under retired general Jimmy Doolittle, he told the general that for all his flaws Allen Dulles was the best director the agency could have.

The dance with journalists could be done to any kind of music. Polish-born reporter Tad Szulc developed a special interest in Latin America. Szulc was among the first to follow the activities of Cuban Fidel Castro, whose revolutionary movement toppled the dictatorship of Fulgencio Batista. Szulc developed contacts among both Castro's supporters and the Cubans who went into exile after Batista's fall. The Eisenhower administration, disdaining Castro's migration toward communism, adopted a covert plan to overthrow the Cuban leader. It relied on the exiles. Tad Szulc famously worked his Cuban contacts to discover the plot and wrote about what became the Bay of Pigs invasion plan months ahead of President Kennedy's execution of the operation. Kennedy prevailed upon the *New York Times* to delay Szulc's story and then minimize it. Later, after the disaster, Kennedy called Szulc into the Oval Office to consult him on the desirability of assassinating Castro. Although Szulc had turned against the Cuban regime, he advised against any such move, but the journalist wrote and spoke in support of a coup that might unseat the Cuban leader. In the period after the Missile Crisis of 1962, with the CIA plotting just such a coup, it too consulted Szulc.[34] The CIA, which considered him an adversary, never tried to recruit Szulc, but he discovered from his own agency file, obtained under the Freedom of Information Act, that it kept detailed watch on his movements and writings.[35]

Consultation was—and remains—a CIA standard procedure. Reporters and newspaper columnists seek private briefings when taking up overseas assignments, and the agency might ask favors in return. Some of the intelligence the CIA relied upon to interpret goings-on in the Kremlin came from foreign correspondents on the Moscow beat.[36]

Some of the informed articles reporters wrote benefited from information provided by spooks. The account of the last days of the Vietnam war penned by former CIA officer Frank Snepp clearly shows reporters making extensive use of CIA information.[37]

R elationships could become delicate, with ties close enough to impugn journalistic integrity. The case of Cyrus L. Sulzberger is a good illustration. Sulzberger, the nephew of *New York Times* publisher Arthur Hays Sulzberger, proved quite a good reporter in his own right. "Cy," as he liked to be called, made his reputation reporting from Europe on the eve of World War II and became the chief foreign correspondent for the *New York Times* late in 1944. A couple of years later Sulzberger, based in Paris until 1954, established himself as perhaps the best-informed American journalist, a reputation he sustained as a newspaper columnist until his 1977 retirement. Sulzberger's published diaries make clear that CIA officers, even chiefs of station, were frequent contributors to his knowledge.

Some scholars who have surveyed Sulzberger's private papers found that the agency's connection with Sulzberger was closer than that.[38] The *New York Times* project for an extensive series on the CIA in 1966 led to a break between Sulzberger, who opposed the inquiry, and his good friend Harrison Salisbury, who had written for the *Times* from London and Moscow and worked under chief correspondent Sulzberger's general direction for six years. The Year of Intelligence provoked intense public curiosity about Langley's journalistic connections, and developments that began then threatened Cy's relationship with the agency.

The year ended with the December 1975 murder of David Welch, the CIA station chief in Athens, by Greek revolutionaries. In its zeal to exploit this incident to obtain curbs on the press, Langley openly misrepresented the source of the assassins' information on Welch. American media were given a contrived version, while the CIA suppressed knowledge of its own security failings. The station chief had not only failed to take elementary precautions, and lived in a home that had been used by his predecessors—well known in Athens (even included on tour bus routes)—he had ignored headquarters' warnings to take care. The CIA blamed the magazine *Counterspy* for revealing Welch's identity, but in fact his name and post appeared in an article in the *Athens News* a month before the murder.

Disturbingly, agency officer Duane R. Clarridge later recounted that Langley actually suspected the Greek intelligence service of blowing Welch's cover to *Athens News* reporters. The Greek KYP had been fighting CIA over differences on Cyprus and issues of cooperation.[39] In December 1977 and after, when the House Permanent Select Committee on Intelligence held hearings on the CIA and the press, the agency continued to purvey its *Counterspy* misinformation.[40] The Greek killers were in fact apprehended many years later and confirmed their targeting of Welch had had nothing whatever to do with the leftist magazine the agency blamed. This represented a clear instance of a CIA effort to influence a domestic audience in violation of its charter.

On one level the Welch affair represented a goad to reporters. It invited journalistic counterattack, for the Fourth Estate had often cooperated with the CIA in the past and now the spooks were tarring it. The agency's ties to the media became controversial—particularly in the conventional sense of its using news outlets to disguise officers. The renowned Watergate reporter Carl Bernstein picked up this thread and, after long research, in 1977 published the seminal piece on CIA-media links.[41] Among other things, Bernstein wrote that Cyrus Sulzberger had been a CIA asset. The *Times* asked Cy to issue a denial. He refused. The heat aroused here factored in the columnist's decision to retire.

Whether or not they were CIA assets, good journalists appreciated the value of contacts within the CIA and worked to cultivate agency officers. Richard Helms had been a reporter before he became a spy, his most notable scoop an interview with Adolf Hitler at the time of the 1936 Olympics. Helms's papers, right through his career as a CIA officer and then its director, are full of letters from journalists drawing attention to assorted issues they felt should command his attention. David A. Phillips, a CIA officer who rose to lead its Latin America Division, had also been a journalist before joining, and he had worked under journalistic cover in Chile and Cuba. Phillips would argue there is a natural affinity between spooks and pressmen.[42] He retired in 1975 to form the Association of Former Intelligence Officers expressly to get the CIA some of the positive publicity it lacked during the Year of Intelligence.

The CIA dance with the media went right to the top. Allen Dulles and John McCone exploited their private contacts on numerous occasions. Richard Helms occasionally met reporters. Bill Colby took the practice to a new level, periodically hosting a changing array of them. Colby extolled this openness and used it to shape press coverage, with which he had some success until Sy Hersh blew the whistle on CIA domestic operations. Though Colby issued a regulation on CIA relations with journalism, it was he who would say both in public interviews and privately—for example, to Frank Snepp—that the CIA as an agency needed to "leak from the top."[43] Stansfield Turner, who headed U.S. intelligence during the Carter administration, expanded the previously tiny Office of Public Affairs. Reagan-era spy chieftain Bill Casey quite consciously received *Washington Post* reporter Bob Woodward—Carl Bernstein's Watergate colleague—and treated him to a wide variety of inside information. Indeed, that relationship became notorious when Woodward, in a book on CIA in the Reagan years, claimed to have gotten information from Casey even on his deathbed.[44]

William Webster headed the CIA under the first President Bush. Webster would sit down with the editorial boards of major newspapers for wide-ranging tours of the intelligence horizon. By then the Cold War had begun to dissipate. In this climate his successor, Director Robert Gates, sought advice from journalists, think tank denizens, and political figures on how U.S. intelligence should refashion itself for the new age. Agency officer James R. Lilley, who had worked in Korea, Hong Kong, Laos, and China, felt comfortable admitting to a congressional panel the old Sulzberger truth— that he had had, and continued to have, a range of relations with journalists. It fell to John Deutch, one of President Bill Clinton's several intelligence directors, to hold a rare public news conference by a CIA chief. Predictably, that openness came with the agency again under assault, this time for allegedly running a covert operation that had imported drugs into Los Angeles.

As agency director, Bill Colby first codified the CIA relations with the media. After final massage, George Herbert Walker Bush issued that directive when he took charge in 1976. The instructions were renewed by Stansfield Turner. They remain on the books today. While the regulations prohibit the agency from using journalists for operational purposes, they explicitly *permit* open relationships with journalists and news media "to provide public information, answers to inquiries, and assistance in obtaining unclassified briefings on substantive matters."[45] Defining the point where public information ends and influence attempts begin is the question that will forever remain.

Meanwhile, the spooks also kept up their dance with historians and book authors, naturally including many journalists. Activity here invokes the question of influence. The CIA's formal book publication program aimed ostensibly at a foreign audience, but by their very nature, books potentially affected the opinions of Americans who happened to read them, and some had quite a pronounced domestic impact. Among these was *The Penkovskiy Papers*, purported to be the reflections of Oleg Penkovskiy, a Russian intelligence officer and one of the agency's most damaging spies inside the Soviet Union. Langley actually hired one of its own assets, the Soviet defector Peter Deriabin, to edit the manuscript, which was published in 1965. A book on Indochina was commissioned by CIA's Far East Division as early as 1954. Certain publishers in their 1950s and 1960s incarnations, such as Frederick A. Praeger (the company has moved on now and is an imprint of a different house), were CIA favorites in this publishing game, a subtle feature of Langley's political and psychological warfare venture. The Church Committee determined that "well over a thousand" books were subsidized by the CIA through 1967, with 200 that year alone, a quarter of them written in English. Publication in the United States then ceased. At least 250 more books appeared in foreign languages before 1975.

The agency was quite clear on its purposes in publishing operations. These were defined by the chief of the CIA Covert Action Staff in a 1961 paper:

Books differ from all other propaganda media, primarily because one single book can significantly change the reader's attitude and action to an extent unmatched by the impact of any other single medium. . . . this is, of course, not true of all books at all times with all readers—but it is true significantly often enough to make books the most important weapon of strategic (long-range) propaganda.

The agency also had a fine understanding of the value of its contributions:

> The advantage of our direct contact with the author is that we can acquaint him in great detail with our intentions; that we can provide him with whatever detail we want him to include and that we can check the manuscript at every stage.[46]

The Church Committee investigations did not end the publication program—literature smuggled into the Soviet Union and Eastern Europe had a role to play in the upheavals that confronted communism in the 1980s—but the program for the United States itself had ended during Lyndon Johnson's presidency. Yet the same principles that had governed formal propaganda efforts were subsequently applied to American writers on intelligence subjects. Those authors considered friendly got help, ones viewed as more critical were obstructed.

During the early 1970s, for example, author John Barron was given privileged access to intelligence case files for his exposé of the Soviet KGB, a book that may not have been part of the agency's publications program, but differed little from those that were.[47] Barron's work proved so helpful the U.S. government later put him in touch with a defecting Soviet pilot, Lieutenant Viktor Belenko, and gave the author the information necessary to craft an authentic account of a top-secret Russian aircraft U.S. intelligence had been seeking to understand.[48]

The Church Committee era, meanwhile, had featured charges regarding CIA counterintelligence chief James Angleton, whose fears of a Russian spy at Langley had roiled the CIA. Once the committee packed up its files, the CIA opened its—to journalist David Martin, whose requests for documents under the Freedom of Information Act were met with amazing rapidity compared to the waits to which other requestors were subjected. Martin's account of the spy wars became the most revealing yet.[49] Threatened with lawsuits, Martin nevertheless produced an account that has stood the test of time.

Late in the decade, Langley favored author Edward Jay Epstein, though the project actually began, again, with John Barron. The latter wanted to do a book on Soviet defector Yuri Nosenko, but had too much on his plate. Barron convinced Epstein to take on the project. The CIA gave Epstein direct access, making Nosenko available for a series of four interviews.[50] But beforehand, the CIA's Office of Security investigated Epstein. Not much impressed by the Russian—something seemed off with him—Epstein inclined to the views of Angleton and his crowd, from whom the author received inside information on CIA interest in Lee Harvey Oswald. Langley itself became much less cooperative. Though it had no approval role in the manuscript, the agency's Publications Review Board opened a file on Epstein's book. This went to press with the same outfit that had handled John Barron's works. In all, the Epstein book proved a bit of a backfire for the CIA, but nevertheless was born of its own efforts.[51] Langley's lesson was that it might be able to turn the spigot on or off, but it could not control the product.

During the late 1980s the agency made actual operational records available to Jerrold Schecter to reprise the Penkovskiy case. A journalist who had been National Security Council spokesman in the Carter White House, Schecter had cooperated with the CIA on such matters as propaganda strategy following the Soviet invasion of Afghanistan, and the public relations aspects of the cases of disaffected CIA officers Frank Snepp and Philip Agee (see Chapter 8). Langley clearly considered Schecter persona grata. It gave him access to actual audiotape recordings of its debriefing sessions with Penkovskiy, and teamed Schecter up with Peter Deriabin, editor of its earlier book on the Russian spy and advisor to the Nosenko inquisitors. Their work was suitably impressive.[52] In 1986, only months before becoming enmeshed in the Iran-Contra affair, Director Casey indulged David Wise, who had been so actively persecuted by John McCone, with a couple of hours-long conversations about CIA turncoat Edward Howard, on whom Wise was writing a book. The author had gained new cachet at Langley.

Over the next decade the agency made a number of its secret internal histories available to at least two reporters. Langley regards these "clandestine service histories" as "operational records," exempt from release under an amendment to the Freedom of Information Act obtained in 1984. Former *Newsweek* stalwart Evan Thomas used these and other records for his history of the early CIA through the eyes of major figures in the clandestine service.[53] After that the retired *New York Times* reporter Peter Grose gained the agency's confidence with a biography of Allen Dulles, and then he, too, was given the monographs for a study of early CIA covert operations.[54] More recently a CIA official historian has utilized the same records in a series of papers on agency covert operations. In yet another sally of this kind, Langley provided journalist Benjamin Weiser with case files and clandestine message traffic—certainly operational records—to write the story of Polish agent Ryszard Kuklinski, who had been instrumental to the agency in discovering Soviet intentions in Poland during the last decade of the Cold War.[55]

There is a marked contrast between these grants of privileged access and the CIA's relationship with the larger community of authors and historians. Those on Langley's good side are coddled just as the agency's Covert Action Staff laid down in 1961. The most favored writers may submit their manuscripts to review, CIA scrubs them, and the result looks pretty. As for the others, they struggle to obtain the declassification of records for their research. And CIA is among the most zealous guardians of its secrets, both in its responses, or the lack of them, under the Freedom of Information Act (FOIA), and in what Soviet apparatchiks of an earlier age would have called "active measures." Agency FOIA processors refuse to confirm or deny that records even exist. Or they call up historians and tell them what they seek will never see the light of day. Or they stall—a favorite tactic. For example, in the early 1990s, in preparation for a biography of William E. Colby, this author filed an FOIA request for a variety of Vietnam-era records, including agency histories by or about Colby. My book eventually appeared in 2003. *After* the book was out, CIA staff inquired as to whether I was still interested in the documents requested under FOIA a decade earlier. This is not the only time this has happened. Naturally I was still interested in the material. It was never released, at least not to me. In August 2011 the CIA declassified its official history of Bill Colby as CIA director in response to another researcher. It had been finished and published in 1993.

It needs to be noted, to take another example, that it took the statutory powers and authority of the John F. Kennedy Assassination Records Review Board to spring free even a few paltry excerpts of the documents Evan Thomas and Peter Grose had used. The agency continues to maintain that this whole category of materials—*histories* by its own writ—are actually operational *records*. Equally distressing, the CIA obtained its 1984 FOIA operational records exemption using the argument that in exchange it would expedite the release of *histories*—which it now claims form part of the operational record. Moreover, the specific language of the 1984 exemption provides that operational records, no matter what they may be, are no longer exempt once used or cited in a declassified monograph or study. Such studies from the CIA have now appeared but the source documents remain secret, and, in the face of FOIA requests, the agency as of this writing has yet to apply the statute except to insist it has a blanket exemption.

The Kennedy review board actually had unique advantages in opening up secret records. Under the law creating it, the board had the authority to make the actual release decisions, which put CIA in the position of having to explain why something needed to remain secret, instead of peremptorily denying requests to declassify material. The board required the CIA to certify, *under penalty of perjury*, that it had supplied all records relevant to its requests. But Langley played games even so. It was reluctant at first to make materials available, then disputed access to full files for investigators to check compliance, then resisted actual declassification. The board finally had to go to CIA Director George Tenet to obtain a formal directive ordering all elements of the agency to cooperate. Despite those orders, some officers of the operations directorate did all they could to impede the process and prevent compromises. In 1998, with the board winding up its work, it uncovered evidence that called into question the thoroughness of supposedly comprehensive inventories the CIA had carried out six years earlier. Board members satisfied themselves in the end when Tenet's executive director swore under oath that the agency had complied fully with the Kennedy Assassination Records Act.

To get the flavor of this, consider the word "station," the term of art for the unit of agency officers assigned to any country. The usage was very familiar. CIA stations were everywhere—in movies, novels, and histories. They were even in declassified documents. "Station" appears in official reports on the CIA and Watergate. In the Year of Intelligence, Langley objected to the appearance of the word in the Church Committee assassination report, that was released by the Senate. As a matter of legal record, CIA stipulated the existence of "stations"—and certain specific ones—in the trials that came out of the Iran-Contra affair (see Chapter 9). Here, nearly a decade later, Langley fought the Kennedy records board over "revelation" of the word station. This was at the same time that CIA official statements on the Guatemala death squad controversy openly used the word. The agency lost its fight—and the Kennedy board's determinations carried the force of law. Yet ten years *after* this defeat should have changed declassification practice, agency censors typically delete mentions of CIA stations when releasing documents, and frequently when approving texts for publication by former officers.

Langley's active measures have been even more disturbing. When the Rockefeller Commission was on the point of releasing its findings, CIA's Office of General Counsel ordered the destruction of the files from Project Chaos. In the late 1970s and early '80s, a historian used a combination of materials, including legally required archival "withdrawal sheets"—which specify papers kept secret in open files—to identify the particular White House meetings in which President Eisenhower decided to move ahead with reconnaissance satellites (today the CIA officially brags about these programs). Agency security officers subsequently visited that archive and literally razored out the identifying information on the sheets. Defacing a government document is a Class C felony in the United States Code. Another time a historian wrote about the Truman administration's Psychological Strategy Board based upon properly declassified documents held in a government repository. The CIA sent an armed security team to that archive and repossessed the entire set of documents—the first known instance in U.S. history in which a full archival collection open for research at an official facility had been "reclassified." It has taken two decades for these documents to dribble back into the public domain.

When historian James Bamford found a set of unclassified National Security Agency newsletters at a university library and relied on them for his NSA history *The Puzzle Palace*, a security team went there and seized the material. Under the Freedom of Information Act, Bamford received documents delineating NSA's legal vulnerabilities for its domestic surveillance programs in the 1960s and after. Once the material appeared in his book, the author was threatened with arrest for possession of classified documents. In 1990 CIA attorneys intervened again to mandate destruction of the files on the controversial mail-opening Project Lingual. Even quite recently, when the family of deceased CIA officer Philip Agee donated his papers to a university institute, agency security officers were waiting on the dock when the shipment arrived. They extracted whatever they wanted from the Agee papers.

Active measures can go beyond attempts to fiddle with the documentary record. Frank Snepp has written about how senior officers at Langley warned employees that he was at work on a CIA book and cautioned them against speaking to him. At least Snepp was a former CIA officer, but the agency applied the same logic in the late 1980s to a private individual, author Douglas Valentine, who was researching a book on the notorious "Phoenix" program during the Vietnam war. The historian collected numerous interviews for his research, and at first Langley had been cooperative, with CIA's Retirement Division even forwarding his letters to former officers, and a number of them speaking with him on the strength of his early contacts with William E. Colby.

Valentine's initial interviews proved the most productive. Elements at Langley became uncooperative after one retiree asked CIA lawyers, in the summer of 1986, what things were safe to talk about. When a Publications Review Board lawyer checked to see whether Phoenix was off-limits (the Board had previously cleared Phoenix material in works by Colby himself and agency officer Ralph McGehee), he was advised to caution interviewees not to talk to Valentine. The lawyer pointed out that the most he could do was warn veterans against unrehearsed, unprepared interviews and suggest that they "obtain the questions from Mr. Valentine in writing in advance and draft a written response for the Board to review." Board lawyers gave this advice repeatedly, noting in an April 1987 instance that when Valentine's questions were solicited and answers reviewed by the Board, "virtually all were found to be classified." Some months later the same lawyer complimented an agency veteran for refusing to be interviewed.

By April 1988 the Publications Review Board was advising clandestine service officers of a concern that Valentine's "forthcoming book will contain so much detailed information about Agency operations and officers that . . . it may cause damage," and asking that senior management of the Directorate of Operations have the entire matter brought to their attention. Spooks, including some in the ostensibly impartial Inspector General's office, were ranging the halls telling each other that the author was bad news and hoping they might escape his attention. Valentine eventually discovered this stonewalling due to the reticence of CIA veterans— and the materials quoted here emerged in the course of legal discovery in the lawsuit Douglas Valentine brought against the Central Intelligence Agency.[56]

It would be a relief to write that this type of behavior represents ancient history, but the opposite, unfortunately, is the case. The experience of James Scott is typical. Scott, who had worked for the U.S. government for thirty-four years, much of that time as a public affairs officer for the navy, was the son of journalist Paul Scott, whom the CIA had wiretapped in its Project Mockingbird back in 1963. When the Family Jewels documents were finally declassified, Jim Scott quickly discovered its mentions of his father's case and applied under the Freedom of Information Act in January 2008 for release of text that had been deleted from the Jewels or was never mentioned in the report—in other words, the details of this affair. The CIA stalled, first by considering the request as one for a personal file rather than for the subject "Paul Scott." Given a copy of the death certificate, in December 2008 the CIA reported that it had completed a thorough search of its files—and then declassified a few documents that had nothing to do with the Mockingbird wiretapping.

James Scott appealed. In the summer of 2009 the CIA summarily rejected his request. The reporter's son waited almost a year and then used a different release procedure called "mandatory declassification review" to request that the redactions be removed from the specific pages of the Jewels that related to the Mockingbird affair. Scott enclosed copies of the pages to make sure there was no mistake. A month later the CIA sent Scott copies of his own pages, no changes made, terming them the result of a recent review of the documents. The reporter's son thought the CIA was simply acknowledging his request; after all, in its letter the agency had assigned it an index number. But when nothing happened, in early 2011 he checked with the agency's information and privacy coordinator, only to be told that CIA's June 2010 letter had been its final response to his declassification request.

Thoroughly frustrated, James Scott wrote to then-CIA director Leon Panetta criticizing the agency's entire record on release of the Mockingbird records. A subordinate signed the reply in which the CIA reaffirmed the decisions it had made on the documents, inviting Scott to submit a fresh request after another interval or take his case to an interagency appeals board. In the meantime, James Scott never even received acknowledgment of a separate declassification request—required by regulations—he had made for unexpurgated versions of the documents it had partially released in 2008. During this time the FBI declassified to Jim Scott more than half of its own file on his father and, in January 2011, sent fifty more pages to the agency for its check on CIA "equities." Langley has completed no action on the material as of this writing. The presidential executive order that controls government secrecy explicitly forbids the use of classification to shield illegal activities—which the Project Mockingbird wiretaps certainly were.

More often than not the manipulations remain invisible. But this record clearly shows an atmosphere in which maneuvers to affect information are considered business as usual. Public relations and spin doctoring were only minor resources in a toolbox that includes such energetic Central Intelligence Agency measures. Provision of materials to shape products, behind-the-scenes tampering with research, interventions to quash some coverage or encourage something else, surveillance of "dangerous" journalists, and retaliation against both officials and private citizens thought to have harmed the agency in some way are domestic activities and have not ceased. Meanwhile, CIA friends received preferential treatment. This was not protecting national security, but playing with "security" to show the agency in the best possible light. Langley's media activity manifests an arrogance of power similar to that exhibited in other areas documented here. The journalists were fortunate in that they were not agency employees and thus less vulnerable to its mailed fist. The most exposed victims would be the Central Intelligence Agency's own rank and file.

8

≡ PLUGGING THE DIKE ≡

A disturbing episode in the CIA's war on books concerned one of its own, Victor Marchetti, who resigned in frustration during 1969. A fifteen-year veteran, Marchetti had wide experience, including as a photo interpreter and as special assistant to the CIA director. In retirement he wrote a novel called *The Rope Dancer*, portraying CIA machinations in a harsh light. Then Marchetti teamed up with John D. Marks, a former State Department intelligence analyst, to offer publishers a nonfiction exposé of the agency's roles and missions, *The CIA and the Cult of Intelligence*.[1] Meanwhile, in conjunction with the appearance of his novel, Marchetti had given a highly critical interview to the wire service United Press International, printed in the newsweekly *U.S. News and World Report*. That put him on Langley's radar screen. In late 1971 the Marchetti interview became a point of contention among agency officials concerned the CIA had become excessively involved in domestic activities.

Director Helms ordered Marchetti placed under surveillance on March 23, 1972. Under Project Butane, Howard Osborn's Office of Security kept the Marchetti watch up for a month. Hysteria increased another notch in early April when the former spook put an article in *The Nation* depicting the CIA as the loyal tool of presidents. Again, Langley saw national security damage where, just a couple of years hence, it would come under wide attack as the infamous "rogue elephant" careening out of control. More reflective officers must later have wished Marchetti's arguments had survived CIA's attempts to discredit him. Meanwhile, Langley soon learned the agency veteran and his coauthor Marks were planning a more ambitious manuscript.

Worried sick, the CIA acquired a copy of Marchetti's book proposal. Helms secured the cooperation of Nixon's White House, enlisting the Department of Justice for a Pentagon Papers–like effort at prior restraint. Agency lawyer John S. Warner went to U.S. District Court with an affidavit from deputy director Tom Karamessines, arguing the CIA's special duty to protect "sources and methods" under the Central Intelligence Act of 1949. Warner obtained a court order compelling Marchetti to submit his manuscript to prepublication review. The filing was made without even notifying the defendant, and the temporary restraining order of April 18, 1972, would be the first Marchetti knew that his writing was at issue.

The authors, so far at work for only a few months, subsequently encountered numerous roadblocks. Marchetti had to clear each piece of his work with Langley, which slowed down John Marks as well. The agency called for deletion of roughly 20 percent of the entire text. Marchetti's lawyers tried to quash the injunction and suppress the demands. The Justice Department argued it was enforcing the contract Marchetti had signed as a CIA employee, not abridging Marchetti's First Amendment rights. A hearing took place on May 15. Karamessines appeared in a wheelchair, demanding his testimony be taken in secret, and the federal judge went along. Historian Angus Mackenzie obtained the trial transcript and reports Karamessines "insisted that Marchetti had to be censored so the other U.S. intelligence agencies' foreign allies would continue to trust the CIA. At stake, he said, was the CIA's reputation among the world community of spies."[2] Judge Albert V. Bryan, Jr., granted a permanent injunction. Bryan did provide for a review process, however. Forced to justify its national security claims, the CIA abandoned half its demands, compromising on 168 deletions that still subtracted vast amounts of material. Melvin Wulf, the authors' lawyer, recalls as very painful the night they met to scissor out swaths of text. Among passages the CIA claimed would "damage" national security, but later relented upon, was one noting that Richard Nixon had mispronounced the name of a country at a meeting, the comment that Henry Kissinger was the most powerful figure on the unit that approved CIA covert operations, the remark that spy satellites were very expensive, plus notes on CIA activities in Tibet and Chile, including the fact that national intelligence estimates had cautioned against the kind of scheme mounted against Salvador Allende. Since the Marchetti-Marks book appeared in 1974, after Allende's overthrow, these passages were of historical note but had no operational significance.

The authors had already appealed the court order, and their hearing before the Fourth Circuit took place on May 31, 1972. On the eve, presidential counselor John Ehrlichman forwarded to Mr. Nixon a letter from Richard Helms thanking the White House for its assistance. Ehrlichman reminded Nixon of their provision of "the necessary help to file an action against Marchetti" and observed that agency lawyers were confident of the outcome on appeal. The president scribbled "Good" in the margin.[3] The Helms letter itself, sent a week earlier, expressed his pleasure at the help "in what I consider historic litigation on behalf of the Central Intelligence Agency."[4]

Judge Clement F. Haynsworth, whom Nixon had nominated for the Supreme Court several years earlier, and who had failed to obtain Senate confirmation, headed the circuit court panel. In mid-September Haynsworth issued the panel's decision, which continued the permanent injunction, merely requiring the CIA to respond "promptly" to anything Marchetti might submit for approval, since the effect of its order was to impose a prior restraint on Victor Marchetti's freedom of speech. Marchetti and Marks appealed again, now to the Supreme Court, which declined to hear the case. The writing—and final negotiation of deletions—delayed the book for two years. Even though the American Civil Liberties Union provided its legal services for free, the case cost publisher Alfred A. Knopf more than $630,000 (in 2012 dollars).

Undoing the damage—not to national security but to citizens' national interest—took many years and remains incomplete. A first edition of *The CIA and the Cult of Intelligence* was published with graphic representation of the deletions. Litigation went on for years, and the courts finally judged legitimately secret only 27 of the 339 passages the CIA had originally excised. In the meantime officers who might have written about the agency were dissuaded. Langley looked pathetic anew when some of the things it had insisted seriously damaged national security appeared: the "secrets" were completely routine descriptions of CIA offices, functions, and activities. Similar descriptions had long been in print from authors like Harry Howe Ransom and David Wise. None of the material seemed especially sensitive with respect to the CIA's alliances with foreign services. The Marchetti and Marks book contained notes on CIA operations too, but these went only a short way beyond what the public already knew. Apparently what was sensitive was an agency veteran speaking authoritatively on allegations previously made by authors or journalists. National security was an instrument wielded to inhibit public discussion, avoid inquiry, and evade accountability.

Richard Helms was right. The Marchetti case cannot be overemphasized as a milestone in the expansion of CIA dominance of discussion of its business, intelligence matters. Until *United States v. Marchetti* there was no requirement for formal review of public writings by CIA officers and no mechanism to accomplish that. Agency officials like Allen Dulles, George Carver, and Miles Copeland had put out books and articles with, at most, cursory once-over from a busy special assistant, a quick look by the Office of Security, and often with nothing but encouragement. The Marchetti case marked construction of the first pillar in what became an edifice of information ascendancy, restricting discussion by means of limiting the knowledge available from the most authoritative commentators—former intelligence officers.

I f Langley wanted a truly dangerous adversary, it had not long to wait. The enemy would be one of its own, Philip Agee. In the CIA pantheon he became something close to the devil incarnate. In fact, Agee ultimately became the poster boy for the agency's brand of suppressive maneuvers. What is not so well known is that Langley helped create this enemy and then exploited his existence for its own ends. The Agee case put in place the second pillar of the CIA's fortress of secrecy. Its reverberations were heard once again even as the finishing touches were put to this manuscript, as will be seen later in the experience of John Kiriakou.

A Florida boy, product of Catholic schools straight through Notre Dame, and raised in comfortable circumstances, Phil Agee was considered prime CIA material. He turned down the agency when it first approached him, before graduation, but joined after all in 1957, when law school did not suit Agee and the alternative was the draft. Over a dozen years, Philip Agee served honorably in what was then the Western Hemisphere Division of the clandestine service, participating in almost every kind of operation, primarily in Ecuador and Uruguay, but with short stints in other nations as well. After a tour on the Mexican desk at Langley his last assignment was to Mexico City, slated to host the 1968 summer Olympics, with cover as the ambassador's special assistant to the Olympic commission. Agee recollects that he began with idealistic hopes—reinforced by John F. Kennedy's Alliance for Progress—that Latin America would reform and the CIA could be part of that solution. He became disillusioned in the mid-'60s, realizing that agency efforts to neutralize the Latin American left played into the hands of oligarchs by reducing political pressures on them to reform. Agee writes that he did that last tour in Mexico already having the intention of leaving the agency. Marital problems exacerbated by his service, plus disaffection, were major concerns. A Mexican girlfriend who wanted no part of the CIA sharpened that intention— and when superiors insisted she be investigated before they marry, that sealed Agee's determination to resign.

Beyond that origin story, nearly everything about Philip Burnett Franklin Agee is controversial. That is because he wrote a book highly critical of the CIA that revealed how it worked in Latin America and identified over 250 agency officers—the beginning of a long crusade against U.S. intelligence. Former colleagues dispute how good a spy Agee had been; whether he was a whistleblower or an agent for Cuban (or Soviet) intelligence, hence a traitor; whether he was a communist. Critic or villain? Forests of trees could probably be slaughtered in disputing the "truth" about Phil Agee. The more interesting—and more important—question is discovering the degree to which CIA suppressive maneuvers made Agee into the thorn he became, just as agency training had turned him into the spy he had been. There is an element of meanness in the CIA's efforts to track Agee and then counter him that had to have had an effect. Agee died in 2008 and can no longer speak to his motives, but the record of suppressive maneuvers against him can be established. The CIA not only battled Philip Agee, it used him.

The Mexico City Olympics came and went. Philip Agee left the agency in 1969. According to later CIA director William E. Colby, Agee's resignation letter was not negative at all, but a text expressing esteem for the agency and regret at leaving it. By Agee's own account, he had political reasons for leaving—he opposed the Vietnam war and saw CIA actions there as cut from the same cloth as those in Latin America—but he had no intention of speaking out, writing a book, or anything else. He worked in a commercial firm for a year and attended the Autonomous University of Mexico City. It was there, exposed to Latino perspectives on the Americas, to fellow students who had suffered at the hands of CIA-backed military juntas, and to even more vociferous opposition to America in Vietnam, that Philip Agee began toying with writing a critique of U.S. policy in Latin America, expressed through CIA actions, framed in relation to the Vietnam war. The idea was vague and inchoate, and Agee recalls it took form slowly and without his ever making a concrete choice.

The difficulties were research and writing. At a certain point Agee exhausted the material available in Mexico City, still without having found much of the socioeconomic data he needed for background, as well as files of the Uruguayan and Ecuadoran newspapers from when he had been assigned to those places. And once Agee quit his job and turned to writing, he lost his salary and had to depend on savings. A writer friend counseled the former spook not to draft his anti-CIA book in Mexico, a country the agency had wired up tight. The friend put him in touch with the French publisher François Maspero, who advanced Agee some money and arranged to get him into Cuba. Phil Agee spent some time there, returned briefly to Mexico to wind up his affairs, and returned to Cuba for more research. Eventually he had gone through everything available in Havana and moved on to Paris, leaving behind requests for additional data that were going to take time to compile, plus a paper on CIA methods to be forwarded to Allende's Chile and a letter to the editor of an Uruguayan leftist journal. The Cubans warned Agee not to publish those things, but he did not care.

These details are important because of what happened later. In Mexico, there had been a very active MH/Chaos branch at the CIA station, but Agee's spiral into opposition never came to its attention. It was publication of Agee's letter in the Uruguayan magazine *Marcha* that raised warning flags at Langley. Some time later in Paris a knock came at Agee's door, and he opened it to find a CIA colleague, a man who had been with him in training and also in Latin America. The former colleague happened to be visiting London, he related, and thought to pop over and see how Phil was doing. Agee knew the man's story of getting the address from his estranged wife was impossible. Once they were alone, the fellow admitted that he had, in fact, gotten the address from the agency's Paris station. Langley knew of Agee's letter in *Marcha*, the CIA man said, and added, "Helms sent me to ask what this is all about."[5]

Philip Agee answered by criticizing CIA covert action, added he was writing a book, and, foolhardy or defiant, let drop that he had been to Cuba and was in touch with Maspero. No doubt Helms's eyebrows rose when he heard that. François Maspero was the publisher of Che Guevara's Bolivian diary, and CIA regarded Cuba as an archenemy in league with the Soviets. Director Helms initiated a full-scale operation to penetrate Agee's activities. Not long after, at the café Agee frequented, he met a young American, a man with New Left journalistic credentials who had arrived in Paris in September 1971. Sal Ferrera had been groomed by the Project Chaos project and had infiltrated the antiwar movement (Chapter 3). Ferrera now ingratiated himself with Agee. He found the budding author a typewriter, and won his trust by spotting a CIA surveillance team and helping Agee evade it. Later Ferrera steered Agee to a bar where a pretty woman picked him up. She found common ground with Agee, waxed enthusiastic about his work, and, claiming to be from a monied family, began to supply him cash. Agee photocopied his draft manuscript for the woman, who wanted to read what he had written. Dollops of money, an offer to stay at her apartment, and the loan of another typewriter followed. At a certain point Agee discovered the typewriter had been bugged. No doubt the apartment was too.

Phil Agee eventually decided that both Ferrera and the woman were CIA plants. Other friends agreed. But Agee dallied with them at length, perhaps desperate for money, even making plans for them to help him in London during the final stage of his research. There were repeated instances of surveillance by CIA teams, including one, Agee recounts, when the watchers were caught right outside his apartment. Meanwhile, in the United States, Agee's father was confronted by an agency lawyer who said he came on behalf of Director Helms. The lawyer, John Greaney of OGC, left behind copies of Agee's signed secrecy agreement and the court decision in *United States v. Marchetti*. After that, the father's tax returns were audited by the Internal Revenue Service. Greaney next saw Agee's estranged wife, encouraging her to refuse him visits with their children.

Apart from the heavy-handed aspects of all this stands the fact that the agency, in effect, supported and financed the very book it feared so much. By these means Langley even obtained a copy of an early draft. Naturally, Philip Agee discovered the CIA's maneuvers—and a decade later he obtained a modicum of proof in the form of documents released under the Freedom of Information Act. To the degree that these antics outraged the former spook, the CIA helped create its own bogeyman.

That Langley actually had Agee's book can be confirmed.

In May 1972 the Western Hemisphere Division was taken over by Theodore Shackley, who had once led operations against Cuba and had more recently been a secret warrior in Laos and Vietnam. Shackley initiated a wholesale shakeout of the division, a program that had its own cryptonym and cost untold millions. The purpose was to realign operations and terminate anything that Philip Agee knew about. At the Mexico City station, officer Joseph B. Smith spent his final year pensioning off agents and shutting down projects as part of this effort. Smith objected to its enormous destructiveness and recounts actually using the Agee manuscript to check whether given CIA officers or spies were mentioned. His objections proved futile. Another who objected was Tom Gilligan, an officer assigned to Portugal, where spies were also being discharged. Gilligan took his concerns to his station chief, but protests were to no avail.

By the fall of 1972 Phil Agee had completed two-thirds of the manuscript and shortly made the connection with the British publisher Penguin, which would ultimately bring out his book. He completed the draft in January 1974. Richard Helms had left Langley, ultimately succeeded by Bill Colby. Despite Helms's departure, the effort to counter Agee continued unabated. The FOIA documents released later revealed that CIA planned a dual-track strategy, one being propaganda to neutralize the book—as had been done with works on the Kennedy assassination, *The Politics of Heroin*, and *The Invisible Government*. The second track was to attempt to discredit Agee by painting him as a lousy spy and an enemy agent. The propaganda strategy would be mooted by the depth of Agee's revelations, but the collusion charges were rather more successful.

Depicting Philip Agee as a turncoat and a Cuban or Soviet agent was an incendiary charge. Nothing could have been more calculated to redouble his determination to strike back. But the CIA might have been right. The importance of this demands some attention. By 1974 Agee had been in Cuba at least three times, had met with Cuban officials in London, and had left queries in Havana that apparently were subsequently investigated and answered for him. Agee's account is vague enough on his research in various places to leave the door open for the Cuban agent charge. Yet the former spook had always been frank about his goal of exposing the bankruptcy of CIA methods and classist basis of American foreign policy. The Cubans were sophisticated enough to understand any connection with their service would taint Agee's critique of the CIA.

On the other hand, former Soviet intelligence officer Oleg D. Kalugin has written and said that Agee *was* a Cuban agent, and that the KGB was chagrined because Agee had gone to the Soviet embassy in Mexico City in 1973 to offer his services and had been turned down, only then going to the Cubans. In a 1974 interview with an American journalist, CIA Director Bill Colby offered that identical date and embassy visit to substantiate the same charge. These claims are problematic. First, Agee had been assigned to Mexico and saw the surveillance of the Soviet and Cuban embassies there. When he initially went to Havana, Agee had avoided both and instead got his Cuban visa in Montreal. Second, Agee was gone from Mexico by 1973. Third, there is no evidence of a Cuban effort—an operation—to support this alleged agent. Had Agee had Cuban support, he would not have needed CIA money to write his book. Most important, Agee's crucial connections with the Cubans, his "research," took place earlier. It is more likely the Cubans regarded Philip Agee as a friend working along parallel lines, not a Havana agent. Finally, Oleg Kalugin and Bill Colby became friends and, later, business associates, collaborating on the design of a computer game. It is entirely possible that Kalugin was simply rehashing what he had read in the British press, which was based on an interview Colby had given to plant this story. Once they knew each other, Colby would have repeated his original allegations.

As for whether the Cubans contributed identifications of CIA officers for Agee to use, that was possible no matter what his status was. But Cuban data were not crucial for Agee's crusade to expose the CIA. Having been with the agency in Latin America for a decade, he knew hordes of these people. Moreover, there was a kind of secret code—for want of a better term—in those days, based on standard State Department publications that listed persons assigned to U.S. embassies and profiled the backgrounds of diplomatic personnel. Since most agency officers served in posts under diplomatic cover, their job titles fell within a narrow range, and their ranks were commensurate with their CIA standings. They were not hard to identify. Agency officers on post looked each other up all the time. My guess (and it is only a guess) is that if the Cubans were helpful, it was in discovering for Agee the office numbers and spaces within Latin American embassies (that the CIA man had never been in) that served as agency premises. The offices and diplomatic lists, taken together, would have permitted assembly of a profile of station chiefs, their deputies, and other senior officers with fair accuracy.

In any case there was precedent—on both sides—for exactly this kind of exposure. The Russians had assisted East German writer Julius Mader in assembling the book *Who's Who in the CIA*. Mader, to judge from the job titles he gave American officers, utilized precisely the method Agee would rely upon. The CIA struck back with John Barron, mentioned earlier (Chapter 7). A former naval intelligence officer turned *Reader's Digest* editor, Barron was given identities of KGB and GRU personnel for a fifty-page list of them included in his book *KGB: The Secret Work of Soviet Secret Agents*. Joseph Smith writes, "I am certain Barron's book and Philip Agee's are related. When Agee contacted the Cubans, it is a small wonder the abused Soviet intelligence service through their Cuban surrogates returned the compliment."[6]

The CIA's back-alley campaign against Philip Agee escalated in the summer of 1974, when articles began appearing in the U.S. press depicting him as a drunkard and womanizer who had hooked up with the KGB somewhere in South America to spill his guts. The stories were clearly based on CIA information, but they lacked crucial details that would have been required for a spin of "truthiness." Agee looked at one story and saw that it corresponded exactly to one of his talks with CIA agent Sal Ferrera—right down to the date of the alleged exchange—except that the real conversation took place in Paris, and with a CIA operative. Ironically, one of the beneficiaries of this agency disinformation was John Crewdson, who then wrote for the *New York Times* and had previously been tabbed at Helms's staff meetings as among the objectionable reporters. Langley now went to Crewdson to retail its allegations against Agee. Another story that enraged Agee came from the *Manchester Guardian*, which picked up a piece that Murray Seeger wrote for the *Los Angeles Times*. This actually never appeared in the newspaper to which it was attributed. Seeger later explained that his editor had killed the story—he was convinced, at the agency's request. The height of the absurd came when an old comrade visited Victor Marchetti, in exactly the same "coincidental" way as the CIA had first approached Agee directly, and tried to induce Marchetti to steal a copy of Agee's manuscript in its current form. Langley must have been desperate.

Philip Agee's book finally appeared in the summer of 1975, published in the United Kingdom. *Inside the Company: CIA Diary* was an instant best seller, though not initially in the United States, where long-standing law precluded importing English-language books written by American authors. Bill Colby threatened lawsuits to prevent the book's attracting an American publisher, but eventually lost out to the marketplace. The Agee FOIA documents reveal that in 1975 the CIA went to the Justice Department to ask for a criminal indictment against him. But when Justice looked into the matter it was stymied—by the CIA. Agee could not be indicted without disclosing Langley's illegal actions against its former employee. The agency was not willing to expose its own crimes. The inquiry closed at the end of 1976. In fact, during 1977–1978, the Department of Justice considered whether to indict CIA officers for their actions. It was a Mexican standoff. The CIA stalemated itself.

Publication of Agee's book marked the onset of a long period of much more open struggle. The former CIA man denounced agency actions and revealed more names. He worked closely with the journal *Covert Action Information Bulletin* (an intellectual successor to *Counterspy*), which became a bête noire to the spy community. Agee collaborated on two edited books that focused on CIA activities in Europe and Africa and revealed more names. The agency sued to enjoin his income from those projects and obtained a general decision that Agee's writings were subject to CIA review, though the courts refused to award Langley any proceeds. Philip Agee began submitting his writings for review, but at the same time sued to obtain records of his case under the FOIA. In the new reality, Agee stopped writing much, but he traveled from country to country giving talks that exposed CIA agents and misdeeds.

Yet Langley was *still* not out of tricks. The 1975 murder of Athens CIA station chief Welch was laid at Agee's door, as well as that of the *Counterspy* people. The next ploy was to challenge Agee's domicile and agitate for revocation of his American passport. As the Ford administration gave way to that of Jimmy Carter, the United States pressured Great Britain to expel Philip Agee. The British issued such an order in January 1977, and Agee failed in all efforts to nullify it. He was then denied admission to France, and expelled from Holland after a brief stay. Agee's name was on a list to be denied admission to Germany at the same time as his application for residence in Hamburg was in the hopper. A suspicious shooting at the home of the CIA station chief in Jamaica—which may actually have been a CIA provocation—was blamed on Agee. At the end of 1979 the United States went ahead and canceled his passport. No American had *ever* had a passport canceled over a political matter, even where attempts were made to punish citizens who visited North Vietnam at the height of the Southeast Asian war, and there were several strong legal precedents against revocation. Agee sued for restoration of his passport and won in both the district court and on appeal, but the Supreme Court went against precedent and found against him. Philip Agee ended up carrying a passport from the nation of Grenada.

In the meantime, Langley used the Agee case to argue that the simple naming of undercover officers endangered them, as well as national security. This position gained the support of the Carter administration. The CIA proposed legislation that would make it illegal to reveal the name of a clandestine services officer on mission. That bill ultimately passed early in the Reagan administration, resulting in the Intelligence Identities Protection Act of 1982. Despite the fact that the law specifies it is for protection of *covert* officers, Langley now uses that authority quite frequently to shield the identity of *any* CIA officer, including senior officials whose identities have always been a matter of public record, even ones subject to Senate confirmation. For example, during the second Bush administration, the identity of Jose Rodriguez as chief of the National Clandestine Service was kept secret for longer than the law provides. This pillar of secrecy has become a double-edged sword. While it performs a good function in protecting officers under cover, it can be used as a tool against whistleblowers.

A new exemplar became the key in laying the final pillar for the foundation of the agency's fortress of secrecy. Agee's erstwhile CIA colleague Frank Snepp was also used by the secrecy mavens, who built their edifice on the foundation of the Marchetti case. Having established a role for prepublication review, what happened to Snepp gave the agency leave to use breach of contract legal grounds to overcome First Amendment rights. Here, Langley zeroed in on CIA officers' earnings from writing about their experiences. Frank Snepp was an agency analyst, one of the best and brightest on Vietnam, on his second tour at the Saigon station toward the end of the war. Snepp stayed on past the Paris ceasefire agreement and until the fall of Saigon in April 1975. During that time he became the leading analyst in situ. What Snepp saw during those last months and weeks of the Vietnam war scandalized him. Snepp's targets centered not on the CIA—which would receive his deep attention nonetheless—but the American ambassador and his superior, Secretary of State Henry Kissinger.

Phil Agee was no model for Frank Snepp. He regarded the Latin Americanist as a turncoat. Despite Langley's efforts to lump them together, Snepp began in channels, filing reports through CIA from Bangkok, later speaking of his experiences to agency audiences and at the Foreign Service Institute. He agitated to obtain high-level review of his charges. Snepp determined to write about what had happened only after efforts to follow procedure failed to produce a meaningful post mortem or any reforms, and began by actually asking permission to write a book on the end in Vietnam. Superiors turned him down primarily to avoid having a strong critique of Kissinger and company emerge from the Central Intelligence Agency.

As it became clear to Snepp that he would never be permitted to tell his story inside the CIA, intermediaries began to approach publishers on his behalf, and a deal was soon made with Robert Loomis at Random House, the same editor who had handled *The Invisible Government*. Snepp resigned from the agency in January 1976 to write his book without interference, and he decided not to submit the manuscript to CIA review. Supplied with chapter and verse on how Langley had sought to interfere with the Wise and Ross project, Snepp handled the writing process much like a spy operation. There were telephone codes, secret meetings, cutouts to hand over portions of the material, and so on. By these means Frank Snepp successfully contrived to get his book, *Decent Interval*, into the bookstores without Langley learning its contents.

Snepp reached his goal in the face of CIA's efforts to block him. As had happened with Agee, an active surveillance program was proposed, this time by Ted Shackley, now in the exalted position of head of CIA's operations directorate. The Office of Security refused to go the whole way, but it allowed "volunteers" to keep track of Snepp's comings and goings. This began within a month of the officer's resignation. Moreover, watch officers and agency group chiefs were put on the lookout for Snepp, alerted that he was writing a book that would not be put up for review. People were warned not to talk to the former officer. One who did was Bill Colby, now retired, who had been a close friend of Frank's father in law school. But Colby—who would have his own little problem with CIA publication review—saw Snepp to counsel him not to rock the boat. Former friend and Saigon station chief Tom Polgar, and CIA deputy director Hank Knoche, also met with Snepp to talk him down. Knoche informed agency director George H. W. Bush that Frank Snepp's revelations had the potential to damage the CIA. By the fall of 1976, Snepp was being looked at as a counterintelligence problem, which, as Snepp writes, "meant I was to be treated as a hostile foreign spy."[7]

At this point Joseph Smith's *Portrait of a Cold Warrior* suddenly hit the bookstores, triggering a new flap. Smith too had evaded prepublication review, and in his case the CIA had been completely unaware of the book until it appeared. Security officers quickly found fault with it. Agency lawyer Anthony Lapham tried to get Smith's publisher, Putnam, to pull the book for a CIA review, and while Putnam was amenable, so many copies had already shipped that no censor's pen could prevent its contents becoming known. Langley then considered suing Smith for breach of contract à la Marchetti, but CIA lawyers decided that would merely draw attention and ensure even more people read the book. The net result was the agency abandoned any action against Joseph Smith. Then the CIA was further embarrassed by the revelations of former contract officer John Stockwell, whose article on shoddy covert work in Angola was scathing. Langley's fury was white-hot. Snepp and Stockwell, their books yet to appear, became the targets.

In October 1976 OGC lawyer John Greaney—the same fellow involved in both the Marchetti and Agee affairs— sent Snepp a letter demanding access to his work. Greaney insisted the agency veteran was violating secrecy agreements and enclosed copies. By Snepp's account, this was the first time he'd seen his 1968 contracts since signing them, and he had been assured when leaving the agency that a less-demanding end-of-service agreement was the only one that applied. Moreover, in the original contract a CIA employee was assured the agency's Inspector General was ready to hear any complaint. In addition, five of Snepp's six secrecy agreements constrained only *classified* writings, and he intended a popular account, one that was not secret. Snepp and his publisher considered that the CIA had nullified the original contract by failing to let him air his grievances, and none of the other contracts applied. The agency primed its own guns, enlisting Admiral Stansfield Turner, its new director, to seek legal action. In March 1977 that recommendation went to the Justice Department.

Decent Interval appeared in November 1977. By then Bill Colby's memoir *Honorable Men* was in the hands of its publisher, and Colby, too, had violated CIA protocol by sending it in ahead of the agency review. Worse, Colby's manuscript was being translated for a French edition, and pieces the CIA demanded be lopped off the English-language narrative survived in French. The agency took no action at all against its former director. Nor did authorities act against former Saigon ambassador Graham Martin, whose car, recovered after being stolen, was found with a trunk full of authentic secret documents. But the full weight of the law descended on Frank Snepp, who had used phony names to protect agency colleagues and taken other measures to safeguard secrets—though he had given an unvarnished account of the intelligence reporting flowing in and out of Saigon, embarrassing as it was, and going to his central point. Simultaneously with the first rush of media attention, the CIA issued statements misleading the public that the veteran had reneged on an express promise to submit for review. By the time Snepp appeared on the television program *60 Minutes*, Langley had put it out that Director Turner was discussing prosecution with DOJ attorneys. The CIA also resorted to the now-standard tactic of cabling all stations instructions on how to handle Snepp's revelations—in this case he should be painted as an embezzler, someone who had *stolen* information.

The government filed suit in February 1978. Allegations about avoiding CIA publication review or disclosing secrets were not even pursued—either avenue would have enabled the defendant to contrast the action against him with the government's complete failure to act against Colby, Martin, or Joseph Smith. So the legal complaint against Snepp stipulated that it did *not* consider that *Decent Interval* contained *any* classified information. Instead, the Justice Department argued that Snepp had *profited* from CIA information—so that income from his book should be seized—and for the future he should be subject to a formal legal stricture to clear his writings. At base, the effort to cast this case as a contract violation shifted the ground. Although normally a showing of actual monetary damage is required by contract law, here the "national security" argument was employed to equate damage to the full amount of the author's earnings, whatever they might be. In July 1978 a judgment was rendered against Snepp that accepted all the government's arguments. Eight months later the federal Circuit Court for the District of Columbia affirmed the finding in every important respect. Snepp petitioned the Supreme Court to take his case on First Amendment grounds. In February 1980, without ever hearing arguments, the Supreme Court issued a summary judgment against him.

In the meantime, the CIA used Frank Snepp, as it had Philip Agee, this time in a campaign to further reinforce its ability to restrict information access on grounds of protecting intelligence sources and methods. One aspect was to seek new exemptions from the Freedom of Information Act. The other was to tighten secrecy agreements, even though Admiral Turner conceded that the Justice Department believed existing criminal statutes gave it all the authority necessary in this area. As Turner put it to Zbigniew Brzezinski in an October 23, 1979, memorandum, "It is imperative that some visible action be taken promptly in this area."[8]

By the summer of 1980, the CIA had completely reworked the texts of existing agreements, creating an "APEX" family of contracts it believed airtight. The agreement that applied at the highest level, "sensitive compartmented information," provided that even if the courts invalidated one or more provisions of the APEX, the others would remain in full force, and specified that once access was given to an employee, she or he was bound for life to agency review, regardless of whether the actual information was subsequently declassified. Agreements had text implying that anything employees saw was "damaging" to national security—regardless of whether it was, in fact, classified—and the CIA would later argue in courts that the contract language alone was a sufficient demonstration of damage to national security of whatever information was in an employee's writings. The contract even had a provision assigning to the United States all income an individual might earn if the CIA had not approved his writings in advance.

By the time the Carter administration ended, the spooks had built their fortress of secrecy. A full set of cloaks was available to conceal the daggers. Basic relations with journalists were mediated by agency spin doctors, who paid specific attention to image. In combination, the Marchetti, Agee, and Snepp cases completed the lock box. Marchetti established prior restraint in the form of prepublication review. The Agee affair led to the Intelligence Identities Protection Act and powerfully reinforced demands to curb FOIA provisions. Snepp established the "principle" that the CIA could seize the income of whistleblowers and added to the arguments against FOIA. All three cases set very unfortunate precedents—for American democracy, if not the wizards of Langley.

Despite Langley's intense interest in scouring the writings of those who had held security clearances and therefore signed secrecy agreements—a group that ranged far beyond the agency itself—the CIA had never bothered to create a unit to review manuscripts. Until the mid-'70s, that had been done informally by the Office of Security. That mechanism was established in June 1976 and would be called the Publications Review Board (PRB). The Publications Review Board was actually a *product* of the selfsame series of embarrassing disclosures that bedeviled the CIA through the Year of Intelligence and after. The agency's motives are apparent in its location of this staff in its *public relations* office, within the inner sanctum of the CIA director. The public relations chief headed the Board. The unit had barely gotten desk space when Stansfield Turner took up the reins, and the admiral brought with him what the professional spooks viewed with suspicion as a "mafia" of naval officers. One of them was Herbert Hetu, a retired navy captain who had been the PR guru for the United States Bicentennial Commission, and made his career before that as a navy spin doctor, doing public relations for the Pacific Fleet, two chiefs of naval operations, and the navy's central public information office. Hetu was best known for his liaison with movie producers, having worked on the navy side of the productions of *South Pacific*, *The Enemy Below*, and *In Harm's Way*. He had come to Admiral Turner's attention when Turner headed the U.S. fleet in the Mediterranean—the post from which he was appointed to the CIA—and Hetu did PR for Commander, Naval Forces, Europe. As a Turner acolyte and a Johnny-come-lately at Langley, Hetu had little trust from the spooks and, lacking any background in intelligence, had no way to judge what was truly sensitive when line officers complained that manuscripts before the PRB contained flap potential. The Board under Hetu became a zealous guardian of secrets, many of them real, but an equally large number fanciful.

The Publications Review Board never overcame its origins. For a decade and a half, until relocated to the CIA's administration directorate, it remained an artifact of Langley's public relations machine. Wearing his PR hat, Hetu would tell the *Washington Post* in 1980 that the Board had cleared nearly two hundred manuscripts and had had to negotiate changes in only three. One of the three was, of course, William E. Colby's book. The other former agency persons who published during the period were Vernon A. Walters, Peer de Silva, Cord Meyer, and Harry Rositzke. Walters mentioned the CIA almost exclusively in connection with Watergate, a subject too hot for the censors to touch. Meyer deliberately set out to craft an unrevealing account and without doubt had no difficulty with the Board. The remaining books were clearly affected by review. Put another way, the majority of major CIA memoirs of the era were combed out.

Wielding the clout of the Marchetti standard, sanctifying its authority to intervene, and the Snepp precedent, which permitted retaliation against those who went off the reservation, the Publications Review Board reigned supreme. It was regularized as an entity comprising a representative of each of the CIA's directorates, a legal advisor from OGC, and detailees from units dealing with personnel security and clandestine cover. To avoid problems, CIA authors had preliminary conversations with the monitors to gain their trust, self-censored their manuscripts, and then suffered through Board review. The various court decisions had set a timeliness requirement, eventually interpreted as a thirty-day interval within which to scrub a manuscript. That rubric was honored in the breach, and delay emerged as a weapon in PRB's bag of tricks.

Former director Stansfield Turner became an early victim. He made a start with opinion pieces for the newspapers. The Board held on to the urgent, timely ones and let pass those on general, nondescript organizational topics. When the admiral spoke up the agency came down on him. On March 8, 1985, for example, a car bombing took place in Beirut that aimed at a Muslim cleric and brought down an apartment building, killing eighty people. The incident was linked to the CIA by *Washington Post* reporter Bob Woodward (it is now generally credited to Saudi intelligence, but the agency had dropped a similar project, which Bill Casey may have handed over to the Saudis). When Admiral Turner made a comment to *Newsweek*, CIA's public relations chief, George V. Lauder (Hetu's successor), insisted in a letter that "it's a bum rap," declaring

Langley had no direct or indirect contact with the Lebanese officer who had masterminded the bombing, and cautioning Turner about what he said in public.[9] The admiral shot back a letter referring Lauder to the "presidential finding" for a covert operation that seemed to sanction the initiative. Lauder stuck to his guns.

All this took place while Stansfield Turner was trying to finish and publish his CIA memoir, and the lesson was that the more vapid the prose, the better chance of agency approval. Turner's efforts to squeeze his book through the PRB were lengthy and frustrating. The admiral's book was even a subject at Lauder's staff meetings. On March 16, 1984, the PRB assistant was reporting that the Board had cleared two "more" of the former director's chapters subject to various deletions.[10] Turner had been a key actor in establishing the publication review system—and he had the advice of Herb Hetu and former CIA lawyer Anthony Lapham, both of whom had had key roles in the Snepp case. Despite Turner's self-censorship, the agency demanded over a hundred deletions. Admiral Turner appealed many, but received just three concessions. The CIA told him to proceed as he felt "appropriate," but reserved the right to take any action *it* felt appropriate. The mailed fist inside the glove was evident.

Turner records that Board members were friendly, but preliminary review on each chapter consumed three weeks and adjudication another three or four. With many chapters being rewritten multiple times, and reviewed at each pass, the net impact felt both unreasonable and unnecessary.[11] Ten or 15 percent of his time evaporated in meeting PRB demands, and the former director said so in his book, which finally appeared in 1985. On April 26, 1985, the CIA issued a statement denying Turner's charges. But his book was gutted. Subordinates calculate that Admiral Turner made his way through—and extensively marked up—five briefcase-loads of paper every day. That added up to more than two million shelf-feet worth of documents. Virtually none of that knowledge is reflected in the Turner memoirs.

The *Fort Lauderdale News* noted the Publications Review Board's arbitrary standards for what had to remain secret. Public relations chief Lauder hit back hard: "The charges leveled by Admiral Stansfield Turner, suggesting that the CIA insisted that he remove unclassified material from his book, have no validity."[12] When the *Miami Herald* reviewed Turner's book, it mentioned that the narrative had been "picked apart" by agency censors. Public relations chief Lauder sent the paper a letter that insisted "the review process . . . exists solely to identify and delete classified material."[13] The stalling of Admiral Turner continued. In the Beirut bombing affair, Turner complained of the PRB's dilatory handling of his opinion pieces. Lauder passed Turner's letter to the Board, but told the admiral the fault lay with National Security Council staff aides.

George Lauder's missive to the *Miami Herald* also asserted baldly that "The CIA's record in avoiding any kind of partisan stance in its review process is a matter of record."[14] That was a falsehood. In fact, there existed no public record at all of the Publications Review Board's performance. If Lauder was referring to the Inspector General's audit of PRB in 1981, that was not public; was produced in-house by a unit that aimed at efficiency, not oversight; and had been done during an era when the CIA became politicized on Bill Casey's watch. A decade passed before the Inspector General returned to review the Board.

Stansfield Turner's experience proved the norm, not the exception. Another example is *Mole*, an account of and reflection on an important CIA spy in Russia published in 1982 by William Hood.[15] The retired clandestine services officer had had some involvement with the case and knew intimately those who had run the Russian agent. The case was publicly known. This was a feel-good situation for Langley, which had obtained some of its best intelligence on the Soviet military in the 1950s from this spy. Even the Russians got into the act, putting out their own account of trapping this CIA spy. Hood had no objection to the review system, was a respected officer, and cleared his idea of a book with a CIA deputy director even before starting. He adopted pseudonyms for his CIA characters except well-known persons or dead agency heroes. After twenty months writing, he entered the wilderness of mirrors of publication review—to discover the agency would have preferred this case remain buried. Hood was bewildered—spy tradecraft, like arithmetic, had been known for centuries. He had avoided sensitive matters and had been protective of identities. Hood met Board objections by lopping off offending passages and hiding dead men. In May 1981 his book was finally cleared to go.

Avoidance strategies became standard. Russell Jack Smith, actually a CIA deputy director, mentions hardly anyone below the level of publicly known officials, and referred to his own foreign assignment as a station chief by his State Department cover identity.[16] Agency lawyer Scott Breckinridge avoided using names and where obliged to do so went with given ones only.[17] Operations officer Tom Gilligan made up names for people and even for the countries where he had been assigned.[18] In his account of the CIA in Vietnam, Orrin Deforest altered names, dates, places, *and* particulars to protect individuals.[19] Shortly before Richard Bissell's February 1994 death, his coauthors submitted chapters of his memoir concerning his time with the CIA—and only those materials—to the Review Board.[20] By way of contrast, CIA spy Miles Copeland, who published a gossipy memoir in 1989 and prided himself on *not* submitting his manuscripts, visited agency lawyers to tell them what he intended to include. Rather than sue him, Copeland recounts, the CIA said he would have to go out and get his own publicity.[21]

The Publications Review Board, empowered simply to

protect classified information, has been wielded as a cudgel to regulate free expression. That is the meaning of interventions, and the effect of self-censorship. During the 1980s the agency worked to restrict discussion of its secret wars in Central America and Angola, and to minimize the research of an author investigating its activities in the Vietnam era. There was improvement, but also fresh evidence of CIA's caution. Procedures became routinized, and the agency gradually moved to uncloak matters once shrouded in secrecy. But indications of self-interest remained. In the late 1980s, the CIA's Family Jewels were, of course, the evidence of its involvement in the Iran-Contra affair. The Board had to restrain itself with the reports of the joint congressional committee and independent prosecutor who investigated the scandal, but it got a crack at the book by prosecutor Lawrence Walsh—naturally he had been given a security clearance. It also got a look at the memoir of President Ronald Reagan. When Iran-Contra CIA principal Duane R. ("Dewey") Clarridge penned his own CIA book, the PRB initially sent him a nineteen-page, single-spaced letter of redactions it demanded. Then cooler heads prevailed. Board chairman John Hollister Hedley viewed himself as a broker, adjudicating between the demands of agency operating divisions and the larger public interest. In what amounted to a bid to take the high ground of history, PRB made special efforts to allow a maximum amount of material when Dewey Clarridge told his story in 1997.[22]

By the late 1990s, the volume of texts had risen to over eighteen thousand pages a year. The concessions to Dewey Clarridge were taken as precedent, and a more open approach became the hallmark. Notable works followed on the CIA in the Cuban Missile Crisis and in Berlin, and several on the wartime Office of Strategic Services. During the millennium year, several hundred texts crossed the PRB transom. Approaching retirement, John Hedley could write optimistically in *Studies in Intelligence*, the CIA journal, that PRB procedure was well established and improving, its "interpretation of damage is not absolute and unchanging," and, despite change toward openness, the CIA was not headed down a slippery slope to "diminished capability to function as a secret organization."[23] Those were pious words, but the bright future Hedley described no longer exists and possibly was morphing even then.

In October 1997 the Board was finally moved to a newly created agency entity, the Office of Information Management, where it was retitled the "Publications Review Division," though the name change never stuck. The new office was buried in the bureaucracy, far from the director's office, and, with a different division, also in charge of CIA responses to the Freedom of Information Act. The effect was a recrudescence of the culture of secrecy. A brief on the PRB's work issued in 2000 by its then-chairman, Scott Koch, noted that the Board relied upon "voluntary compliance" and specified that the "CIA can eliminate information from nonofficial publications only if the text is classified and the Agency can demonstrate the damage to national security that disclosure would cause." This document, never classified, deletes passages supposedly "damaging" to the national security. The regs explicitly said that the Board *could not* deny permission simply because information was critical of or embarrassing to the CIA. But that was nullified by the stricture that agency directorates, as government employers, can prevent publication of even unclassified information if this would affect their ability to function or be detrimental to the foreign policy or security of the United States.[24]

By 2004 the number of pages reviewed was up to thirty thousand, and requests for permission to write had quadrupled. Langley worried that Board review could be overinterpreted. The Publications Review Board countered with what has become a standard notation in CIA memoirs—that PRB sanction means neither approval of a work nor authentication of its contents. Richard L. Holm, an officer with key roles in the Congo, Laos, and Lebanon, used both pseudonyms and single initials for senior officers. Holm's book contains such a statement.[25] So does the Robert Baer memoir, which has names and short pieces of text, along with a few more extensive passages, deleted.[26] Ted Shackley's posthumous account contained a similar notice in its acknowledgments.[27] Frank Holober's book follows this model. Holober's account of CIA covert missions along the China coast—by then dealing with events three decades in the past—was held up for months by the agency's FOIA office and cover representatives on the Board, who demanded pseudonyms for long-departed persons.[28] It is worth noting that the Intelligence Identities Protection Act has the purpose of protecting the names of clandestine officers (only) serving in active operations *within the last five years*. Holober credits then–Board chairman John H. Hedley with helping him overcome these objections. Any Board representative can block a manuscript, and representatives do so from the parochial positions of their divisions. Floyd Paseman, a clandestine service division chief, thanked the Review Board for helping him navigate the obstacles posed by his own unit, the Directorate of Operations.[29]

Stuart Methven, an agency operative prominent in the Southeast Asian wars, made up countries, people, languages, and more with such aplomb that his book hardly qualifies as a memoir, but fully justifies its title, *Laughter in the Shadows*.[30] Though treating his readers as fools, Methven nevertheless includes the standard CIA disclaimer. One who does not is former Congo station chief Larry Devlin, whose memoir protects colleagues by using only their given names (except for senior officials).[31] Devlin notably uses the term "station." Devlin's former subordinate David Doyle refers to himself simply as a CIA representative, with self-censoring throughout.[32] Milt Bearden, a general in the secret war in

Afghanistan and chief of the Soviet Division at the triumphal moment the Berlin Wall fell, made deletions requested by Review Board chairman Scott Koch, but his coauthor James Risen, not a CIA person, did not submit his portion of the text to censorship.[33]

Among CIA directors, several of whom have told their stories, there has been strong support for the Publications Review Board. Stansfield Turner has been mentioned, and he affirms the appropriateness of review despite the trouble it caused him. Robert Gates thanks the Board's Molly Tasker for cooperation and prompt action and pictures his review as "eminently fair and consistently reflect[ing] good common sense."[34] Similarly, former director George Tenet has kind words for Hedley's successor, Richard Puhl.[35] There are no deletions in Richard Helms's memoir, and he equably notes that "in keeping with CIA regulations, some of which I instituted, this manuscript was submitted to the Agency for security clearance."[36] Ironically, Helms's editor at Random House was Bob Loomis, the man the CIA had threatened at the time of *The Invisible Government*, and who had shepherded Frank Snepp's cri de coeur into print.

In the recent past the secrecy mavens have wavered. The CIA worked to inhibit public knowledge of its operations in the war on terror—from the Afghan campaign to secret prisons, to hostile interrogation—but also such historical subjects as the 1970s project to salvage a Soviet submarine using novel technology. In a book on the agency's first training class following the September 11 attacks, author T. J. Waters falsified names, places, dates, times, activities, and sequences of events to satisfy secrecy preferences.[37] One who had a positive experience with the PRB was John F. Sullivan, a longtime polygrapher.[38] So did Melissa Mahle, whose account of her recent CIA experience was critical but evenhanded.[39] Michael Scheuer, who gained fame as the anonymous author of a book on America's hubris, told a reporter, "I think it is going to be very difficult to publish a book on anything except cooking or Civil War history."[40]

Other important books go directly to intelligence "sources and methods," where the Board demonstrates considerable ambivalence. Not long after 9/11, CIA disguise experts Antonio and Jonna Mendez came out with a volume on their specialty and thanked the Board for helping them avoid the shoals of secret information.[41] As CIA director in 2005, Porter Goss initiated a revision of Board regulations. Goss, of course, was the man who countenanced the destruction of videotape evidence in the CIA torture scandal. In 2006 a retired agency counterintelligence chief, James M. Olson, published a study that framed a variety of espionage dilemmas as moral questions, solicited the comments of a range of persons from inside and outside the agency, and elaborated on the commentaries.[42] Olson noted the Review Board as cooperative, although several pages of his text would be blacked out.

At the time that tome was in press another book, on espionage tradecraft, was before the Board. By Robert Wallace, retired director of the CIA's Office of Technical Services, and H. Keith Melton, a historian of espionage gadgetry, the work would cover the waterfront of technological wizardry and show how such devices had figured in the spy wars. The authors cleared their project with the Board and got sample chapters approved in July 2004. Wallace himself, on active service, had participated in PRB clearances, and he wrote with a view to protecting sensitive information. The manuscript crossed the Board's transom in the fall of 2005. Wallace heard nothing for half a year. In March 2006 the authors were told that just the parts of their narrative that dealt with World War II were approved. The rest, including even the sample chapters, 95 percent of the work, was to stay secret.

Wallace hired a lawyer and appealed, leading to another eight-month hiatus. Before taking the agency to court, the authors appealed to a senior official, and in February 2007 most of the manuscript was suddenly cleared, and much of the rest followed that summer. The resulting book lauded CIA technologists.[43]

A different experience awaited Ishmael Jones, a clandestine service officer who had labored for the CIA under deep cover starting in 1989 and became so frustrated he left the agency to encourage reform of what he saw as a Soviet-style bureaucracy. The pseudonymous Jones incorporated his views in a manuscript that noted many ways in which agency management had acted in counterproductive, even silly, ways to cover its ass or pursue careerist goals. Jones sent his text to the Review Board in April 2007. A month later he was told clearance had been denied. Jones, who had read dozens of CIA memoirs more revealing than his, and had taken pains to avoid including anything secret, was stunned. He asked PRB to identify any places where the text contained classified information and promised to remove it. Several exchanges took place on this matter, and court records from both sides indicate no secrets were actually involved. Rather, the Board apparently indicated that the manuscript might be acceptable if rewritten in the third person, but once Jones had done that, PRB approved the release of just a few paragraphs. In January 2008, when Jones protested the extent of the excisions, the CIA took that as an appeal of the Board's decision, and said nothing further until the frustrated officer proceeded to publish. Jones's highly critical account of hidebound and creaky methods appeared at midyear.[44]

Langley filed suit against Jones for breaching the fiduciary trust implied by secrecy agreements, charging he failed to seek prepublication approval—because he had not waited for final agency action or sued the CIA himself—and therefore damaged the United States by "undermining of confidence

and trust in the CIA and its prepublication review process."
Using the Snepp precedent, the agency demanded it be
awarded Jones's earnings.[45] The court rejected the defendant's efforts to change venue, request for a jury trial, and
argument that Vietnam-era judgments of national security
damage cannot be applied at this late date. Jones's contention that the CIA had gone beyond its mandate and was acting as censor was also rejected. In November 2011, without
court trial, the federal judge awarded the CIA everything it
had sought. But Jones had arranged to donate all proceeds to
a fund for disabled agency veterans, and there were no proceeds to seize.

Other recent illustrations concern the emerging literature of the war on terror. Writing a preemptive defense of
his actions on renditions and torture tapes, and with former
agency PR chief Bill Harlow at his side, Jose Rodriguez had
pretty clear sailing. Not so the critics. Not even the initial
U.S. invasion of Afghanistan—where the agency has a proud
story to tell—escaped scrutiny. Henry A. Crumpton, the CIA's
top field commander, found the Board members courteous
and timely, "although incorrect in some of their excisions."[46]
He did not dispute them. Gary C. Schroen, whose account
of leading the first CIA operational group into Afghanistan
is a testament to a heroic agency, had to fight over much of
his account, including such silliness as identifying the type
of Russian-built helicopter that conveyed his team into the
country—readily apparent from photos that appear in the
book. Like others before him, Schroen contrived aliases for
everyone who accompanied him and obscured the identities
of those at headquarters. He recalled the review as long and
tedious, noting, "I had no idea . . . that so many of the details
that I included in the first draft . . . would be considered sensitive and would be marked for exclusion." But he decided the
process, which ultimately cleared most of his text, had been
fair. The Review Board told Schroen his book was the most

detailed account of an agency covert operation ever approved for publication.[47]

One who took heart from Schroen's experience was Gary Berntsen, his colleague and successor as the CIA's Afghan team leader, whose bout with the censors was even less pleasant. Berntsen was an experienced officer, loyal to the agency, and had already self-censored his narrative. Yet the clearance, he recalled, "turned out to be the most surreal and frustrating experiences [*sic*] in my life." After repeated delays he filed suit, and a federal judge ordered the CIA to liberate his manuscript, acceding to forty pages of deletions, including items such as the mileage between cities in Afghanistan— measurable on any map—and the name of William Buckley, a CIA officer murdered by extremists in Lebanon in the 1980s, whose case has figured in many writings. Berntsen had to file suit again and obtain an injunction before the CIA would respond to his appeal to restore some of the material, and adjudication of those deletions was yet to be completed when his book went to press.[48]

Those CIA officers for whom national security became the God That Failed, who sought to write about their disillusion, have had their works parsed ruthlessly at the Publications Review Board. Their substantive reporting has been dealt with elsewhere, but the CIA reaction to their narratives has not. John Kiriakou is the newest poster boy. He survived prepublication review after not one but several appeals. The agency veteran credits PRB for permitting those appeals, and he accommodated Langley by changing names, disguising or eliminating some locales, and blurring certain true events.[49] But Kiriakou spoke to reporters, divulging the name of an agency colleague and commenting—inaccurately, as it turns out—on waterboarding. His wife, a fellow CIA officer, was forced to resign. John Kiriakou was indicted for breaching

the Intelligence Identities Protection Act and for other transgressions. One of the four counts in the government's bill of
particulars charges Kiriakou with lying to the Publications
Review Board. No one has ever been indicted for such a
crime. The potential chilling effect is incalculable. If former
CIA persons can be sent to prison for their dealings with the
PRB, there is no end to the mischief this will cause. Defense
lawyers in the Kiriakou case informed government attorneys that at court they would present evidence on, among
other things, the arbitrary actions of the Publications Review
Board, which had, in fact, approved Kiriakou's manuscript.
But the CIA's interest in avoiding public testimony on PRB
operations cannot yet be demonstrated. Intent on obtaining a result that would at least add weight to the Intelligence
Identities Protection Act, prosecutors offered a plea bargain. Kiriakou took the deal. In October 2012 he pled guilty
to revealing the name of a covert operative. Several months
later he was sentenced to thirty months in prison. John
Kiriakou's case may become a brick in the fortress of secrecy.

Glenn Carle became another casualty of the agency's drive
to minimize flap potential. Carle's account of the CIA's way-
ward path encountered fierce obstruction, with demands for
redaction of 40 percent of his manuscript and the final excision of about a third. He "literally" rewrote the book a dozen
times to meet the censors' demands. Carle fought for months
to be able to mention a urinal and had to scrap for passages
that described the color of fog, indicated that agency officers
disagreed, or commented that someone spoke authoritatively
or another seemed a fool. Quotations from the poet T. S. Eliot
were suppressed, as was his use of the word "kidnap" from
a previous book the CIA itself had cleared. The agency prevented Carle's using numerous details, leaving surviving
pages laced with deletions.[50]

Valerie Plame, a clandestine service officer who worked
to prevent nuclear proliferation, was victimized by Bush

administration officials intent on evading accountability for their disastrous decision to attack Iraq. Plame's undercover status as a CIA officer, supposed to be guarded under the Intelligence Identities Protection Act—ironically a product of the agency's frantic appeals after the Phil Agee fiasco—was revealed by aides to Vice President Richard Cheney. Her husband, retired ambassador Joseph Wilson, had published an opinion piece revealing the lack of evidence for the administration's charge that Iraq was buying uranium from the African nation of Niger. Cheney sought to retaliate. Cheney's national security deputy, I. Lewis Libby, was prosecuted and convicted for Plame's outing. Her cover blown, Plame felt obliged to leave. But when she attempted to write about her career, the CIA drained Plame's memoir, refusing clearance for her to include numerous details that formed part of the Libby trial record or had been widely discussed in the press. Review Board chairman Richard Puhl even denied Plame's mention of the dates of her service at CIA, which had been the subject of routine, unclassified correspondence with its retirement office that had been printed in the *Congressional Record*. Publisher Simon & Schuster sued in an attempt to compel the Publications Review Board to approve the material, but the courts succumbed to the CIA's usual dark claims of national security "damage." Simon & Schuster eventually commissioned reporter Laura Rozen to write an afterword with elements that had been cut from Valerie Plame Wilson's manuscript.[51]

The CIA has even reached beyond Langley, applying its scissors to manuscripts from employees of other agencies, like State Department nation-builder Peter Van Buren, who participated in the Iraq war with the so-called Provincial Reconstruction Teams. This diplomat, who had served in many posts in close cooperation with the military and other agencies, shepherded his manuscript through State's clearance. Shortly before publication, the department's censors informed him that the CIA was asking for changes to his text. Van Buren decided to go ahead anyway.[52]

Then there was FBI interrogator Ali Soufan, who had worked with the agency in questioning Al Qaeda captive Abu Zubaydah. He broke with CIA counterparts when it became a matter of torturing the man. Soufan's manuscript survived FBI's clearance process only to be stalled, just weeks from publication, by CIA demands for a host of cuts. Langley's faxes ordering revisions totaled 181 pages, nearly a third of the length of the text itself. The CIA's official spokesperson, questioned about these demands, termed it "ridiculous" that the agency's basis for action was that it did not like the content of Soufan's book, and reiterated the standard boilerplate that the Review Board only sought to protect classified information.[53]

According to Soufan, the FBI had no obligation to clear the book with Langley, since he had no contractual relationship with the CIA and had never reported to it. When he demonstrated that the demanded cuts concerned information in the public domain, were FBI material, or consisted of previously declassified CIA data, the Publications Review Board withdrew its demands but came back with an even more extensive list. Committed to a certain date for publication, Soufan made the cuts. Among them were quotes from unclassified testimony presented in public before Congress and broadcast live on national television, material drawn from the 9/11 Commission reports, the words "I" and "me," and use of the word "station" for the contingents of CIA personnel assigned to U.S. embassies abroad. Soufan believes that he was required to delete from his own book details appearing in Jose Rodriguez's memoir. He asked the FBI to review the deletions. Not satisfied, he sued.[54] The Soufan suit is now in an early stage in the courts, and he intends to see it through.[55]

Secrecy is compromised when everything is deemed

secret—more so when what is deemed classified is manipulated, whether for political purposes or any others. It was
inevitable that the record of the Publications Review Board
would eventually come under scrutiny. In the late 1990s,
when Board chairman John Hedley published the first real
examination of the unit in the agency's in-house magazine,
the PRB had been moderating its approach, and Hedley could
offer an optimistic view. In the war on terror, that is no longer
possible. Members of the Senate Select Committee on Intelligence wrote CIA Director General David Petraeus in the
spring of 2012 to express concern at the Publications Review
Board's behavior. Press reports at this writing indicate the
CIA has begun an internal investigation of the PRB. While
such an inquiry may be a move forward, it could also represent a tactical maneuver. The Board's actions and methods
will be central to the Soufan civil suit. Langley needs to be in
a position to offer some kind of substantive evidence, if only
to avoid a deeper probe into its Publications Review Board.
Substantial stakes ride on the outcome.

The CIA's fight to avoid accountability has had the effect
of producing a fractured history populated by books that
resemble Victor Marchetti's—pages littered with black ink
that obscure known facts, embarrassing incidents, and outright illegalities, along with literally stupid deletions, all with
a combination of real and fraudulent claims to secrecy, now
to be enforced by criminal sanction. The net result will ultimately drain CIA history of any credibility, if not worse. Yet
the agency behaviors that have moved former intelligence
officers to write, even when excised from their books, do not
disappear simply because censors succeed in suppressing
their mention. And as often as not, the controversies leave
a paper trail that will one day furnish guideposts to investigators. Rather than avoid flap potential, actions like these

create time bombs that will one day explode with the greater force of pent-up pressure.

Meanwhile, in its own terms—and despite the pious affirmations of agency practitioners—the CIA publications review process has exceeded its mandate. In fact, it is difficult to avoid the impression that the Publications Review Board has run wild. Designed simply to ensure the secrecy of properly classified national security information, the system operates in knee-jerk fashion with the arrogance of a star chamber. The shadow warriors have profited from the reluctance of U.S. courts to interfere in matters of national security, but they risk putting the entire system into bankruptcy the moment its excesses become so blatant they can no longer be denied. When that happens the loser will be the Central Intelligence Agency. And even if the break never comes, the distortions in the record of U.S. intelligence induced by this approach will ultimately rebound to the detriment of the CIA.

Had it then existed, the CIA's publications review apparatus would not have prevented the Year of Intelligence, because government actions, not the mention of them, are the key determinant. Secrecy can be counterproductive, as in the case of the Family Jewels, increasing pressures toward revelation and magnifying the public's horror when transgressions are revealed. Secrecy did not contain the Iran-Contra affair in the 1980s—and the resulting political crisis sapped the power of the Reagan administration. Secrecy did not prevent the revelation of the CIA's cozy relationship with Central American torturers in the 1990s, with detrimental consequences to the agency even though it succeeded in avoiding a full-blown disaster. With the tip of another iceberg of malefaction already evident today, and Americans themselves in the role of kidnappers and torturers—and, with the drone war, executioners—the agency erred in resisting a full airing of these allegations in 2009, and President Barack

Obama made a serious misstep in acceding to CIA demands. When it comes, the efforts of the Publications Review Board will not avert this flap. Better would have been to blow off the steam, take the public's reprimand, and move on. As the secret warriors know better than anyone, there are *always* Family Jewels. When the next crisis arrives, the unanswered charges that have been so cleverly suppressed will arise anew and add their force to the flap of the moment, ensuring spooks' misery.

9

≡ CIRCLING THE WAGONS ≡

P residents and spies. Responsibility, loyalty—and calculation—flow both up and down the chain of command. There is a kind of symbiotic relationship between the White House and the Central Intelligence Agency. Presidents who demand questionable sorts of operations have some responsibility to defend the agency once it comes under fire. Even where the issue is activities carried out under previous chief executives, the president who wishes to protect his prerogatives has an incentive to rise to the CIA's defense. Agency directors seeking to maintain their freedom to act in the face of mounting criticism have an analogous inducement to call upon White House protection. "While the heat from the Church committee was on the CIA, the White House told us not to cooperate," Bill Colby would recall, "but when the heat began to move toward the White House, they began to give up papers."[1]

Gerald Ford's responses during the Year of Intelligence are good examples. The president sought to get ahead of the controversy and preserve his political position, calculating that he could protect capabilities by making certain interventions. Creation of the Rockefeller Commission had been one such measure. Richard Cheney held the reins as long as he could, but later, when Donald Rumsfeld moved to the Pentagon and Cheney rose from deputy to chief of staff to the president, he no longer had the time to ride herd on the proliferating aspects of the intelligence crisis. Cheney took a hand in creating the basic system and then watched the paper flow, jumping in where he saw a need to do so.

Once the Senate and House established panels for independent looks at intelligence, President Ford knew his strategy of limiting damage through the Rockefeller Commission had failed. The administration needed a new approach. Cheney was on board in late February, when Henry Kissinger told Ford they needed a White House "CIA steering committee." The good doctor even suggested that the president appoint Lawrence Silberman to replace Colby at the CIA, but Ford was not prepared to go that far then (he would fire Colby, bringing in George H. W. Bush, but not until November). The steering group indeed formed, headed by White House counsel Philip C. Buchen. A week later President Ford met the ranking members of the Church Committee in the Oval Office. His talking points were to promise full cooperation but emphasize the sensitivity of the matters under investigation. Disclosures would be disastrous. Ford's aides cautioned him to *promise* cooperation but not *commit* to it. Everything would be done on a case-by-case basis, which effectively meant that Phil Buchen took a look at every request before the CIA, or any other agency, was permitted to respond to it.

Over the long year that followed, it was the White House, not necessarily CIA, that stood at the center of the storm. The White House approved the CIA's basic arrangement for dealing with the congressional committees, as well as the schema for how Langley would provide documents to the investigators. The Church Committee, encouraged to put its requests in writing, sent them to the White House, where Phil Buchen reviewed them for political sensitivity and Robert C. McFarlane, then a junior NSC staffer, did the same for substantive content. Richard Cheney wanted a more coherent approach for responding to Church Committee requests. Buchen provided it. It was Buchen who signed off on the document lists, Buchen who considered committee requests for access to the President's Foreign Intelligence Advisory Board, he again who wrote talking points for Henry Kissinger's meeting with Bill Colby in May. Phil Buchen manipulated David Belin over the Rockefeller Commission's assassinations report, and got that key document to Kissinger for the NSC staff to "edit." Later Buchen broke up Bella Abzug's effort to inquire into the National Security Agency's Project Shamrock by keeping General Lew Allen from testifying. Once it became a matter of legislative proposals for what became the Foreign Intelligence Surveillance Act, Phil Buchen took the lead there too.

When the Church Committee began looking into covert operations, the White House argued the subject was so sensitive that Colby should *only* meet with the committee leadership, and *brief* only, not *testify*. There would be no questions. In the face of public outrage over CIA domestic covert activity, that gambit could only fail. The fallback would be that CIA compiled testimony for Colby that was approved by the White House. President Ford's talking points for the meeting where that happened—written by Phil Buchen—suggested that Colby say the least amount possible and when getting down to the nitty-gritty demand to go into executive session with only the committee's ranking members. That attempt to revive the failed gambit also did not fly.

In the middle of this controversy the public learned that Richard Ober, the CIA officer who had notoriously run Project Chaos, was at the White House on the NSC staff. Dick Cheney was furious. He demanded a rundown on all CIA people working at the White House. When Cheney got the list Ober's name was on it—and he had been at the White House since March 18, 1974—earning over $150,000 a year (2012 dollars) at a civil service grade of GS-16.

Richard Cheney was also instrumental in Ford's decision to bring John Marsh onto the team. Marsh participated regularly in White House discussions on the CIA quagmire. Anticipating that the congressional investigations would lead to reform proposals, the White House sought to head off the stampede by implementing its own reorganization first. Marsh led the group that created the plan for this, completed and announced in early 1976.

Gerald Ford's actions illustrate the tension that exists between a president's political interests and her or his management of the CIA. There is a temptation for presidents to call upon the agency for extraordinary services, or to hide White House adventures behind the cloak of CIA secrecy. Gerald Ford avoided the adventures, but watched over his interests like a hawk. But an exemplar of the opposite sort is his predecessor, Richard Milhous Nixon, who summoned the Central Intelligence Agency to assist his political machinations. Nixon's maneuvers led to the Watergate scandal. The political storm that followed the unraveling of Watergate conditioned the atmosphere in which the Family Jewels revelation took place. The agency's participation in Nixon's Watergate plots, however limited, injected an element of vulnerability into its position from the outset, and colored it sinister to the public. Watergate is a good place to start.

The Watergate scandal began on a June night in 1972 when the security man on duty, making his rounds, found access doors taped open. A check of the Watergate office building, in downtown Washington, led to the discovery of intruders inside the Democratic Party's national headquarters. Police were summoned and the men arrested. Within days of the June 17 incident, the burglars were revealed to be hires of Richard Nixon's electoral campaign staff and their bosses, Nixon campaign intelligence officials, former White House employees. Worse, two of the key Nixon staffers, E. Howard Hunt and James McCord, were former CIA officers, and the Watergate burglars themselves were anti-Castro Cubans who had worked for the agency.

Though Watergate in those early days aroused little public concern—nothing resembling the huge political crisis it became—the Nixon White House was immediately aware of its vulnerabilities, and the president initiated a plan to cover up the scandal. The early disclosures pointed at least some suspicions toward the CIA. Nixon, worried that he could not control the FBI investigation, sought to use the CIA to quash it. The most important single piece of evidence in the Watergate saga was what President Nixon told his chief of staff, H. R. Haldeman, on the morning of June 23, 1972. Recorded on an audiotape system the president had secretly installed in his office, the chronicle of that conversation became known as the "Smoking Gun Tape," and its forcible disclosure through a Supreme Court decision led to Nixon's resignation before he could be impeached. In their actual talk, Nixon and Haldeman discussed how to stop the FBI. Haldeman suggested they have CIA chiefs call the FBI director and tell him to drop lines of inquiry that were uncovering White House involvement. The president not only agreed, he suggested directions they might take with the CIA, and wanted Langley to put it on the basis that the FBI investigation would blow open the whole Bay of Pigs affair. Mr. Nixon's celebrated comment that "we protected Helms from a hell of a lot of things" was likely an allusion to his help in suppressing the Victor Marchetti–John Marks book *The CIA and the Cult of Intelligence*.[2]

Armed with the president's instructions, Haldeman summoned Director Helms and his deputy, General Vernon Walters. They met with Haldeman and colleague John D.

Ehrlichman early that afternoon. Richard Helms repeated what he had already told the FBI—the agency had had nothing to do with Watergate—and added that the Bureau knew this as a result of his telephone call. Haldeman persisted and declared it was the president's wish that General Walters inform acting FBI director L. Patrick Gray that CIA wanted the Bureau to drop its inquiries in Mexico, ostensibly because they might touch on CIA activities. Helms stood his ground, repeating that no CIA operations were implicated. Ehrlichman piled on. General Walters finally agreed to talk to the FBI, and did so later that day.[3] Walters saw Gray alone at FBI headquarters afterwards, saying he had come from the White House. While he was aware of Director Helms's affirmation of noninvolvement, Walters added that FBI inquiries "might lead to some [CIA] projects." Gray responded he would have to think about that, but he looked forward to cooperating with the agency.[4] Walters exceeded his boss's instruction by reminding the FBI that under a long-standing agreement the Bureau had to inform Langley whenever its inquiries uncovered CIA operations. The general did so, he recounted, because he suspected the president's chief of staff must be privy to information not available at the agency, thus Haldeman's message should be passed along as given.[5] Equally possible was that Walters, who had worked closely with Nixon on Vietnam over several years, was not as yet fully aware of its implications and therefore willing to go along with his scheme.

President Nixon's attempt to use the Central Intelligence Agency to cover up the Watergate scandal unraveled over the next ten days. Deputy Director of Central Intelligence Walters had second thoughts about his careless entry into the conspiracy, while FBI Director L. Patrick Gray, seeking ironclad evidence he had been ordered to stand down, demanded a written affirmation the CIA was calling him off. Meanwhile, the White House escalated its demands. Presidential counsel John Dean had Walters back on June 26 and fished for a clear admission that the Watergate break-in could not have occurred without Langley's knowledge. Dean pressed for the CIA to bail out the burglars. General Walters refused and pointed out the scandal would get ten times worse if such an act were revealed. On June 28 John Dean tried again, and Walters, not budging, reassured the White House aide that scandals in Washington blew over quickly, soon to be replaced by spicier ones. Walters counseled patience, but returned to Langley to offer his resignation. Helms refused to accept it. The CIA, if not the White House, would ride out the storm. Mr. Helms now put to paper orders that there was to be "no freewheeling exposition of hypotheses or any effort made to conjecture about responsibility or likely objectives of the Watergate intrusion."[6]

Efforts to enlist Langley in the Watergate cover-up collapsed on July 6 over the FBI's demand for a document that would insist it stand down. General Walters met Patrick Gray, instead handing him a memorandum that summarized the CIA links of all the Watergate burglars plus its lack of connection with two Mexicans whom the FBI suspected of laundering drug money. Walters repeated that no CIA operations were involved and added the agency was not willing to affirm any endangerment of national security.[7]

Despite this record President Nixon made a public effort to pull the CIA cloak around himself. In a speech on May 22, 1973, he referred obliquely to the "smoking gun" conversation, maintained that worries of compromise of CIA operations had led him to act, and, within that context, confirmed he had told Haldeman and Ehrlichman to have Walters and Gray ensure that the Watergate investigation not uncover either CIA or White House activities. In June 1976 George Herbert Walker Bush, at that time the head of the Central Intelligence Agency, proposed that the highest honor existing in the intelligence field, the National Security Medal, be awarded to Vernon A. Walters. One of the four grounds given for that award was "his key role in 1972 just after becoming Deputy Director of Central Intelligence in preventing CIA from being improperly used in a domestic policy matter."[8]

So far this record shows a president intent on hiding behind CIA secrecy, plus an agency that —save for Walters's momentary lapse—had refused to be drawn into the cover-up. There might have been nothing more said of the CIA and Watergate except that this story had layers. The agency was on top of Watergate from the beginning. The burglars had been arrested on a Saturday. First thing Monday morning, Director Helms mentioned the burglary to his barons, discussing both Howard Hunt and James W. McCord. By his account and that of Cord Meyer, attending that day in place of Tom Karamessines, Helms asked each man whether they had anything to do with Hunt's cabal. All replied in the negative. Helms instructed them as to what would be said and who could say it. The director himself noted the FBI inquiries, saying, "We have no responsibility with respect to an investigation except to be responsive to the . . . request for name traces."[9] Next day, security chief Howard Osborn briefed on the CIA's relations with Bay of Pigs veteran and agency operative Bernard L. Barker. Helms asked that "future inquiries be met with a response confined to the fact that, now that we have acknowledged that both McCord and Hunt are former Agency employees, we know nothing more about the case."[10]

Actually the CIA's knowledge went deeper than that, and suspicions that Langley's role was more ominous made the agency a target for any number of politicians on the make or conspiracists determined to prove their case. Howard Hunt had been a subject at Helms's staff meetings before—almost a year before—when Hunt's White House outfit had drawn the

CIA into illegal domestic activities yet again. The immediate rationale was the old bugaboo of leaks. In June 1971 there was a huge leak in the form of Daniel Ellsberg's release of the Pentagon Papers. In the wake of abject failure to suppress that Vietnam material by court order, the Nixon White House formed a special unit to counter disclosures. Hunt, whose day job was with the public relations firm Mullen & Company, had been hired as a consultant for that unit, soon known as the "Plumbers." Walters's predecessor, marine General Robert Cushman, informed the CIA barons at their morning meeting of July 8, 1971, that Hunt had become a White House security consultant.[11] Nixon officials wanted CIA cooperation with the unit, which Helms approved.

The agency assembled a study of Nixon-era leaks for the Plumbers, and CIA officials met with Hunt and his White House colleague, David Young, seconded from the NSC staff, on leaks and on administration schemes both to protect information and arrange provisions for declassification of documents. Nixon aide John Ehrlichman asked the agency to help Hunt. Two weeks after his name had come up at Helms's meeting, Hunt was at Langley to see Deputy Director Cushman. Howard Hunt requested disguise material and "pocket litter"—cover identity items—to conduct certain meetings anonymously. The request typified Nixon White House duplicity; one of those missions concerned checking the plausibility of doctored "official" documents that would have more directly linked President Kennedy—and the CIA—to the 1963 assassination of South Vietnamese leader Ngo Dinh Diem. That was a Nixon political project to gain advantage against Democrats for the 1972 election.

On July 28 Hunt suggested to Nixon political operative Chuck Colson that the CIA be tasked to assemble a psychological profile of American citizen Daniel Ellsberg. It could be used to identify weak points to discredit the leaker. Langley had previously done profiles only of foreign leaders. More illegal domestic activity. Nevertheless, the next day, having discussed the request with Helms, Howard Osborn asked Dr. John R. Tietjen, chief of CIA medical services, for the paper. The profile was completed in early August and handed over in David Young's office on August 12. It is not clear what advance word the Plumbers had of the Ellsberg profile, but they were not at all happy with it. Hunt later recounted that he had seen much better products on such people as Cuban Fidel Castro or Iranian Mohammed Mossadegh, based on even less data than available here. In any case, on August 11, *before* the CIA turned in its paper, Ehrlichman approved a covert break-in at the workplace of psychiatrist Dr. Lewis J. Fielding in order to copy Ellsberg's private medical records.

Meanwhile, pocket litter led to other Plumber demands. Hunt's colleague G. Gordon Liddy wanted a false identity of his own, and that was provided at a CIA safe house on August 20. The agency also furnished two miniature cameras and a tape recorder concealed in a briefcase. Director Helms was furious when he learned that his people had given pocket litter to a non-CIA employee. Hunt went over the top when he asked that his former agency secretary, now assigned to the Paris station, be brought back to work for him. According to CIA records, on August 25 Helms ordered cooperation with Howard Hunt to cease. But it was the next day that Hunt and Liddy scouted Dr. Fielding's office, and the photos from that California trip were then developed at Langley. The actual burglary took place on September 3. In addition to Hunt and Liddy standing outside, it involved Bernard Barker and Eugenio Martinez, either former or current CIA agents and both future Watergate defendants.

Despite Mr. Helms's purported orders, more help for Hunt's Plumbers followed. On October 12 Hunt met with Tom Karamessines regarding concerns about Mullen & Company, which the agency used for disguising some of its operatives and as an intermediary with Howard Hughes, and for which Hunt still formally worked. Langley put Hunt in touch with a proprietary that could furnish him physical security and telephone monitoring services in a Las Vegas operation connected with Mullen. There were more discussions with Hunt that October regarding the White House's pursuit of Vietnam documents. Any doubts this remained a key Nixon concern must have evaporated after November 16, when John Ehrlichman had CIA's number three man, William E. Colby, to the White House. He pressed Colby for the agency to declassify the Diem assassination documents. Colby refused. Helms backed him up. Meanwhile, Hunt again approached an agency officer in connection with a break-in plan that seems to have fallen through. In December 1971 the CIA performed a name trace at Howard Hunt's request.

If not exactly an agency domestic operation, the CIA's support to the Fielding break-in made it complicit in the commission of a crime. The other contacts at a minimum contradict CIA's position that it knew nothing about Hunt's activities. Worse, Langley actually did a fresh version of the Ellsberg psychological profile based on the private medical records. It was finished early in November—*and* Dr. Teitjen, with his lead analyst, wrote explicitly of their concern the CIA role might become known. They put this to Helms in a November 9 memo. The profile *was* an illegal activity. Later, when Hunt and Liddy moved over to the Nixon campaign staff and crafted its plan to gather political intelligence, the briefing boards illustrating the scheme were produced at Langley. As late as the spring of 1972, when Hunt wanted the help of an expert lock picker, the CIA put him in touch with an agency retiree. In short, there were multiple instances, some involving crimes, in which any standing order to refuse cooperation was honored in the breach.

Later it became apparent that Langley had even more fore-knowledge of Hunt-Liddy political sabotage activity. Senator Howard Baker, who made the CIA his special portfolio as vice-chairman of the congressional panel investigating Watergate, developed this evidence. It came from the agency and through Cuban exile channels. Hunt's request for a lock picker was a dead giveaway. Meanwhile, he recruited operatives for nefarious schemes, among them the same Cubans who had helped with the Fielding break-in. One, Eugenio Martinez, *was still on the CIA payroll* (at $550 a month [in 2012 dollars] for his information about the Miami Cubans). Martinez told his CIA case officer, as well as Jake Esterline, the agency's Miami station chief, of his connection to Hunt not long after the Fielding break-in. In March 1972 Hunt recruited Martinez again, and the latter informed a new case officer. Martinez worried whether the Hunt operation had CIA clearance. He approached Esterline to ask whether the station chief was, in fact, aware of all agency activities in the Miami area. Esterline checked with Langley. On March 27 Cord Meyer, Karamessines's assistant, sent Esterline word to "cool it" and pay no attention. Hunt, Meyer informed Esterline, was on unknown White House business.[12] Meyer wanted no information about Hunt from the CIA operative: "It seemed clear to me that it was outside the Agency's charter and a violation of our legal authority to use one of our part-time paid informants to report secretly to us on what the White House might be doing in the field of domestic politics."[13] Eugenio Martinez's most recent meeting with his CIA case officer had occurred in Miami ten days before the Watergate break-in.

The assertion that the CIA knew nothing of Nixon administration dirty tricks could only be sustained by drawing the narrowest possible definition of what constituted "knowledge." It is clear that Langley knew of the special equipment it had itself provided the Plumbers—and it had to be aware of the typical uses for those items. Howard Hunt's various demands for help further illuminated the direction in which the Plumbers were headed. The Ellsberg psychological profiles crossed the line—and Director Helms had personally been made aware of subordinates' concern. Langley certainly knew enough that when Eugenio Martinez queried his CIA chain of command, Cord Meyer surmised the agency should keep its distance.

Once it came to the actual investigation of Watergate, there were instances of apparent foot-dragging at Langley, as Senator Baker also documented. Martinez's case officer was ordered to Washington but directed to go slow—drive, not take a plane. Another Miami source told Esterline that Martinez's car had been left parked at the airport and contained compromising materials. The CIA held on to this information for two days before informing the FBI. It is not clear if the time was used to get rid of evidence. In Washington that *did* happen—a colleague of former officer James McCord entered the suspect's home and did the deed. This officer's identity was withheld until February 1974. Meanwhile, Robert Bennett, the president of the Mullen company and a CIA source, fed Langley a diet of inside information on Watergate and served as a conduit to incarcerated former officers Hunt and McCord. Senator Baker established that Richard Helms was apprised of Bennett's information.

Information about these matters emerged piecemeal over many months. The net effect was to keep the CIA under the microscope despite Langley showing it had resisted the cover-up. Director Helms quickly decided he needed a point man to handle Watergate. For that he selected agency executive director William Colby. The marching orders, as Colby recounted them, were to "stay cool, volunteer nothing, because it will only be used to involve us, just stay away from the whole damn thing!"[14]

That proved difficult to do. Colby's first task was to liaise with the FBI's Alexandria field office, which led its Watergate investigation. At first this was a matter of name checks, but that soon evolved. The discovery of the Martinez car at the

Miami airport led the Bureau to wonder what else Langley was holding back. The Howard Hunt contacts were another case in point. The southern California locale of the Fielding office photographs and their purpose for planning a burglary were recognized only inadvertently by Cord Meyer. Handing them over became somewhat delicate. Once congressional investigators got involved, the situation became even more complicated. Colby defended the CIA, and he later maintained the agency had given Congress more than seven hundred documents and permitted two dozen of its officers to testify. By its count the agency had as many as 160 objections to Howard Baker's report—it must have grated not to have the authority to censor Watergate materials.

But Langley's unhappiness at how it came out in Watergate reporting had plenty to do with Colby and Helms and their reticence. Investigators repeatedly asked for all the 1971–1972 papers documenting Eugenio Martinez's contacts with agency personnel, but CIA provided only excerpts of the early ones. Colby refused to give up the debriefing record covering Martinez's CIA case officer. Documents regarding Mullen & Company, requested in February 1974, were still pending when the Watergate committee went out of existence. The records of technical support for Hunt were denied. As for materials concerning the Ellsberg profiles, Colby only offered to show them to the (friendly) congressional committees that usually dealt with CIA matters. Similarly, only the House Armed Services Committee got to see records related to Lee Pennington, the agency officer who had entered the McCord home after James McCord's arrest. There was a lengthy list of other evidence which Bill Colby never produced to the investigators.

The most egregious tampering took place with Richard Helms's records. Watergate investigators learned from Victor Marchetti of the possible existence of an audiotaping system in the offices of senior CIA officials. By letter on January

16, 1973, Senator Mike Mansfield asked the CIA to safeguard all evidence including tapes. Within days, maintaining his actions were mere housekeeping before leaving for his new post as ambassador to Iran, Director Helms ordered the destruction of all tapes and transcripts, plus written records concerning them. More than four thousand pages of documents were apparently involved—there had never been such a mass expurgation of records at Langley. The CIA gave investigators only summaries of logs and denied the Office of Security logs related to the taping.

Tape questions led to one of the CIA's biggest Watergate embarrassments. Once Colby informed Howard Baker the Cushman-Hunt tape had been destroyed, the senator asked if there were others. The CIA man confirmed a taping system had existed, said there might be some audio recordings left, and agreed to review any remaining tapes and provide the relevant ones. Colby later had to admit the materials had been destroyed. But at the Watergate hearings General Cushman testified on his contacts with Hunt and produced a transcript of their July 1971 conversation. Bill Colby explained that his secretary—who had previously worked for Cushman—made the record from memory, because Colby had encountered no tapes when looking for Watergate-related records in 1972. After that two Cushman tapes—one of them the talk with Hunt—had been found after all.

Vernon Walters's executive assistant rediscovered the tape in May 1973. Senator Baker demanded it be reviewed, which consumed seven months, and he arranged to listen to the tape. By then it was February 1974. Suddenly, the day before Baker was to hear this conversation, CIA deputy legislative counsel Walter Pforzheimer produced a new transcript, plus one of John Ehrlichman's side of his original approach to Cushman regarding Howard Hunt. It was all too convenient.

President Nixon had invoked the CIA and national security to cover up his Watergate transgressions, and he had failed. But because there *was* a record of CIA activities that touched on White House dirty tricks, and because the agency *did* drag its feet in the investigation, Watergate tarnished Langley. Meanwhile, in the midst of the preliminaries, when Richard Nixon still looked to be the victor and had won reelection, he banished Richard Helms to Iran. The agency's official historians of Helms's time offer this comment: "Helms's dismissal was not the result of his or his agency's involvement in the Watergate mess, but instead may have been influenced by his resolute refusal to permit the White House to use the CIA as an instrument in its elaborate coverup of the crime."[15]

Fast-forward a dozen years. Starting in October 1986 there began a new scandal, one directly rooted in intelligence activity, a scandal that again had the executive branch of government circling its wagons. This was the Iran-Contra affair. Like Watergate, Iran-Contra opened with an incontrovertible event, not an arrest this time, but the shootdown of a transport plane that had been supplying Nicaraguan antigovernment rebels formerly supported by the CIA. One member of the crew, Eugene Hasenfus, parachuted from the flaming aircraft to be captured by government forces. Taken to the Nicaraguan capital, Managua, Hasenfus told a news conference that the men who employed his air company belonged to the agency. The charge was not exactly right, though it was close to being true. Those who coordinated the air operation—former CIA contract officers indeed—were actually with a private corporation that worked in cooperation with President Ronald Reagan's National Security Council (NSC) staff. In one of its corporate guises, the "private benefactors," as they would soon be called, had already been revealed by the Costa Rican government as controlling an airstrip in that country.

The shootdown in Nicaragua set off alarm bells. Officials of both the CIA and the State Department denied knowing anything about the plane or its flight. The president's national security advisor, Vice Admiral John Poindexter, and the principal NSC staffer involved, marine Lieutenant Colonel Oliver North, kept quiet. During a brief press appearance on October 8, President Reagan asserted the United States had absolutely no connection with the Hasenfus airplane. But the press stayed on the story, which did not go away. For a month or so Reagan stuck to his strategy of mere denial, but then the scandal blew wide open.

The Nicaraguan adventures did not exist in a vacuum. They were but one facet of a wider initiative, in which the Reagan NSC was selling weapons to America's archenemy, Iran. The weapons were unloaded at inflated prices and the difference used to pass money along to the Nicaraguan rebels. Thus, the "Iran-Contra" appellation stuck to the affair. Its origins lay in twin problems that bedeviled President Reagan. On the one hand, the CIA had overreached in Reagan's project to overthrow the Marxist government of Nicaragua by supporting *contra* rebels, leading Congress to ban further military or CIA efforts. On the other hand, Islamic fundamentalists in Lebanon, associated with Iran, had taken to kidnapping westerners, including Americans and even CIA officers, and Reagan faced a dilemma on how to respond to that. He had ordered the NSC to do whatever required to keep the *contras* together, hoping to convince Congress to reverse itself and vote new money for the CIA covert operation. That was in June 1984. The following year President Reagan had been encouraged to try an opening to Iran in hopes that Teheran might order the Lebanese to free American hostages.

These two tracks involved the Reagan administration in a variety of ill-considered actions that strained the boundaries of legality if they were not actually criminal. Officials solicited money or weapons from foreign nations—Saudi Arabia,

Brunei, Taiwan, South Korea, Israel, South Africa—to be used for U.S. policy purposes not approved by Congress. Law on weapons sales to foreign countries that required congressional notification was skirted in the arms deals with Iran. In addition to legal strictures, the deals violated a specific arms embargo the United States had in place against Iran. The NSC staff conducted an outreach program encouraging *contra* support that verged on illegal solicitation of funds. The intelligence oversight system put in place after 1975, which provided that "presidential findings" back every covert project, was violated in both principle and detail, with portions of the Iran-Contra project never so justified, and knowledge of the finding Reagan actually issued withheld from the responsible congressional committees. Private citizens were enlisted to conduct the arms sales, move the weapons, and funnel money to the *contras*, violating statutes prohibiting individuals conducting foreign policy. Former national security advisor Robert C. McFarlane, together with retired CIA and military officials, indeed had made a trip to Teheran in May 1986, carrying weapons with them, and negotiating in behalf of the United States. Their essential purpose was to trade arms with Iran in exchange for American hostages. Money for the *contras* was a side benefit. Once again, in addition to being violations of law, these talks breached an official U.S. policy of refusing to negotiate with terrorists— by an administration that had attempted to equate "state-sponsors" with terrorists themselves. In short, the Reagan administration had a lot to hide—and the emerging Iran-Contra story threatened President Reagan's leadership.

In the early days of the crisis, both CIA and State Department officials were called before congressional committees and denied knowing anything about the airplane shot down over Nicaragua. Meanwhile, behind the scenes, NSC staffer North and his boss, John Poindexter, intervened with the Justice Department to halt an investigation of the background of the plane, which could be traced to Southern Air Transport—a former CIA proprietary—and which had previously been used by the Drug Enforcement Administration in a sting operation aimed at linking Nicaraguan government leaders with drug trafficking. Air crewmen were discovered to have CIA backgrounds, flying in Laos for another CIA proprietary, Air America. At every turn the U.S. government connections of this shadowy operation seemed more substantial.

Disclosure of the Iran side of the operation also loomed. Reagan's Director of Central Intelligence, William J. Casey, was approached by a business associate whose connections included persons who had helped finance the Iran arms transfers and had not been paid. Casey's associate warned the men were ready to leak the story. The CIA director met with John Poindexter and with senior agency officials to cobble together a course of action. They had yet to do anything when, on November 3, the Lebanese magazine *Al-Shiraa* printed an account of the McFarlane trip to Teheran and the Iran arms deals. Media speculation rose to fever pitch.

Following the *Al-Shiraa* account, Secretary of State George Shultz sent Poindexter a message advising that the administration get ahead of the story by admitting its essential truth while insisting it had been a onetime deal to free hostages. Shultz believed the denial strategy had become untenable. Admiral Poindexter resisted his recommendation. According to Poindexter, Casey, Vice President George H. W. Bush, and Secretary of Defense Caspar Weinberger all agreed on the need for continued secrecy. The perseverance of the press led President Reagan, given the need to say something, to make an offhand remark in response to a question as he ceremoniously signed an immigration reform bill on November 6. In it Reagan acknowledged "a story that came out of the Middle East," but insisted it was completely without foundation.[16]

At a White House reception the next day to introduce freed hostage David Jacobsen, the president referred to comments the previous evening (possibly at a photo opportunity with officials of a radio network, but there seems to be no record of what was said, only references to it). Mr. Reagan had evidently denied the report that McFarlane visited Teheran, rejected the contention that the U.S. had traded arms for hostages, and reiterated that the United States did not negotiate with terrorists. With Jacobsen the next morning, President Reagan tried to squelch speculation, saying all his advisors agreed with his Iran policy. He could not comment further since, in hopes of returning more hostages, there were continuing exchanges with foreign nations.[17]

Even today Ronald Reagan's role remains ambiguous. The independent prosecutor who would investigate Iran-Contra proved unable to obtain any evidence of the president's direct participation in the events of the actual conspiracy. The president denied approving any transfer of funds from Iranian arms deals to the *contras*, though he admitted issuing orders to help the Nicaraguan rebels. President Reagan had received the king of Saudi Arabia after a meeting at which the Saudis had agreed to make a huge cash contribution to the *contras*, and he had approved at least one—possibly two—presidential findings authorizing the weapons sales to Iran. Mr. Reagan had also approved not informing Congress of the Iranian initiative. Given his daily national security briefings, it is hardly conceivable that the president did not learn something of the military deliveries made to the *contras* by the private benefactors.

In his personal diary, on the other hand, Ronald Reagan seemed bemused the stories did not just go away. He wrote nothing of the Hasenfus plane downing. When the Iran story broached in Beirut, Reagan waited several days until noting, on November 7, failure of the no comment strategy, then posed his alternative—to refuse answers on the grounds it would endanger the lives of the hostages. That weekend at Camp David, Reagan found the media "giving credence to every rumor and supposed leak," with the talk shows hammering at the Iran arms story. Returning to Washington on the following Monday, the president convened his principal advisors specifically to deal with this. In his diary Reagan for the first time acknowledged a "press storm" and went on, "They quote as gospel every unnamed source plus such authorities as a Danish sailor who claims to have served on a ship carrying arms from Israel." The next day the president groused that the media were "largely ignoring" the administration's nonexplanations. By November 12 Mr. Reagan was complaining, "This whole irresponsible press bilge about hostages & Iran has gotten totally out of hand."[18] The problem for Mr. Reagan was that there was fire behind the smoke.

The president and his advisors had concluded on November 10 that a more active strategy was necessary. On November 12 there was a White House briefing at which four congressional leaders were given a picture of the Iran initiative. Among them on the House side was Representative Dick Cheney. Mr. Reagan would give a nationally televised speech the next night, as he put it to his private diary, to "reply to the ridiculous falsehoods the media has been spawning."[19] In his speech the president denounced the "rumors" that had been circulating. These had become so extensive the risks of remaining silent now outweighed those of speaking out. He explicitly said the United States had made no concessions to those who held hostages, that the policy of refusing to negotiate with terrorists remained in effect. "The United States has not swapped boatloads or planeloads of American weapons for the return of American hostages," Reagan added. He then said that he had authorized "the transfer of small amounts of defensive weapons and spare parts," that, together, could fit into "a single cargo plane." Mr. Reagan admitted that he had himself asked Robert McFarlane to visit Teheran. He went on to assert that neither Congress nor executive branch officials had been circumvented and that "the relevant committees of Congress are being, and will be, fully informed."[20]

This text repeated what the congressional leaders had been told and was very narrowly drawn. For example, Congress had been informed only to the extent of what its leaders had been told just the previous day, and Admiral Poindexter at that briefing had mentioned only about half the weapons that had been shipped, and only one of the presidential findings. He had abstained from any reference at all to an entire shipment of weapons carried out in November 1985, or to participation by Israel in that operation. Nor had congressional committees been told of the single presidential finding—already ten months old—that Poindexter *had* referred to. In his speech Ronald Reagan had affirmatively declared that no laws had been violated and no arms traded for hostages. Both those categorical assertions were false.

Administration officials were unable to make this new version stick. In various press appearances Poindexter and presidential chief of staff Donald T. Regan gave conflicting versions, some also contradicting the president. Poindexter, for example, admitted that the Joint Chiefs of Staff had not been told of the arms deals. Don Regan affirmed that Israel had sent arms to Iran in September 1985. Neither would account for the freeing of a hostage at that time—coincident with the Israeli shipment, on behalf of Washington, which promptly replaced the antitank missiles it had sent with a more modern model. Secretary Shultz pressed for an iron-clad statement there would be no more arms sales, only to be stymied by his colleagues. Shultz then went public with his position. By now Mr. Reagan was writing in his diary about the media "harping" on the Iran situation, putting out "pure fiction," and its "lynch mob attitude."[21] By November 19,

Reagan felt, America had its own Dreyfus Affair and fresh public comment had become unavoidable. He held a news conference that night.

In the opinion of historian Theodore Draper, this encounter with the reporters was "the most disastrous in President Reagan's presidency."[22] Mr. Reagan opened with a brief statement that had been extensively reworked by McFarlane and Poindexter, and he had been prepped for the appearance by both of them, Secretary Shultz, and others. He still made a hash of it. Reagan asserted he had a right "under the law" to defer reporting to Congress. He admitted the arms deals—he still insisted there had been only one—had been "a waiver of our own embargo." The president could not account for how individual hostage releases had coincided with weapons shipments. The journalists were now ahead of the president, repeatedly pushing him on Israel's role while he still stammered vaguely about third countries. Reagan denied that sending weapons to Iran amounted to giving them to the Ayatollah Khomeini, the Iranian leader and America's sworn enemy. Now Mr. Reagan described the Iranian interlocutors as a faction, which can only have weakened their position in Teheran. Finally, Reagan's denials of Israeli participation were so strongly at odds with what had become known that, within the hour, a White House clarification admitted that, indeed, one "third country" had been involved.[23]

After the news conference it was clear the facts were not as President Reagan had presented them a few days earlier, and also that his position on his legal obligations differed substantially from widespread understanding of certain laws and regulations. Congressional investigation became unavoidable. The administration initiated an internal investigation by Attorney General Ed Meese. On November 23, in Oliver North's office, Justice Department officials discovered an April 1986 paper describing a procedure for taking money from the Iran arms deals and sending it to the *contras*. The "diversion memo" made a season of deep inquiry inevitable. The intelligence oversight committees of both houses of Congress had already held hearings focused on the Nicaraguan rebel angle; now there would be a joint committee to look into all aspects of Iran-Contra for a full year. In due course there would be an independent prosecutor, as there had been a special prosecutor for Watergate.

The Central Intelligence Agency was a convenient scapegoat, from the Reagan administration's perspective, for the excesses of Iran-Contra. A CIA proprietary had carried some of the weapons shipments to Teheran. The McFarlane mission had traveled on another proprietary aircraft, accompanied by a senior CIA officer and equipped with agency communications gear. Money from the arms deals had been funneled through CIA bank accounts. On the Nicaragua side, the CIA station chief in Costa Rica had worked closely with the private benefactors, the involvement of the agency apparatus in Honduras was in question, and CIA had had a prime interest all along in seeing the *contras* through until its covert operation could be ramped up again—which was authorized anew as of October 1, 1986.

Even more to the point were the knowledge and actions of senior CIA officials, particularly Director of Central Intelligence William J. Casey. The spy chieftain had his finger in every pie. It was Casey who had originally suggested soliciting money for the *contras* from other countries. He had advocated this at the National Security Planning Group, President Reagan's NSC unit for managing the Nicaragua program. Bill Casey had recruited Oliver North as principal action officer for the private benefactor operation. The director interceded with Ed Meese to use his influence as a senior official to induce the Marine Corps to extend Lieutenant Colonel North's assignment to the NSC staff so the latter could do this work. Casey and North had had two dozen one-on-one meetings during Iran-Contra, and, according to the spy chief's daybook, they spoke on the phone 165 times.

Director Casey took North to a meeting of CIA station chiefs active in Central America and introduced him to the players. Casey met with the private benefactors too. On another occasion he passed a willing donor along to North to be solicited by the White House–connected *contra* fund-raising apparatus. When Congress became restive at signs something was going on with the *contras*, Casey stage-managed an event, more like a séance, where he gave North phony orders not to operate in Central America. In the face of allegations the CIA had given the *contras* some $50 million during the 1984–1986 period, in September 1986 Director Casey sent the Senate Intelligence Committee an official reply that maintained the agency had scrupulously followed restrictions and had not provided any assistance whatsoever that was not authorized by Congress. He did not mention that he had prodded CIA lawyers to identify ways the agency could help the *contras* while adhering to the letter of the law.

The spy chief commissioned the original paper pointing out the potential for an Iran arms ploy and circulated it in the White House. Casey then pressed for a fresh NSC policy paper based on the CIA opinion. He watched with favor as the Israelis executed the first Iranian deal in August–September 1985. Director Casey sanctioned without a presidential finding the use of the CIA proprietary for the November Israeli arms shipment, facilitated by a subordinate CIA officer. The CIA prepared a draft presidential finding only after that episode—and after Casey's deputy insisted that one was necessary. Incidentally that document—never found—described the Iran initiative as a straight arms-for-hostages trade, and it was supposed to apply retroactively. In January 1986 Casey personally outlined two methods by which the United States could sell arms directly. The spy chieftain furnished support, including NSA monitoring, for Oliver North's contacts with Iranian intermediaries, and sent CIA officers along on the trips. The arms sales yielded a surplus of roughly $18 million. The private benefactors took much of that as profit, but they passed along a couple of million plus several more weapons shipments to the Nicaraguan rebels.

When the Iranian side began to unravel, it was Bill Casey who sounded the alarm, warning North to begin destroying documents, and meeting with Poindexter to find a way to prevent revelation. Even then, during the final month before Iran-Contra broke into the open, Casey had backed another North negotiating mission to a new Iranian channel. The mission carried a Bible personally inscribed by Ronald Reagan. When the president finally decided to give a speech on the Iran affair, Casey huddled with Poindexter and others to massage the text, right up to the morning before Mr. Reagan spoke. When Secretary Shultz went public with objections to Iran arms sales, the CIA director wrote President Reagan a letter demanding he be fired: "You need a new pitcher!"[24] The diversion memo was discovered the next day. According to Donald T. Regan, who made an unprecedented visit to Langley late that afternoon to inform the CIA chief privately, Director Casey evinced no surprise at this development.

An enduring mystery of Iran-Contra is whether Casey had approved North's diversion scheme. There is a fair likelihood that he did, though the only substantiation of that is the NSC staffer's own testimony, and North's representations seemed questionable in certain other respects. Within the CIA a senior analyst had developed suspicions of a diversion based on discrepancies in pricing, and Casey was told this in early October. Deputy Director of Central Intelligence Robert M. Gates, who participated in this conversation, relates that Casey seemed surprised then. In a closely reasoned analysis contrasting the paucity of proof for Casey's knowledge of the diversion with inferential plus some real evidence against that hypothesis, Gates concludes the CIA chief probably did not know of the diversion.[25]

Nevertheless, the spy chieftain became a natural target for Iran-Contra investigators, beginning with his appearances before both the House and Senate intelligence committees on November 21, 1986. The basic CIA cover-up of the Iran side of this affair resides in that testimony. Casey concealed the U.S. involvement in the 1985 Israeli arms shipments; failed to disclose the so-called "retroactive" finding, the CIA's primary role in it, and the arms-for-hostages terms of the approval; failed to disclose the extent to which Congress had been left uninformed; hid the money diversion; and misled the legislators on the extent of NSC staff involvement. Casey's testimony also overstated the degree of accountability and control afforded by CIA bank accounts, suggesting that the Iranians were paying the United States directly and not through Swiss banks; stated that the U.S. had obliged the Israelis to take back a shipment of antiaircraft missiles rather than admit the Iranians had refused to accept them; misrepresented the results of the McFarlane mission to Teheran; and retailed what became an Iran-Contra chestnut—that the CIA believed the November 1985 shipment had consisted of oil-drilling equipment, not weapons.

The chief of staff to both Casey and Gates at the time was James McCullough, who would retire after thirty-four years of service on both the clandestine and analytical sides of the agency. His unit had the primary responsibility for compiling Casey's testimony. It was a time of pandemonium and confusion, McCullough recalls, with the director exhausted and soon to succumb to the brain tumor that would kill him. The staff director attributes much of the misguided testimony to Casey's poor health and distraction, barely allowing that the CIA chief might have been purposeful in his actions.[26] Robert Gates had the office next door to the director and, of course, worked intimately with Casey. He did not see the boss the same way. "In contrast to allegations later made by others," Gates writes, "I had seen no particular change in Casey's behavior in the preceding weeks or months that might suggest he was ill."[27]

The idea that Director Casey had compartmented Iran-Contra as his private, off-the-shelf covert operation barely intrudes into McCullough's version of events. Bob Gates, who agrees with the chief of staff that there was no private covert operation, ironically informs us that Casey's style throughout the Nicaragua operation had been to rely upon this kind of close-to-the-vest activity, and concedes that "Casey probably also was instrumental in moving operational management of the *contras* from CIA in the summer of 1984 to the NSC, to North. And there seems little doubt that he advised and helped North during the period CIA was proscribed from involvement."[28] Colleague David Gries, present at the same meetings as the head of the agency's congressional liaison staff, is on the point where, reflecting on McCullough's account, he notes that "vertical compartmentation is a sure prescription for trouble whenever officers are called to account for actions."[29]

In any case, that exact thing happened in preparing Bill Casey's congressional testimony. McCullough returned from a vacation to be put on this task, problematical because he knew nothing. To get up to speed, the chief of staff attended a briefing given by Clair George, deputy director for operations, for the congressional aides before whose committees Casey would be appearing. There was enough there already for the congressional staffs to warn of tough hearings, but afterwards McCullough found George's assistants apoplectic that their boss had completely omitted the Israeli arms shipments. That marked the start of a nightmare. From the beginning, accounting for the Israeli arms shipments and the lack of a presidential finding to cover them was an insuperable obstacle for Langley. The CIA's struggle to craft a chronology for the November 1985 shipment went on interminably and led to major disputes with the State Department. Its legal experts saw the draft and concluded that Casey was about to perjure himself, leading to one revision. The same text worried Oliver North as implicating him, and he intervened to obtain a different emendation, also a falsehood. Knowledge of the initiative, as well as the celebrated "oil-drilling equipment," were both at issue. Casey made changes to a draft opening statement reviewed at the White House, but never incorporated them in his testimony. Meanwhile, word of the controversy became a factor in Edwin Meese's decision for a Justice Department inquiry, forcing the scandal into the open once the diversion memo emerged.

Clair George apparently adopted marching orders consonant with how he thought Director Casey would respond under such circumstances. George's misleading briefing to congressional staff was of a piece with his approach from the moment of the crash of the Hasenfus plane. Due to his CIA position, George had constant access to intelligence on the private benefactors' *contra* resupply operations, as well as agency contacts with the network. At one point he affirmatively instructed a subordinate not to become involved in activities that were being handled by North at the White House. Some of the CIA personnel most directly involved, like the chief of station in Costa Rica, worked for George. Yet in two October 1986 appearances before congressional committees, Clair George denied knowledge of the network, representing that he knew only what was in the newspapers. In testimony during November and December, George's denials included any knowledge of the role of Oliver North, *contra* funds, or the private benefactors. At several of these appearances, the deputy director for operations was accompanied by the chief of CIA's Central America Task Force, Alan D. Fiers, who joined Clair George in misleading Congress. George would later tell the joint congressional committee investigating Iran-Contra that William J. Casey would never have countenanced a private off-the-shelf covert operation.

The deceptions of Bill Casey, Clair George, and other CIA officers aimed at protecting the Reagan administration and the CIA. But they left Langley vulnerable to being left to flap in the wind while others ran for cover. The wholesale destruction of documents at the White House, including all copies of at least one—possibly two—presidential findings, made it impossible for the CIA to demonstrate that its covert activities had been authorized. The Israeli deliveries to Iran posed a significant accountability problem, while complicity in *contra* operations threatened to derail the reconstitution of the long-standing effort against the Sandinistas in Nicaragua. White House and other Reagan administration officials made no attempt to deflect allegations against the CIA. The agency's effort to protect this Family Jewel only did it harm, while the Iran-Contra faults overall were so large that no effort to scapegoat the CIA actually could protect the White House.

In December 1986 Director Casey appeared again, at a pair of House hearings, one before its appropriations committee, the other before armed services. There he denied knowing of the diversion—and later adverted it might conceivably have been cooked up by North and Poindexter—withheld information about the private benefactors, and disclaimed any knowledge of Saudi Arabia's contributions to the *contras* other than what *he* had read in the papers. Despite Ronald Reagan's complaints, it seemed the newspapers were everybody's source now. Casey was scheduled before the Senate Intelligence Committee again on December 16. The previous day, returning to Langley to prepare his testimony, Bill Casey collapsed in his office. Lawyer John Rizzo was standing outside the door. Taken to a hospital, Casey was found to have a brain tumor. Operated on, Casey was then treated for prostate cancer. He never returned to CIA. William J. Casey passed away on May 6, 1987, taking the Iran-Contra secret to the grave.

Congressional investigators, a presidential commission (the Tower Board), and, after December 1986, an independent counsel all struggled to get to the bottom of this affair. The latter two proceeded with a degree of comity, but the congressional investigation did not. As it happened, the ranking minority member of the House of Representatives contingent on the joint committee was Representative Richard Cheney. Since leaving the White House with his Ford administration colleagues, Cheney had returned to his home state. He stood for office in the next election, announcing his candidacy in December 1977, and had been elected from Wyoming in 1978. Mr. Cheney rose rapidly in the House. By the mid-'80s he had become the minority whip and was a member of, among others, the House Permanent Select Committee on Intelligence.

Iran-Contra erupted just after the 1986 elections, which had returned Dick Cheney to office. He had actually been expecting some post-electoral relaxation. Cheney had planned an elk hunt, obtained the necessary hunting license, and was packing his bags for the flight home. Then the call came to attend a White House briefing. It was the November 12 event where President Reagan insisted everything had been above board and Admiral Poindexter then misled the congressional leaders. Elk hunting forgotten, Representative Cheney became enmeshed in the Iran-Contra affair as he had been—from the White House side—in the Year of Intelligence.

President Reagan, falling precipitately in the polls, began to understand that his own veracity on Iran-Contra had become an issue. At the beginning of December he created the Tower Board to review the affair from the NSC perspective. Reagan also instructed Attorney General Meese to arrange for the appointment of an independent counsel. On December 2 he hosted another White House function, a Republican leadership meeting in the Cabinet Room. Dick Cheney was present. There President Reagan declared he would welcome congressional inquiries as well as the independent counsel. Mr. Reagan announced that Frank Carlucci would become his national security advisor, succeeding the disgraced John Poindexter. The next day Cheney returned to the Oval Office, again with the Republican leadership, while Ronald Reagan once more explained what he thought he had been doing and asked what had been wrong with that. As they sat, Admiral Poindexter appeared before the Senate Select Committee on Intelligence and repeatedly invoked his Fifth Amendment rights to avoid answering. By December 4 the die had been cast. Congress would move forward with a joint investigating committee; Cheney would lead the Republican side of its House membership.

A month later, on January 5, 1987, joint committee members held an inaugural get-together with newly consecrated independent counsel Lawrence E. Walsh and his deputy. There Mr. Cheney sat, "coldly radiating dissatisfaction," and openly worried that cooperation between the two entities would be a one-way street, with the congressional committee providing data while the prosecutors, with their legal obligations, furnished nothing.[30] That summer, when the committee was going full bore on its public hearings, Representative Cheney interrupted when Oliver North was stepping onto shaky ground under questioning, taking the group into closed session because the subject matter was supposedly sensitive. He reserved some of his own time and used it later to give North leave—in the nationally televised hearings—to present his standard Soviet/Cuban/Nicaraguan scare briefing. And when questioning North himself, Dick Cheney condemned Congress for its numerous changes in "policy" about

Nicaragua, excused NSC covert operations on grounds of presidential frustration with hidebound bureaucracy, and explained Reagan's decisions on Iran as intelligible "when we understand the depth of concern on the part of the President over the fate of a handful of American citizens in the brutal torture and subsequent death of [CIA Beirut station chief] Mr. Buckley."[31] In August, with the American public glued to the television watching the Iran-Contra hearings every day, Cheney telephoned the White House and spoke to President Reagan, who recorded, "He feels the public is fed up with the whole subject of Iran-Contra."[32] Mr. Reagan naturally agreed.

Such cooperation as was forthcoming between the joint committee and the independent prosecutor proved sterile, as Walsh, for fear of tainting his court filings with data obtained by Congress under grants of immunity, felt required to establish autonomously all the same facts discovered by the congressional investigators. The conviction of John Poindexter was thrown out precisely because of such congressional taint.

Independent counsel Walsh nevertheless persevered and eventually obtained indictments, with plea bargains and some convictions, against a number of Iran-Contra players. When Walsh moved to indict former secretary of defense Caspar W. Weinberger for concealing evidence, Cheney, by then himself the defense secretary in the first Bush administration, went on television to denounce the move. He permitted Weinberger special access to Pentagon files. Secretary Cheney advised Bush to pardon Weinberger and the others. On December 24, 1992, President George H. W. Bush did so, Weinberger in advance of his trial; along with Clair George, Alan Fiers, and Duane Clarridge of the CIA; Elliott Abrams of the State Department; and former national security advisor Robert McFarlane.

Within the halls of Congress at the time, Representative Cheney pressed for a quick investigation, assertedly to get the story out, but incidentally ensuring that members would have the least time possible to explore the facts or wear down the individuals who were subjects of inquiry—indeed ensuring that grants of immunity became a major vehicle for obtaining testimony. When public Iran-Contra hearings opened in May 1986, Cheney led off with an attack on *Congress*, not the executive, remarking that a major question to be aired, which had led to the events of Iran-Contra, was the lack of a distinct policy on the part of Congress. This was the same man who, when Congress had debated the legislation that proscribed CIA activity in Nicaragua in the first place, had characterized it as a "killer amendment" designed to force the *contras* to lay down their arms.[33] That seemed pretty lucid, especially since the legislative history of the provision explicitly admitted of no exceptions. What Cheney left unsaid was that in the American system of government, in its classic formulation, the president proposes and Congress disposes—in other words, the executive makes policy, which the legislature accepts or rejects.

Speaking of rejection, once the Iran-Contra investigation had run its course, Cheney led a minority of members who repudiated the committee's report and appended their own tome of 150 pages essentially refuting its findings. Mr. Cheney engages in a modicum of creative storytelling in his recent recounting of Iran-Contra. In his memoir Cheney positions himself with the administration's critics:

> The freeing of hostages was undeniably a good thing, but it was clear to me that the initiative was ill-conceived. It violated the arms embargo that we had imposed on Iran and that we were insisting other nations observe, and it undermined our strict policy against negotiating with terrorists. Congress had not been told about the operation, as we should have been.[34]

These were reasonable points, but they have a sharper edge

than Dick Cheney exhibited at the time, when he essentially functioned as a defender of the Reagan administration.

For example, the Iran-Contra minority report recognized congressional concern at being kept in the dark by the Reagan administration, but excused this on the grounds that Congress had a record of leaking. The Cheney report viewed the legal problems thrown up by the diversion and by violations of the Arms Export and Control Act as minor and technical, the NSC staff's deceits as not intended to hide illegalities, and the excesses of the affair as simple, well-intentioned mistakes, substantially the result of "an ongoing state of political guerrilla warfare between the legislative and executive branches."[35] Violations of the U.S. arms embargo against Iran, and of the policy of not negotiating with terrorists, were hardly mentioned in this Cheney report. Its analysis overwhelmingly credited the idea that the arms deals were an attempt at a strategic opening to Iran, one that more or less haphazardly degenerated into arms-for-hostages trades. There was no effort to explain why, if that were so, any cover-up was necessary. The minority report recommendations aimed almost entirely at Congress, and its body contained several chapters emphasizing the scope and depth of presidential power on national security.

Now to today's Family Jewels. In the second Bush administration, that of President George W. Bush, Richard Cheney had become vice president of the United States. As seen in our chapters on surveillance and on detention and interrogation, Cheney rematerialized as a major player who helped fuel Bush administration excesses. We have not even engaged the *other* set of events of that era, the push to justify an invasion of Iraq. There, too, Cheney played a key role. With aides David S. Addington, his pocket-size Constitution in his jacket, and I. Lewis Libby, who would take the fall for the smear of an honorable CIA officer, the tale was always about presidential power, the very stuff of the Iran-Contra minority report.

So far, the record from George W. Bush's watch is complex but fundamentally similar to earlier periods. After the 9/11 attacks, there were demands for investigation of its antecedents followed by a joint inquiry by the House and Senate. The administration, spearheaded by Vice President Cheney's office, kept critical subjects off the agenda and circumscribed the flow of information to the panelists. The resulting inquiry satisfied few and led to demands for a broader investigation. Cheney opposed this too. When the September 11 Families Association, a group formed of family members of the victims and survivors of the attacks, pressed anyway, its political weight proved formidable. Congress and the Executive agreed to an investigation by a National Commission on Terrorist Attacks Upon the United States. The Bush administration, after promising full cooperation, again sought to restrict the information provided to the commission and impede access to White House aides. Vice President Cheney successfully fended off any questioning of himself or President Bush under oath, limiting their participation to a single, private meeting with the commissioners, and narrowly defining the records that could be made of their encounter.

In the case of the Bush administration's decision to invade Iraq, in the justification of which Bush, Cheney, and all their aides had been active participants, the White House moved heaven and earth to portray itself as the victim of faulty CIA intelligence on Saddam Hussein's alleged possession of weapons of mass destruction (WMD) and links to Al Qaeda. Administration demands for that intelligence—driven by Cheney's personal pressure—and its harping on the false data to create a political basis for war, were hotly denied. Congressional investigations of the underlying facts were obstructed, and the administration changed the subject with its own presidential commission, one that would broaden the focus to include other WMD cases and treat Iraq as simply a matter of analytical and collection methodology.

While the supremely sensitive issue of White House manipulation of the Iraq intelligence remained in play, President Bush still needed the CIA, NSA, and the other agencies to pursue his war on terror. That required smoothing the spies' feathers even while the White House heaped responsibility for the Iraq failure onto their shoulders. George W. Bush did something his predecessors had resisted: when news of the NSA's Terrorist Surveillance Program and the CIA's black prisons burst into public, he stood up to defend these operations and his orders to conduct them. But starting in 2006, when Congress began to zero in on the Family Jewels, the old pattern repeated itself. That September, shortly before President Bush revealed the CIA interrogations and closed the black prisons, the CIA director first briefed the full intelligence committees on the High Value Detainee Program. It was February 2007 when the director, now General Michael V. Hayden, who had moved over from the NSA, focused his congressional briefings on renditions, and that April he was back again to discuss the value of interrogations. In fact, during the fifteen months between Bush's acknowledgment of black prisons and revelation the torture tapes had been destroyed, the CIA met the oversight committees over detainees roughly as many times as it had briefed the Gang of Four during the entire period since 2003—and most of those sessions were led by Hayden personally. The CIA director also issued an extraordinary public statement in February 2007. He insisted the program had been carefully controlled, that fewer than a hundred passed through the system, less than a third of them subjected to aggressive questioning, and only a handful the most extreme techniques.

Langley's attempt to curry the public's favor ended disastrously on December 6, 2007, when the *New York Times* revealed that the CIA had made videotapes of its interrogations and had now destroyed them.[36] Reporter Mark Mazzetti disclosed that the agency had not told the oversight committees of the tape destruction, that it *had* affirmed to courts—*twice*—that no tapes existed, only to be forced to admit that two videotapes and an audio recording had survived the bonfire. The article also noted that staff of the 9/11 Commission were surprised to learn of the tapes. In the firestorm that followed, there were multiple demands for an investigation, editorials condemning the agency, and warnings to avoid the Iran-Contra error of public hearings with immunized witnesses. New details flooded out—Jose Rodriguez was identified, the kabuki play of the cables between Langley and Bangkok emerged, Gang of Four legislators let it be known they had opposed destruction of the tapes, 9/11 Commission members that they had been denied them. Far from disappearing in a few news cycles, the story of the torture tapes stayed on the front pages through the remainder of George W. Bush's presidency. It was a nightmare both at Langley and the White House.

No evasion was possible. On December 11 General Hayden faced the Senate Intelligence Committee, which grilled him for more than an hour. Hayden proved unable to answer key questions about the tapes and stuck to the unsatisfactory excuse they had been destroyed because they were a security risk, not that they posed prima facie evidence of criminal acts. He asserted that White House lawyers had neither advocated nor opposed destruction. Hayden, of course, had taken up the reins at Langley half a year after the tape bonfire, so his knowledge of the backstory was inadequate at best. The general left Capitol Hill for the White House, where he attended Vice President Dick Cheney's Christmas party. Predictably, the general was accosted by a posse of reporters.

After twenty minutes he managed to get David S. Addington to rescue him—Cheney's man physically pulled Hayden away from the journalists.

White House sources let slip that its lawyers had advised against destruction of the CIA's torture videotapes. They insisted that every activity had been within the law. President Bush said that he had known nothing of the tapes' existence or their destruction until General Hayden told him. Bush took credit for shuttering the black prisons and transferring the CIA's detainees to Guantanamo Bay.

In January 2008 Attorney General Gonzales announced the CIA had lost its permission to waterboard. Bush was prepared to let investigations go forward. Justice Department lawyers and the CIA Inspector General began a joint probe into possible destruction of or tampering with evidence. Attorney General Mukasey rejected demands for the appointment of a special prosecutor for the tapes case, but he did authorize a criminal investigation conducted by assistant U.S. attorney John H. Durham. The unprecedented joint inquiry into the NSA eavesdropping by the inspectors general of several agencies was another element of the Bush administration's sudden openness. The spy agencies, not the White House, would take the heat. Jose Rodriguez retained prominent Washington lawyer Robert W. Bennett as his counsel. Bennett immediately demanded immunity for his client, which shielded Rodriguez from the first round of congressional inquiries but not from Durham's prosecutors.

So began a messy and still largely obscure season of inquest, which dragged on into the Obama administration. The Bush Justice Department used its probe to head off the obstruction of justice investigation ordered by the federal court that had been denied evidence. 9/11 Commission staff examined their files and confirmed the CIA had misled them regarding tapes. The congressional oversight committees had their own inquiries, the results of which have never been made public. Agency general counsel John A. Rizzo faced the House intelligence committee all by himself. When a heavily excised version of the CIA Inspector General's report on interrogation was declassified as the result of an FOIA request and subsequent lawsuit, the agency started a counterintelligence investigation against its own internal watchdog. Michael Hayden was responsible for that. Another feature would be Vice President Cheney's repeated declarations that torture had been necessary and had saved lives. Prosecutor Durham ground away on his own criminal probe and eventually convened a grand jury to continue it.

The waters were thoroughly muddied by all this to-ing and fro-ing. By the time the Bush administration gave way to the presidency of Barack Obama, pressure had built for a public examination, a "truth commission" exploring all the CIA abuses of the war on terror. Barack Obama's administration has avoided airing this laundry, still moldering in the hamper. President Obama issued an immediate order to terminate all "enhanced interrogation," and he decided to release a set of key documents bearing on the controversy, including the Justice Department legal authority papers, the subsequent professional reviews of those papers, and a fuller version of the CIA Inspector General's report. Obama took that action over the threatened resignation of his own CIA director.

In May 2009 the Senate Judiciary Committee held a hearing on the need for a truth commission and another on the interrogations themselves. A group of former CIA chiefs contributed a joint letter opposing any such inquiry. In November 2010 Attorney General Eric Holder declared he would not seek indictments of CIA officers in the tape destruction, though prosecutor Durham continued investigating whether unauthorized methods had been used on prisoners, particularly during the period before the Yoo memos existed, when the questioning of Abu Zubaydah had already begun. The following summer Holder announced that two criminal investigations would be pursued and the remainder closed. In 2012 the last remaining criminal inquiries were also dropped. An accounting for the Bush-era excesses has been lacking. The administration may have suffered in the court of public opinion, but no senior official has been held accountable.

"I have been troubled," George W. Bush would write in his memoir, "by the blowback against the intelligence community and Justice Department for their role in the surveillance and interrogation programs."[37] The Central Intelligence Agency is still in the crosshairs. Dick Cheney may have demanded enhanced interrogation techniques, and repeatedly visited Langley to push for more results, but it was CIA officers and contract employees who did the waterboarding, turned up the cold, and held the mock executions. Agency senior officers ordered the destruction of evidence, and subordinates carried that out. It was CIA and special operations people who entered various countries to capture or kidnap individuals, and proprietary aircrews who "rendered" prisoners to a succession of black prisons and finally relocated them to Guantanamo Bay. The agency's officials approved kill orders for targeted individuals, and CIA drones carried out the attacks—until the program became so massive the military got into the act too. At this writing, among participants in the CIA rendition and torture program the only one sent to prison was John Kiriakou—the whistleblower—and not for his actions but for challenging the fortress of secrecy.

Mr. Bush deplores the criminalizing of differences of legal opinion, and the deleterious effect that had on intelligence officers, as if these were merely honest differences, and only about opinion, not people's lives and America's standing in the world. Right behind him are Justice Department lawyers, who insist they did nothing more than furnish opinions on statutes and legal principles. The truth is that those who rendered the opinions were less concerned with principle than with permissiveness, finding rationalizations for what they knew the administration wanted to do. America's currency in international relations was at stake, and the legal memoranda were loaded guns aimed directly at it. The abuses also went far beyond those of interrogation or surveillance, to encompass infringements on the sovereign rights of allies and the inducement of those allies into complicity. That individuals were tortured and died—not just at the hands of Americans—only adds to the tally of shame. When the Family Jewels are exhibited, the CIA will suffer and American intelligence capability will be diminished. Assets important to the survival of the nation will be affected. But on the day when the wagons circle again, no doubt there will be great concern to protect George W. Bush, Richard Cheney, and their successors. White House prerogatives always win through.

≡ CLARITY ≡

We have learned a great deal from studying the Family Jewels. Not simply the documents of the Year of Intelligence, but the entire period since. The lessons can be jarring and the history is often not pretty, but for the sake of control of secret entities in a free democracy and proper accountability for political authorities, they must be faced squarely. Anything less cheapens the coin of the republic and weakens the constitutional framework that was created to ensure liberty and justice for all. All citizens become victims, perhaps less obviously than those whose lives were taken by secret warriors, or crumpled by overzealous inquisitors, or oppressed by hidden surveillance, but victims nonetheless. Democracy is protected only by the vigilance that detects abuse and the courage to stand for real principles. The place to begin is to look at what actually happened—as has been established by this historical inquiry.

In the first place, it is time to dispense with the fiction that the Central Intelligence Agency, the National Security Agency, and their confederates ran around like "rogue elephants." That cute turn of phrase got Frank Church a lot of headlines, but it was ill considered and created more misunderstanding than enlightenment. Intelligence agencies operated under presidential control at all times. That does not mean that presidents explicitly ordered everything the agencies did, or that they knew everything the spooks were up to. Neither Lyndon Johnson nor Richard Nixon ever put his name to a directive ordering the CIA or NSA to watch political protesters. Rather, they made clear what they *wanted*—to discover their opponents and the opposition's ties to others. Ronald Reagan declared the *contras* needed to be supported body and soul. Agencies *interpreted* presidential desires. It was a process of triangulation. Some presidents did issue orders. George W. Bush is a case in point with his Terrorist Surveillance Program.

What agencies *did* with desires and orders was something from which presidents were frequently shielded. Intelligence operatives preserved the chief executive's deniability specifically by *not* informing the White House of some of their activities. There is no evidence that President Johnson knew of Project Chaos or CIA mail-opening. The same is true for Richard Nixon, who in over four thousand hours of unguarded conversation recorded on his audiotapes never once referred to CIA surveillance or mail-opening—at least in the declassified portions of those tapes. Gerald R. Ford, late on the scene, seems to have been surprised to learn of the various Family Jewels that ignited the Year of Intelligence. The evidence is that Ronald Reagan knew things were being done to help the *contras* and that he participated in the solicitation of Saudi Arabia, but no one, including the Iran-Contra independent prosecutor, could establish that he had direct knowledge, and even more certainly not of the diversion of Iranian money to the *contras*. To judge from what has been disclosed so far about the 2004 fracas over reauthorization of the TSP, George Bush similarly did not know of the aspects that so concerned the Department of Justice and FBI.

Management and control of intelligence activities,

however, remained a presidential priority. The trick was to accomplish that without assuming direct responsibility. Just as the NSC Special Group served to insulate presidents from covert operations, chief executives typically had some designated person to go between them and the agencies on the things that would become Family Jewels. Frequently that individual was the national security advisor. McGeorge Bundy's comment on the Castro assassination plots—that he would be surprised had the CIA gone ahead without consulting him—gives the flavor. Henry Kissinger certainly played that role in the Nixon-Ford administrations. Jerry Ford turned to Richard Cheney to supervise efforts to control the fallout from the Year of Intelligence. Vice Admiral John Poindexter in conjunction with a CIA chief, Bill Casey, were the managers of Iran-Contra. Cheney reappeared, in his guise as vice president, as George W. Bush's manager for the activities on the dark side of his watch.

Intelligence operations required positive control. There was a logic to the way Family Jewels evolved. Typically, much was promised at the proposal stage, there were initial results, and then the collection programs failed to be the gold mines advertised. The usual argument was that effectiveness suffered because not enough was being done, and the result was, in effect, escalation. CIA mail-opening became massive in this way. Project Chaos went from simply targeting agency collection elements to employing its own agents. The NSA's Project Minaret expanded its coverage and solicited names for its watch list. Iran-Contra started by accosting allies for contributions in cash or in kind to collecting money from direct arms sales—to enemies. Escalation of the Terrorist Surveillance Program remains hidden, but will no doubt prove to be considerable. When there was a balance to be struck between perceived collection requirements and the rights of citizens, the latter were minimized.

Mission creep has complemented ineffectiveness arguments in accounting for project escalation. A search for useful propaganda themes motivated CIA mail-opening, which turned to watching Americans. Project Chaos aimed at antiwar protesters but expanded to encompass black radicals. The rendition and interrogation program similarly targeted Al Qaeda, but soon widened to include terrorist suspects of all stripes. Successes with NSC activism in aiding the *contras* led to a supposition the same operatives could free hostages in Lebanon. The CIA drone program began with discrete, individual missions and mushroomed to constant aerial coverage over multiple combat theaters. At each stage the programs became more dangerous and an even greater public concern—but secrecy kept the public from learning until the Family Jewel was revealed by leak or by failures in the operational arena.

These attributes of Family Jewels are typical of intelligence ventures, and their importance is magnified by some others. One crucial aspect is that projects are relatively easy to initiate, but then very difficult to shut down. Not only do opponents of continuation have to counter the "do more" argument, they have to overcome the accumulated inertia of the activity. Project Chaos and CIA mail-opening are ideal examples. Chaos endured complaints from an internal management group at Langley, a negative finding from the agency's Inspector General, and the end of the war protests it was intended to counter. Even then it survived into the postwar period by shifting to counterterrorism, finally to demise as it lost focus. Project Lingual, the mail-opening, stayed afloat in the face of knowledge of its illegality from the beginning, two adverse IG reports a decade apart, and two years of the responsible office trying to get rid of the program. In the case of NSA's Minaret eavesdropping, the program continued for more than a year after a court decision rendered it plainly illegal. In the modern era, so far as can be discerned from the Department of Justice legal opinions and the disclosures

made about "enhanced interrogation," the techniques seem
to have become discredited and fallen into disuse by about
2005, yet the Bush administration bent heaven and earth to
preserve the legal authority—if you can call it that—to use
them. The "authority" survived President Bush's acknowledgment of the black prisons and was canceled only after revelation of the destruction of the torture videotapes.

Perhaps the most disturbing aspect of all is that Family
Jewels seem to have a tendency to replicate, suggesting that
abuse fulfills some functional purpose. Vietnam-era surveillance is reprised by war on terror surveillance. Vietnam-era
eavesdropping yields to the Terrorist Surveillance Program.
Harsh interrogation tactics used in the CIA molehunt are
followed by the even greater horrors of the Bush administration's treatment of its detainees. The assassination plots of
the Cold War have been succeeded by the real killings of the
drone program. In all these cases the replication occurred
despite the knowledge among intelligence officers of just how
controversial and painful were the consequences—to them—
of the same kinds of actions in bygone days.

Secrecy cloaks the daggers. Security classification protects legitimate national security information, but as frequently or more so it has been used to evade accountability.
The Central Intelligence Agency's suppressive maneuvers—
and the other members of the intelligence community play
in the same key—attempt to shape public discussion, minimize criticism, and produce an idealized image of the secret
warrior. Friendly journalists are coddled, critics obstructed.
Former agency persons attempting to present their views
to the public have been the special victims of suppressive
maneuvers. The entire concept of flap potential—which first
led to the Family Jewels documents—aims to avoid negative
publicity or, failing that, structure the outcome in the way

most favorable to the agency. This is not to say that every government institution does not engage in similar kinds of public relations—but in the case of Family Jewels, the manipulation of knowledge in the public domain has legal and ethical aspects that elsewhere exist within much narrower boundaries.

This review of the Family Jewels has touched only tangentially on the way in which the CIA complies with its legal responsibility to release records to the public and respond to Freedom of Information Act and other declassification requests, but it has shown in great detail how the agency engages in suppressive maneuvers and has erected a fortress of secrecy to control the voices of its own. Suffice it to say that there is a huge—and exactly parallel—story in Langley's formal treatment of records. Those secrecy practices impinge directly on Family Jewels. Managing flap potential is all about what the public learns and what is denied to it.

Secrecy also has an operational aspect. Not only does secret knowledge have extremely seductive power, when spooks walk on the dark side they experience the greatest invitation to excess, believing that security classification shields their actions from scrutiny. If doing more means threatening the human rights of citizens or foreign nationals, the spooks would prefer the public not know. Under conditions of secrecy the Family Jewels have flourished, and the more secret the activity, the greater the temptation to evade safeguards. The Bush administration succumbed to that allure in the way it handled congressional notification about its eavesdropping, rendition, and interrogation programs.

But abuse festers amid secrecy. The challenge of preserving an intelligence agency in a democracy is precisely that public confidence is required to ensure effectiveness. The compact between the CIA and the American polity is a delicate one—and it is affected by Family Jewels revealed in the past. Dirty laundry that is not aired gets smellier. All secrets are revealed sooner or later, and if citizens know or believe that spooks have kept the lid on their actions so as to avoid accountability, their suspicions of the CIA and its cohorts will only be further magnified.

Presidents and their staffs are some of the most dangerous violators of secrecy, because they know what the public does not. Whenever a Family Jewels crisis erupts, the president is of course enveloped in whatever political situation happens to exist at that moment. A president can respond to a Family Jewels crisis in four basic ways. The first is to leap to the CIA's defense. In the crises surveyed here, no president did that, at least not exactly. George W. Bush held the line for a time, but only so long as he needed to mollify the agency on some level while he cited its flawed intelligence to defend himself against charges of aggression in starting the Iraq war. A second possibility is for the president to lead the charge, professing himself surprised, demanding efforts to get to the bottom of the mysteries revealed. This is not difficult to do, since presidents are not, in fact, familiar with every detail of the CIA's activity. The president takes command, shows himself to be active and responsive to challenge. Thus Gerald Ford, at the outset of the Year of Intelligence, created the Rockefeller Commission. Bill Clinton did the same, quickly assigning his Intelligence Oversight Board to investigate the Guatemala affair. The third option is for the chief executive to do nothing, to leave the CIA flapping in the wind and hope the controversy dies out. Ronald Reagan did that with Iran-Contra, resisting any comment until political upheaval became so intense that the cost of silence became excessive. The final strategy is to manipulate the CIA to ensure that it, not the White House, becomes the main target, which is what Richard Nixon attempted to do in Watergate.

One tactic in any of those strategies is to reveal secrets.

The first the public learned that there had been any question of the CIA intervening to quash Watergate inquiries was when Richard Nixon—whose own conspiracy this had been—outed it. Mr. Nixon's minion Henry Kissinger leaked all the time. Gerald Ford's assassination disclosure was inadvertent, or was it? The effect of that revelation was to turn public attention away from the White House. Leaks proliferated during Iran-Contra. The Bush White House deliberately leaked intelligence to justify the invasion of Iraq—and then outed a CIA undercover officer in a harebrained scheme to discredit a critic. Presidents and staff leak to protect themselves, to deflect attention, or to focus the public in a direction they want.

The complement to leaks is obfuscation and amnesia. Vice President Nelson Rockefeller warned Bill Colby not to remember so much when testifying before his commission. Vice Admiral John Poindexter had a clear recollection that President Reagan had approved a covert action finding, but could not remember where this key document was located. Oliver North's shredding party would be a legendary episode in Iran-Contra too. Alberto Gonzales and Richard Cheney asserted that a group of legislators had agreed to aggressive NSA eavesdropping when the congressmen maintained they had posed objections. The Church Committee could not reach a conclusion as to whether presidents had approved assassinations, because national security advisors Gordon Gray, McGeorge Bundy, and Walt Rostow could not remember ever discussing the topic with them. The combination of leaks and obfuscation is used to shape inquiries and protect the president from accountability. The White House plays the same games as does the CIA.

Before continuing, it is worth spending a little time on some of the ringmasters of the Family Jewels crises

recounted here. Many, many people—officials and operatives—at Langley, at Fort Meade, and in the White House
helped grind and polish the Jewels, but a few figures stand
out as key players. These ringmasters sparked action, pushed
for programs and resisted halting them, or when the crises
came stood against inquiry. Sometimes the ringmasters did
all those things. At some level their actions put presidents,
colleagues, and subordinates all in jeopardy.

Vice President Richard Cheney has to be ranked the leading ringmaster. He exercised a remarkable influence through
the Family Jewels crises described here. Over a period of
three decades starting with the Year of Intelligence, Dick
Cheney remained a central figure. As deputy assistant to the
president, Cheney set up the Rockefeller Commission and
ensured its narrow scope. Promoted to assistant with Donald
Rumsfeld's departure, Cheney spearheaded President Ford's
responses to the congressional investigators. In the Iran-
Contra affair, Representative Cheney was crucial in limiting
the joint committee inquiry and in drafting a minority report
to discredit Congress's findings. In the second Bush administration, the vice president stood at the forefront of those
actually ordering the operations that created Family Jewels,
functioning as George W. Bush's manager for the dark side.
Mr. Cheney was at the heart of rendition and interrogation
as well as NSA eavesdropping, not to mention the invasion of
Iraq. Cheney's involvement in the Family Jewels can hardly
be overstated.

Before turning to the lower ranks, Barack Obama's role
also needs to be considered. A number of President Obama's
actions have damaged America's real interests. Obama effectively quashed the public's push to impose accountability
on former Bush administration officials and CIA operatives.
He lightened that offense somewhat by forcing release of the
"torture memos," the documents that underlay Bush-Cheney
activities, but further clouded the issue by permitting the

prosecution of whistleblower John Kiriakou in a context in which none of the actual transgressors in the earlier abuses had been brought to justice. No doubt President Obama faced a delicate situation—he needed to forge good relations with the spooks. He had taken office with little standing on national security issues. They were under fire. The president coddled the spooks here—and expanded their role by approving intensification of the drone war. It is impossible to escape the impression that Obama bought into the basic premises of the war on terror. But as he showed with his initial push to close the Guantanamo prison camp, the president also had a moral center. Obama's failure to sustain the effort to close Guantanamo and his acquiescence in continued authority for the wireless intercept programs show poorly. He either lacked the courage of his convictions or let himself be led by the intelligence mavens. Unlike his predecessors, however, President Obama did not add new Family Jewels. Obama functioned as an enabler for the jewelers, not as their ringmaster.

The other major ringmaster, at least for the early period, was an agency official. Richard Helms was CIA's spy par excellence. His fingerprints are all over the domestic abuses that formed the early Family Jewels. Helms held sway during the first era much as Cheney has dominated the more recent period. As a division chief and operations directorate official, Helms was present at the creation of illegal mail-opening and mind-control experiments, and he held the top directorate job during the post–Bay of Pigs Castro assassination plots. Though he later issued orders prohibiting assassination plots, Mr. Helms considered he held a field marshal's baton the day he left the Oval Office after Richard Nixon ordered CIA to go after Allende of Chile. As deputy, and then Director of Central Intelligence, Helms presided over the spy wars and harsh interrogation of Yuri Nosenko, the CIA's projects aimed at the antiwar movement, the NSA's Minaret and Shamrock operations, the initial effort to construct a fortress of secrecy by prosecuting Marchetti and persecuting Agee, and the CIA's involvement in Watergate. Dick Helms, though uneasy about Nosenko's treatment, could not bring himself to simply order inquisitors to desist.

Director Helms positively resisted termination of the Chaos and Lingual projects. In fact, Helms solicited customers for the latter, and he went to brief the attorney general in an effort to preserve the operation when the Post Office threatened to blow the whistle on the entire effort. Helms would have gone along with the massive domestic spying entailed by the Huston Plan. At that fateful meeting of January 4, 1975, with President Ford, when Mr. Helms raised the veiled threat of joining the critics in tossing "dead cats" around Washington, Dick Helms had real stock to trade. The president could not afford to let him take the rap for the Family Jewels.

Among the ranks of lesser ringmasters, something similar appears to have happened with Jose Rodriguez. Captain of the Counter-Terrorist Center and architect of the destruction of the torture tapes, the agency veteran also had smelly carcasses to dangle before prospective prosecutors. So did John Rizzo of the Office of General Counsel and White House attorney Alberto Gonzales. James Angleton, notorious CIA counterspy, had an armful of dead cats to purvey, stretching back to CIA mail-opening and its mind-control experiments. And then there was Ollie North of Iran-Contra, whose diversions and manipulations were positively scary. Bill Casey and John Poindexter were right behind him. Philip Buchen, Cheney's loyal lieutenant in President Ford's damage control campaign during the Year of Intelligence, would have understood the need to protect them. So too did Attorney General Eric Holder, who in the Obama administration stayed the sword of justice for John Yoo with his interrogation papers, and the CIA people implicated in those Family Jewels. That does not pass the smell test.

On a table shrouded by a cloak of secrecy lies a pile of Family Jewels just waiting to tumble to the floor. Once that happens, there will be another bloodletting. No one wants that. On the other hand, there must be accountability. America has been shamed by what has been done in its name. There is a price for that. The sword half-sheathed at the outset of Barack Obama's presidency has been drawn again. Obama's refusal to countenance a truth commission will not be the end of the story. Rather, unanswered charges and new ones are likely to renew demands for investigation. If the United States fails to enforce accountability, someone else will, whether in the form of criminal proceedings elsewhere or perhaps even hostilities. The steady implantation and solidification of international human rights law, increasingly bold moves toward cross-national legal enforcement, and the broadening trend toward international prosecution of war crimes ensures that. It would be foolish to suppose that any statute of limitations will protect torturers—and the Nuremberg principles apply to their superiors as well. French officers who participated in torture during the Algerian war of 1954–1962, despite dispensation by that country's National Assembly—and even a presidential pardon—found themselves ensnared in renewed controversy more than four decades later. The underlying acts, not the mumbo jumbo of legal "authorization," will be the controlling factors.

The masters of the Family Jewels do not see it that way. Their view is that enforcing accountability will result in trials that confront the United States government with the unpalatable choice of declassifying dark secrets or foregoing prosecution. Ringmasters have some precedent for that. Richard Helms actually was brought up on charges—though for lying to Congress about Chile rather than any of his other exploits. The Carter administration flinched in the face of the secrecy dilemma. Helms got away with a plea bargain, not contesting the charge, and wore the conviction as a badge of

honor. In 1980 the United States enacted the Classified Information Procedures Act to fix that problem, but during Iran-
Contra Oliver North's lawyers found a counter—demand
release of such a broad swath of secrets that the government
is left in the same place. The most important charges against
North were dropped because he had received congressional
immunity, but the demands for revelations of secrets at trial
certainly affected the prosecution.

This illustrates another aspect of the Family Jewels problem that begs reform: the Central Intelligence Agency's
fortress of secrecy. The question of proper security classification encompasses issues beyond Family Jewels, but these
kinds of activity are a major motivator in Langley's arbitrary
and capricious—indeed self-interested and ultimately self-
defeating—approach to interpreting "damage" to national
security. Current practices risk robbing the agency of credibility and prevent the emergence of a public consensus on
the value of the CIA and, particularly, covert operations in a
free democracy.

It is five decades now since Harry Howe Ransom, an astute
observer of intelligence, published his book titled *Can American Democracy Survive Cold War?*[1] Ransom is renowned
for his work at the University of Texas, of which he eventually became president, but was among the first and deepest
analysts of the American intelligence scene, even a founder
of the field, and was read closely at Langley and elsewhere.
Secrecy is among the primary themes of this book, which,
although it was concerned with the Cold War, could almost
have been written yesterday. "The existence of a large, secret
bureaucracy sometimes pivotally important in making and
implementing national policies and strategies raises special
problems," Ransom notes. He continues:

At the level of democratic ideals, the problem is the existence of a potential source of invisible government. At the level of representatives of the people—Executive and Legislative—the problem is primarily how to control a dimly seen instrument, so hot that if not handled with great skill it can burn its user instead of its adversary.[2]

Ransom believed that an informed electorate was both the ultimate power and ultimate restraint of a democracy, and he ruled out any attempt to assert that intelligence, by its nature, was not an appropriate subject for public inquiry. Instead, Ransom advocated a careful approach distinguishing between legitimate secrets and the mass of material that resides in the secret vaults. This was perhaps a radical position in 1963, but today it is the norm, and the United States has built an entire declassification system around that precise principle, manifested most recently (2009) in the creation of the National Declassification Center. It would not be difficult to find texts that declare commitment to this on Central Intelligence Agency letterhead paper.

The problem with CIA is that principle is not manifest in practice. In fact, as shown here in Langley's suppressive maneuvers, its construction of a fortress of secrecy, and its manipulations of the record, the agency's practice is the opposite of its principle. The fact is that CIA commitment to declassification is almost entirely declaratory. Its actual declassification process lacks objectivity, seemingly even any capacity to discriminate between real national security secrets and embarrassing misadventures; appropriate timeframes within which secrets need protection; any incentive to timely declassification; or, indeed, any desire to reduce the monetary cost of maintaining secrecy. Flap potential is no guide to legitimate secrecy. This strategy invites Family Jewels—and the revelations that create political crises. The CIA process is a discredit to the agency and to its principle.

Given its discredited declassification program, the conclusion is inescapable that the agency is too self-interested to be
entrusted with such a critical function. The most important
reform that can be made to the secrecy system is to take away
the CIA's authority to release secret materials and entrust
this to some other entity. The National Declassification Center, with appropriate addition of staff and funding, might be a
suitable candidate for this role.

Ultimately openness is but a tool of accountability. The
goal is to ensure our secret agencies operate on the basis
of principle. The current system has not succeeded in enforcing accountability. There are many reasons for that. Presidents are zealous defenders of their political interests. On
some level serious inquiries into intelligence operations are
perceived as attacks on the presidency. Once presidents see
themselves as vulnerable, *then* they throw the spooks under
the bus. The CIA itself, jealous of its freedom of action, strives
to avoid any inquiry and to stall those that materialize. The
independent Inspectors General are obstructed and their
credibility impugned, and their powers are limited in any
case. The congressional intelligence committees are actually dependent upon the CIA and other agencies responding
in a frank and honest fashion, leaving them exposed to the
proclivities of the denizens of Langley. Committees' staffs
are too small and too far stretched to accomplish anything
more than broad oversight, and the committees have been
victims of presidents' manipulation of the data made available to them. At the same time, the courts have been overly
solicitous of the intelligence mavens and quite susceptible to
vague assertions of national security damage.

As a result, accountability is administered in bursts—
when abuses of sufficient dimension erupt onto the public
scene. Then comes a rush to investigate, with proliferating

inquiries, hysterical responses from the intelligence agencies, and presidents running for cover. A modicum of reform usually follows, but the system is not fundamentally changed. Much of this pattern, triggered by Family Jewels in the Year of Intelligence, then in Iran-Contra, later in the Guatemalan affair, most recently in the 9/11 Commission review, is driven by short-term calculation. The first thing to notice about all this is its cyclical nature. Another aspect to the phenomenon is that, for all the hysteria, the "truth commission" exercises have had a cleansing, hence positive, effect.

It would be a huge advance in oversight to routinize the process of inquiry. This would make short-term calculation much less useful as a tactic, and remove both agency and White House tendencies to try and avoid any investigation at all, which is a frequent inducement to cover-ups. It would recognize the limited capabilities of congressional overseers and the delicate position of internal watchdogs like inspectors general. Line intelligence officers would then gain nothing by lying in an effort to circumvent investigation. Such regular—public—reviews would become an important device in restoring and then growing citizens' confidence in the activities of the United States intelligence community. This system would air the Family Jewels.

President Barack Obama has rescinded permissions for torture and secret detention, but an unconscionable assassination campaign continues, sometimes targeting Americans, and it has attained the level of a military operation without so much as a nod to the question of war powers. The Family Jewels piled up during the war on terror remain to be examined. A web of measures designed to prevent the cutting of new gems is still to be created. There is much work to be done by presidents, legislators, officials, and citizens. The time to start is now.

<h1 style="text-align: center">☰ NOTES ☰</h1>

INTRODUCTION

1. Readers who wish to explore the drug experiments and mind control issues should consult John Marks, *The Search for the Manchurian Candidate* (New York: W. W. Norton, 1978); or the more recent account, H. P. Albarelli, Jr., *A Terrible Mistake: The Murder of Frank Olson and the CIA's Secret Cold War Experiments* (Waterville, OR: Trine Day, 2009). At this writing the family of U.S. Army scientist Frank Olson, killed in the agency drug experiments, has announced its intention to file suit against the CIA and the United States government.

PROLOGUE

1. Seymour Hersh, "Huge CIA Operation Reported in U.S. against Anti-War Forces, Other Dissidents in Nixon Years," *New York Times*, December 22, 1974, 1.

2. Walter F. Mondale with David Hage, *The Good Fight: A Life in Liberal Politics* (New York: Scribner, 2010), 135–136.

CHAPTER 1. WHERE DID THE FAMILY JEWELS COME FROM?

1. The Directorate of Plans (DDP), very shortly to be renamed the Directorate of Operations (DO), and known since 2005 as the National Clandestine Service, was the unit of CIA mainly concerned

with field activity. The nomenclature thus changes repeatedly over our period, and it is further confused in that all three units were informally known as the "clandestine service," and by the way it was typically abbreviated, with the Deputy Director for Plans (DDP) using the same denotation as his unit. For consistency, except where unavoidable (as in quotations), this text will use the formal name "Directorate of Operations," and informally, "clandestine service."

2. Cord Meyer, *Facing Reality: From World Federalism to the CIA* (New York: Harper & Row, 1980), quoted p. 160.

3. William E. Colby and Peter Forbath, *Honorable Men: My Life in the CIA* (New York: Simon & Schuster, 1978), 338.

4. CIA, Office of the Director, "Memorandum for All CIA Employees," May 9, 1973, Gerald R. Ford Library, Gerald R. Ford Papers, White House Operations Series, Richard Cheney Files, Intelligence Subseries, box 5, folder "Colby Report."

5. Colby and Forbath, *Honorable Men*, 338.

6. CIA, "Reflections of DCIs Colby and Helms on the CIA's 'Time of Troubles,'" *Studies in Intelligence* 51 (3): 12 (hereafter cited as "Colby Oral History").

7. Ibid.

8. See John Prados, *Lost Crusader: The Secret Wars of CIA Director William Colby* (New York: Oxford University Press, 2003), 262–263.

9. CIA, Office of the Inspector General, William V. Broe Memorandum for the Record, May 23, 1973, National Security Archive, Family Jewels Collection, 401–403.

10. Houston's office record of this hearing, along with the Osborn deposition, appears in the Family Jewels Collection at pp. 399–400, 404–409.

11. The record is in United States Congress, House of Representatives (94th Cong., 1st sess.), Armed Services Committee, *Hearings: Inquiry into the Alleged Involvement of the Central Intelligence Agency in the Watergate and Ellsberg Matters* (Washington, DC: Government Printing Office, 1974).

12. Colby Oral History, 13.

CHAPTER 2. THE FAMILY JEWELS: *THE WHITE HOUSE REACTS*

1. Dick Cheney with Liz Cheney, *In My Time: A Personal and Political Memoir* (New York: Simon & Schuster, 2011), 91.

2. Henry A. Kissinger, *Years of Renewal* (New York: Simon &

Schuster, 1999), 320. Publishing this memoir twenty-five years after the fact, Kissinger complains that "Though the headline implied otherwise, the substance of the article, in fact, related to events which had taken place in previous administrations" (310). No doubt he counted on short memories. In fact, a major element in the first Hersh article was the news (accurately reported) that the Nixon White House had initiated a project in 1970 calling for "the use of such illegal activities as burglaries and wiretapping to combat antiwar activities" ("Huge CIA Operation Reported in U.S. against Anti-War Forces, Other Dissidents in Nixon Years," *New York Times*, December 22, 1974, 1). Director Colby reminded Kissinger of this scheme, known as the Huston Plan, in the telephone conversation referenced below. And by noon that day, *the second day of this political controversy*, Dr. Kissinger had also been reminded by NSC aides that he had received at least two major CIA reports on the U.S. antiwar movement that, though couched as studies of possible foreign control over American political groups, had embodied plentifully detailed coverage of those American groups. Our examination in the chapter below on the CIA and domestic surveillance shows clearly that this activity peaked during Nixon's administration and not in, as Kissinger writes (p. 310), "primarily that of Lyndon Johnson." At the time he received the first of those CIA analyses, moreover, then-director Richard Helms had explicitly told Kissinger the document was supersensitive because the underlying CIA spy operations were illegal (see Chapter 4).

3. Kissinger, *Years of Renewal*, 310. Dr. Kissinger's account here is unreliable. On December 23 Kissinger sent a memorandum to Vail for Rumsfeld, cited below, that among other things contained a set of questions that could be expected to come up at news conferences, along with suggestions for how they should be answered. The *second* of these questions was "What was the 'partial information' the President mentioned yesterday that he had about this matter?" The response Kissinger suggested on December 23, 1974, was "This reference was to *advance information that the* Times *would be carrying an article such as the one that appeared yesterday*" (our italics). On the phone with reporter Marvin Kalb on the evening of December 24, Kissinger also stated that two days before the story hit Colby had taken him aside after an arms control meeting and said the *Times* would have a CIA article in its Sunday editions. When Colby expressed the opinion the story was not accurate, Kissinger had told

him not to worry. This record puts beyond doubt the fact that the White House had advance knowledge of the Hersh article.

4. Department of State, TELCON, Bill Colby–Henry Kissinger, December 23, 1974, 9:40 a.m. (declassified February 8, 2005; National Security Archive FOIA 200102979).

5. White House, Cable Donald Rumsfeld–Henry Kissinger, 240307Z, December 1974 (declassified August 4, 1988), Gerald R. Ford Library, Gerald R. Ford Papers, White House Operations [unless otherwise noted, all documents cited here subsequently come from this archival source, collection series information only will be cited], Richard Cheney Files, Intelligence Series, box 5, folder "Colby Report."

6. National Security Council, Memorandum, Henry Kissinger–Donald Rumsfeld, "Public Handling of New York Times Allegations of CIA Domestic Activities," December 23, 1974 (declassified December 23, 1992), Cheney Files, Intelligence Series, box 6, folder "Intelligence—General."

7. Department of State, TELCON, Henry Kissinger–Ted Koppel, December 23, 1974, 11:20 a.m. (declassified January 3, 2005; National Security Archive FOIA 200102979). Koppel persisted in asking about the CIA activities, and Kissinger promised to check. About an hour later aide Richard Kennedy told Kissinger that one of the CIA reports, at a minimum, had been updated to include the American group Students for a Democratic Society (SDS). There is no record of Kissinger supplying Ted Koppel any correction of his earlier assertions.

8. Department of State, TELCON, Henry Kissinger–Marvin Kalb, 5:20 p.m., December 24, 1974 (declassified December 28, 2004; National Security Archive FOIA 200102979).

9. Department of State, TELCON, Henry Kissinger–Barry Schweid, December 24, 1974, 3:25 p.m. (declassified December 27, 2004; National Security Archive FOIA 200102979).

10. National Security Council, Memorandum, Henry Kissinger–Gerald R. Ford, "Colby Report," December 25, 1974 (declassified June 20, 2003), Cheney Files, Intelligence Series, box 5, folder "Colby Report." This memorandum had at least the virtue of sticking to the substance of the Colby Report. Dr. Kissinger's description of The Family Jewels in his memoirs goes far beyond the actual contents of the material. "The 'family jewels,'" Kissinger writes, "alleged as well assassination plots against foreign leaders during the Kennedy and Johnson Administrations and touched on every aspect of covert

and paramilitary activities conducted by the American government during a twenty-five year period" (*Years of Renewal*, 313). In fact, The Family Jewels said nothing whatever about paramilitary action; its coverage of assassinations is defective (and one of the reasons why the National Security Archive decided to create a "real" Family Jewels). The original document is confined to one single narrow aspect of the subject, CIA relations with American organized crime figures; and it covers no covert operations at all except in the sense that the CIA domestic activities were carried out in secret, and thus were "covert."

11. "A New CIA Furor," *Newsweek* magazine, January 6, 1975, quoted p. 10.

12. White House Office, Richard Cheney Notes, "CIA—The Colby Report," December 27, 1974, Cheney Files, Intelligence Series, box 5, folder "Colby Report."

13. White House, Memorandum of Conversation, President Ford–Henry Kissinger, January 4, 1975 (declassified April 20, 2000), Gerald R. Ford Library, Ford Papers, National Security Advisers' Files, Memcon series, box 8, folder "January 4, 1975: Ford–Kissinger."

14. Department of Justice, Office of the Deputy Attorney General, Memorandum, Lawrence H. Silberman–Gerald R. Ford, January 3, 1975 (declassified January 8, 1997), Gerald R. Ford Library, Ford Papers, Richard Cheney Files, Intelligence Series, box 7, folder "Meeting with Richard Helms."

15. White House, Memorandum of Conversation, President Ford–Richard Helms, January 4, 1975 (declassified May 5, 1999), Gerald R. Ford Library, Ford Papers, National Security Advisers' Files, Memcon series, box 8, folder "January 4, 1975: Ford–Former CIA Director Richard Helms."

16. Officially the President's Commission on CIA Activities within the United States. Its product, the *Final Report* (Washington, DC: Government Printing Office, 1975) issued in June 1975, will be cited in several places later as "Rockefeller Report."

17. Chaired by Idaho Democrat Senator Frank Church, the Senate investigators would be informally known as the Church Committee, and technically as the Select Committee to Study Governmental Operations with Respect to Intelligence Activities of the United States (Senate [94th Cong., 2nd sess.]). The Church Committee produced several interim reports, six books of final report, and seven volumes of hearings (all Washington, DC: Government Printing Office,

1975–1976). These will be cited in various contexts in later chapters, always as "Church Committee."

18. The House of Representatives investigatory body was called the House Select Committee on Intelligence, initially under the chairmanship of Representative Lucien Nedzi (D-IL). Nedzi would be discredited when his prior knowledge of The Family Jewels—as related in the next chapter—became known, and the committee would be reconstituted in June under Representative Otis G. Pike (D-NY). Its report was never officially issued, though bootleg copies leaked and would appear in the press.

19. Walter F. Mondale with David Hage, *The Good Fight: A Life in Liberal Politics* (New York: Scribner, 2010), 139.

CHAPTER 3. DOMESTIC SURVEILLANCE

1. Church Committee, *Final Report: Book III: Supplementary Detailed Staff Reports on Intelligence Activities and the Rights of Americans* (Washington, DC: Government Printing Office, 1976), 721–723, quoted p. 723. Also see Frank Donner, *The Age of Surveillance: The Aims and Methods of America's Political Intelligence System* (New York: Random House, 1980), 272.

2. Church Committee, *Final Report, Book III*, 723–729, quoted p. 725.

3. Bill Richards, "CIA Infiltrated Black Groups Here in the 1960s," *Washington Post*, March 30, 1978, A1, A3.

4. Church Committee, *Final Report, Book III*, 681. Helms's testimony to the committee on antiwar dissent and the formation of this project was that "President Johnson was after this all the time. I don't recall any specific instructions in writing from his staff, particularly, but this was something that came up almost daily" (ibid., quoted p. 689).

5. Stokely Carmichael with Ekwume Michael Thelwell, *Ready for Revolution: The Life and Struggles of Stokely Carmichael (Kwame Ture)* (New York: Scribner, 2003), 636.

6. Frank J. Rafalko, *MH/Chaos: The CIA's Campaign against the Radical New Left and the Black Panthers* (Annapolis, MD: Naval Institute Press, 2011), passim.

7. CIA, Memorandum, Thomas Karamessines–James J. Angleton, "Overseas Coverage of Subversive Student and Related Activities," August 15, 1967, EYES ONLY (declassified April 26, 1989), Gerald

R. Ford Library, Ford Papers, White House Operations (hereafter, GRFL, GRFP, WHO), Richard Cheney Files, Intelligence Series, box 5, folder "Colby Report."

8. Richard Helms with William Hood, *A Look over My Shoulder: A Life in the Central Intelligence Agency* (New York: Random House, 2003), 279–280.

9. Rafalko, *MH/Chaos*, 54.

10. Confidential source.

11. CIA, Operational Cable, Director 49260, November 2, 1967 (declassified April 26, 1989), GRFL, GRFP, WHO, Richard Cheney Files, Intelligence Series, box 5, folder "Colby Report."

12. CIA, Memorandum, "Distribution of OCI Paper on Student Dissidents," September 17, 1968 (MORI 145843), declassified as part of the *Family Jewels Documents*, 2007, 173–174.

13. CIA, "Special Information Report: Vietnam Moratorium Day, October 15, 1969," October 1969 (declassified, MORI 18137), Texas Tech University, Vietnam Center Archive, CIA Collection, item 04112155001.

14. CIA, "Special Information Report: Anti–Vietnam War Protest, November 1969," and idem, "II," November 1969 (declassified, MORI nos. 18139, 18140), Texas Tech University, Vietnam Center Archive, CIA Collection, items 04112154007 and 04112155003.

15. Submitting a new copy of the "Restless Youth" study to the president in 1969, Helms's cover memo to Henry Kissinger contained a different warning: "This is an area not within the charter of this agency, so I need not emphasize how extremely sensitive this makes the paper" (Church Committee, *Final Report, Book III*, quoted p. 697). This puts a very different light on the language in the Helms CIA directive. In his memoirs Helms records that "Nothing in my thirty-year service brought me more criticism than my response to President Johnson's insistence." He recounts that when LBJ brought it up, "I explained that such an investigation might risk involving the agency in a violation of the CIA charter" (*A Look over My Shoulder*, 279). Mr. Helms calls his language in the cover note to Kissinger "a similar caution in respect to the Agency charter" (281).

16. Rockefeller Commission Report. The Helms memoir (*A Look over My Shoulder*, 281) asserts that the Chaos files were FBI, not CIA, material.

17. Some of these files were many volumes long. Thus the Rockefeller Commission enumerated these files, but the CIA, in a June 25,

1975, letter, objected that the number of "files" was only 107 (Church Committee, *Final Report, Book III*, fn. p. 695).

18. These and other Chaos personnel were interviewed by the Rockefeller Commission or the Church Committee. Agent numbers appear in the Rockefeller Commission report.

19. Angus Mackenzie, *Secrets: The CIA's War at Home* (Berkeley: University of California Press, 1997), 30–34, 36–41, 55–57.

20. CIA, "Foreign Support for Activities Planned to Disrupt or Harass the Republican Convention," July 26, 1972 (MORI 16753), Texas Tech University, Vietnam Center Archive, CIA Collection, item 04112151002.

21. *Congressional Record*, Extensions of Remarks, April 7, 1971, p. E2911. The entire proceedings of the Winter Soldier Investigation were inserted into the *Congressional Record* by Oregon Senator Mark O. Hatfield.

22. CIA, Management Advisory Group memoranda, "CIA Domestic Activities," March 25, 1971, and November 1971 (declassified, MORI 1451843), CIA, *Family Jewels Documents*, 439–443.

23. Richard Helms Speeches, to the American Society of Newspaper Editors, April 17, 1971; and to employees, "State of the Agency," September 17, 1971, excerpted in CIA, *Family Jewels Documents*, 445.

24. CIA, William Colby Memorandum, "CIA Activities in the United States," April 21, 1972 (declassified, MORI 1451843), CIA, *Family Jewels Documents*, 444–447. In typical CIA fashion the Colby memorandum had already been declassified—in 1985—and lay among Dick Cheney's White House files. It need not have awaited release with The Family Jewels in 2007.

25. Cord Meyer, Jr., *Facing Reality: From World Federalism to the CIA* (New York: Harper & Row, 1980), 215. That Meyer, writing five years after the Church Committee investigation, with an increasingly strong Freedom of Information Act in place, still believed that he could get by with this assertion is a telling comment indeed.

26. Scott D. Breckinridge, *CIA and the Cold War: A Memoir* (Westport, CT: Praeger, 1993), 165.

27. Church Committee, *Final Report, Book III*, quoted p. 706.

28. Victor Marchetti and John D. Marks, *The CIA and the Cult of Intelligence* (New York: Dell Books, 1980), quoted p. 190.

29. Helms, *A Look over My Shoulder*, 279. However, the fact that Helms had previously approved both Projects Resistance and Merrimac puts his assertion here in doubt.

30. U.S. Army, Deputy Chief of Staff for Intelligence, Memorandum, "Collecting Information on U.S. Persons," November 5, 2001, declassified copy held by the Federation of American Scientists, http://www.fas.org/irp/agency/army/uspersons.html (accessed November 12, 2012).

31. Christopher Dickey, *Securing the City: Inside America's Best Counterterror Force—The NYPD* (New York: Simon & Schuster, 2009).

CHAPTER 4. SURVEILLANCE II: *PRIVATE COMMUNICATIONS*

1. Of course it is true that phones existed at the time, and that telegrams and cables were arguably at that time the form taken by today's e-mail, but I believe this characterization is the more accurate one. Long distance telephony was expensive, almost prohibitively so, with telegrams a close second, forcing the bulk of long distance, overseas communications into the mail. In addition, those other forms of communication were also subjected to intrusive monitoring—telephones by FBI wiretaps and telegrams by the National Security Agency. These latter were not CIA projects and thus were not represented in The Family Jewels. The same issues we raise here, however, apply to those FBI and NSA activities.

2. Until the 1970s the Post Office was a Cabinet-level department of the United States government.

3. Church Committee, *Final Report, Book III: Supplementary Detailed Staff Reports on Intelligence Activities and the Rights of Americans* (Washington, DC: Government Printing Office, 1976), quoted p. 568.

4. CIA, Inspector General, Survey of the Office of Security, December 1960 (declassified October 9, 1975), Annex II, p. 1 (Church Committee, *Hearings: v. IV: Mail Opening*, reprinted, Exhibit 1, p. 175).

5. Our italics. To "review first-class correspondence" meant actually opening the letters. Note that (1) Dulles said nothing of opening *U.S.* letters and (2) the precise analogy between 1954 and 2012: foreign mail in transit to Latin America corresponds to global cellphone/e-mail communications transiting U.S. switching centers on their way elsewhere.

6. CIA, Memorandum, Richard Helms–Sheffield Edwards, "SRPOINTER," May 17, 1954 (Church Committee, *Hearings: v. IV*, reprinted, Exhibit 27, pp. 257–258).

7. CIA, 1960 IG Report, p. 8 (Church Committee, *Hearings: v. IV*, reprinted, p. 182).

8. CIA, Raymond Rocca–Sheffield Edwards, "Project HTLINGUAL," February 23, 1962 (declassified August 18, 1980), copy in author's files.

9. Church Committee, *Final Report, Book III*, quoted p. 586.

10. CIA, Memorandum, Richard Helms–Raymond Rocca, "HTLINGUAL," February 16, 1961 (Church Committee, *Hearings: v. IV*, reprinted, Exhibits 8 and 10 [retyped], pp. 205, 210).

11. Church Committee, *Final Report, Book III*, quoted p. 588.

12. Thomas Powers, *The Man Who Kept the Secrets: Richard Helms and the CIA* (New York: Alfred Knopf, 1979).

13. This might be the place to note that Project HT/LINGUAL was not the only CIA mail-opening program. There was a yearlong effort in Hawaii in 1954–1955; an experimental activity, Project SETTER, in New Orleans in 1957; and an episodic exploitation of mail to the Far East at the San Francisco post office, KM/SOURDOUGH, between 1969 and 1971. These have been left aside here, though SOURDOUGH figures in one document in the original Family Jewels, because the first two clearly fall outside the period of domestic surveillance, while SOURDOUGH never attained the level of HT/LINGUAL, processing only about 16,000 letters throughout its existence. Each of these efforts nonetheless involved the same criminal act embodied in the original program.

14. Church Committee, *Final Report, Book III*, quoted p. 574.

15. Columnist Tom Wicker makes the appropriate comment regarding the Helms testimony: "Mr. Helms' 'assumption,' for example, not only emphasizes the fact that the C.I.A. was scarcely accountable to anyone, and that its power to operate in secrecy was, in fact, the power to do virtually anything it wanted to do. It also suggests the arrogant, expansive and dangerous habits of mind officials can develop when they can act in secret and without accounting for such acts" ("The Mail Cover Story," *New York Times*, October 24, 1975).

16. Richard M. Helms with William Hood, *A Look over My Shoulder: A Life in the Central Intelligence Agency* (New York: Random House, 2003), 439–440.

17. Church Committee, *Hearings: v. IV*, 30–31.

18. "Reflections of DCIs Colby and Helms on the CIA's 'Time of Troubles,'" *Studies in Intelligence* 51, no. 3 (September 2007): 21.

19. Ibid., quoted p. 6.

20. Ibid., 7.

21. Robert M. Hathaway and Russell Jack Smith, *Richard Helms as Director of Central Intelligence, 1966–1973* (CIA: Center for the Study of Intelligence/History Staff, 1993; declassified July 2006), 126.

22. Church Committee, *Final Report, Book III*, 578.

23. Ibid., 574.

24. Ibid., 586–591. Also Church Committee, *Hearings: v. IV*, 202.

25. For 1971–1972 Angleton claimed to have identified thirty-one Soviet students "academically active" in the United States as civilian or military intelligence agents or sources, about half the total of sixty-seven. Based on his own data for letters copied, that amounts to 1 identification per 619 mail intrusions. Without doubt the collection ratio was much higher for U.S. persons on the watch list, as all the Soviet students—whose identities were already known to the U.S. government—certainly were. Also note the discrepancy between Angleton's claims in 1973 and those made retrospectively by Richard Helms (*A Look over My Shoulder*, 439–440).

26. CIA, Office of Legislative Counsel, "Journal," March 20, 1975, 6. Compare at the National Archives and Records Administration (CIA CREST Files) the agency's 2005 redaction of this page (CIA-RDP77M00144R000600120042-0) with the same page as released in 2006 (CIA-RDP77M00144R000600070040-8). It is worth noting that the original classification level of this information (in 1975) was merely "Confidential," and also that CIA censors considered the document's marking as "CIA Internal Use Only" as worthy of national security protection.

27. Church Committee, *Final Report, Book II: Intelligence Activities and the Rights of Americans*, quoted p. 109, fn. 512.

28. National Security Agency, Assistant Director, Establishment of Sensitive SIGINT Operation: Project MINARET, July 1, 1969 (Church Committee, *Final Report, Book II*, reprinted pp. 149–150).

29. National Security Agency, Memorandum, Gayler–Laird/ Mitchell, January 26, 1971 (Church Committee, *Final Report, Book II*, reprinted pp. 156–157).

30. Department of Justice, "Report on Inquiry into CIA-Related Electronic Surveillance Activities," SC-05078-76 (declassified FOIA), quoted p. 107, copy courtesy of James Bamford.

31. *United States v. United States District Court*, 407 U.S. 297 (1972). This case law, the fact that the government had relied upon the national security exception, the unanimous decision, and the tight

Supreme Court opinion that admitted no exceptions are crucial to understanding the legal status of NSA phone monitoring. The Court found the national security exception in the 1968 Act "is not a grant of authority to conduct warrantless national security surveillances." The decision essentially meant that NSA programs were legal only during the interval between entry into force of the act and its clarification by the Supreme Court in June 1972. It is highly significant that in his 1975 testimony before the Church Committee, NSA Director General Lew Allen attempted to avoid any reference to "Keith," as the case is known for the originally presiding federal district court judge. Certain NSA lawyers during the Year of Intelligence professed to believe that the ruling did not constrain the NSA. That is simply not true. The attorney general explicitly referred to Keith in terminating FBI collaboration in the fall of 1973. Moreover, the Department of Justice referred to Keith as a "watershed" in its 1976 review of the legal vulnerabilities of the NSA, CIA, FBI, and other agencies resulting from these domestic operations, and devoted considerable space to contriving arguments for possible defenses against criminal prosecution under the statutes.

32. Frank van Riper, "Find U.S. Agencies Spy on Embassies' Cables," *New York Daily News*, July 22, 1975, 1, 24. Britt Snider credits a different press story with breaking open the issue, one in the *New York Times* in early August (Nicholas M. Horrock, "National Security Agency Reported Eavesdropping on Most Private Cables," *New York Times*, August 8, 1975, 1), but it will be apparent here that by August 8 the only new element in public knowledge would be that the NSA was monitoring "most" cables (L. Britt Snider, "Recollections from the Church Committee's Investigation of NSA," *Studies in Intelligence*, Winter 1999–2000, p. 45 and fn. 4, p. 50).

33. Nicholas M. Horrock, "Colby Says N.S.A. Tapped Phone Calls of Americans," *New York Times*, August 7, 1975.

34. CIA, Letter, William E. Colby–Gerald R. Ford, September 18, 1974 (declassified February 6, 1995), GRFL, GRFP, Philip W. Buchen Files, box 26, folder "National Security Chronological File."

35. CIA, Memorandum, "Electronic Intelligence Legislation," May 27, 1975 (declassified January 8, 1992), GRFL, GRFP, Robert K. Wolthius Files, box 1, folder "Central Intelligence Agency."

36. Quoting from the decision in *Zweibon v. Mitchell*, DC Circuit No. 73-1847.

37. Loch K. Johnson, *A Season of Inquiry: The Senate Intelligence*

Investigation (Lexington: University Press of Kentucky, 1985), quoted p. 92. From the NSA side see James G. Hudec, "Unlucky Shamrock— The View from the Other Side," *Studies in Intelligence*, no. 10 (Winter 2001): 85–94.

38. Walter F. Mondale with David Hage, *The Good Fight: A Life in Liberal Politics* (New York: Scribner, 2010), quoted pp. 148–149.

39. Department of State, Memorandum, Robert S. Ingersoll– Gerald R. Ford, "Attorney General Levi's Proposed Bill on Electronic Surveillance," March 16, 1976 (declassified May 13, 1997), GRFL, GRFP, Presidential Handwriting File, National Security Series, box 3, folder "Intelligence (14–15)."

40. George W. Bush, *Decision Points* (New York: Crown Publishers, 2010), 163.

41. Dick Cheney with Liz Cheney, *In My Time: A Personal and Political Memoir* (New York: Simon & Schuster, 2011), 350.

42. General Michael V. Hayden, "What American Intelligence and Especially the NSA Have Been Doing to Defend the Nation," National Press Club Address, January 23, 2006, Office of the Director of National Intelligence Release, http://www.dni.gov/files/documents /Newsroom/Speeches%20and%20Interviews/20060123_speech _content.htm (accessed January 25, 2006).

43. Scott Shane and David Johnston, "Mining of Data Prompted Fight over U.S. Spying," *New York Times*, July 29, 2007, 1, 17.

44. Interagency Inspectors General (Department of Defense, Department of Justice, Central Intelligence Agency, National Security Agency, Office of the Director of National Intelligence), "Unclassified Report on the President's Surveillance Program," July 10, 2009, 21–24, copy in author's files.

45. Cheney, *In My Time*, 351.

46. Condoleezza Rice, *No Higher Honor: A Memoir of My Years in Washington* (New York: Crown Publishers, 2011), 115.

47. Cheney, *In My Time*, 353.

48. Harold H. Bruff, *Bad Advice: Bush's Lawyers in the War on Terror* (Lawrence: University Press of Kansas, 2009), 152.

49. Dan Eggen, "Bush Warned about Mail-Opening Authority," *Washington Post*, January 5, 2007, quoted p. A3.

CHAPTER 5. DETENTION AND INTERROGATION

1. United States Congress, House (95th Cong., 2nd sess.), Select

Committee on Assassinations, *Hearings, Volume IV* (Washington, DC: Government Printing Office, 1979), p. 22 for the specific assertion, pp. 20–28 for the full discussion and meeting records.

2. Richard Helms with William Hood, *A Look over My Shoulder: A Life in the Central Intelligence Agency* (New York: Random House, 2003), 238.

3. CIA, "KUBARK Counterintelligence Interrogation," July 1963 (declassified January 1997), 6–9, 90–104, copy in author's files. KU/Bark was the agency's acronym for the CIA itself.

4. In 1954 O'Neal had opposed the CIA project for a coup to overthrow President Jacobo Arbenz and had been sent home to get him out of the way. He subsequently became the first chief of the Special Intelligence Unit within the Angleton staff, which was elevated to the status of a "group."

5. Helms, *A Look over My Shoulder*, 244.

6. Tennent ("Pete") Bagley, a case officer in Bern, Switzerland, when Nosenko first appeared, was mobilized to meet him. Pete Bagley had also conducted the initial CIA debriefings of Deriabin in Salzburg after that officer defected in Vienna in 1954. Angleton, who once tried to recruit Bagley for the CI Staff, later gave him access to the Golitsyn file. By the mid-1960s Bagley was counterintelligence chief within the Soviet Division, and later rose to be deputy chief of division, over the ruined careers of his main competitors for that job, who were successively fingered as the possible Soviet mole. Some felt Bagley a ruthless opportunist. By 1973, CIA reviewers of the Nosenko affair were accusing Bagley himself of being the mole. In any case, Pete Bagley was a knowledgeable and sharp analyst, though his fluency in Russian is reported to have been limited.

7. Robert M. Hathaway and Russell Jack Smith, *Richard Helms as Director of Central Intelligence, 1966–1973* (CIA: Center for the Study of Intelligence/History Staff, 1993; declassified July 2006), quoted p. 107.

8. Tennent H. Bagley, *Spy Wars: Moles, Mysteries, and Deadly Games* (New Haven, CT: Yale University Press, 2007), 263.

9. Ibid., quoted p. 107.

10. U.S. Congress, House Assassination Committee Hearings, *Hearings, Volume IV*, reprinted p. 46.

11. This was also Mr. Helms's recollection in the May 1984 interview the director gave for the CIA's official history of his tenure (Hathaway and Smith, *Richard Helms*, quoted pp. 110–111).

12. James Angleton, "Report to the Presidential Commission on CIA Activities within the United States," no date (June 1975 [declassified May 24, 2000]), Gerald R. Ford Library, Ford Papers, White House Operations, Richard Cheney Files, Intelligence Series, box 7, folder "Report by James J. Angleton, 6/75," p. 6.

13. On Angleton see Tom Mangold, *Cold Warrior James Jesus Angleton: The CIA's Master Spy Hunter* (New York: Simon & Schuster, 1991). Among the early accounts of the whole issue of the defector wars is David C. Martin, *Wilderness of Mirrors* (New York: Harper & Row, 1980). The best single study is in David Wise, *Molehunt: The Secret Search for Traitors That Shattered the CIA* (New York: Random House, 1992). For a biography of one of the CIA officers involved see *CIA Spy Master* (Gretna, LA: Pelican Publishing, 2004). The most detailed bill of particulars presented against Nosenko is Pete Bagley's in *Spy Wars*. For John Hart's view see *The CIA's Russians* (Annapolis, MD: Naval Institute Press, 2003).

14. Stansfield Turner, *Secrecy and Democracy: The CIA in Transition* (Boston: Houghton Mifflin, 1985), 45.

15. CIA, Memorandum, Stansfield Turner–Deputy Director for Administration, April 19, 1978 (declassified November 23, 2005), National Archives and Records Administration, CIA CREST files.

16. L. Britt Snider, *The CIA and the Hill: CIA's Relationship with Congress, 1946–2004* (CIA: Center for the Study of Intelligence, 2008), 244. The notes reflecting Alpirez's participation in the DeVine interrogation were apparently among a compilation of ten CIA reports prepared for presentation to Senate committee staff for a meeting on June 16, 1992, according to the CIA Inspector General's investigation of these same events. Because of the extent and character of "national security" deletions from the IG report, however, the text that is in the public domain states that the information was actually "shown" to Congress (CIA, Inspector General, "Report of Investigation: Guatemala, v. I: Overview," 95-0024-IG, July 15, 1995 [declassified December 2001], 26). The entire subsequent evolution of the Guatemala affair indicates this is not accurate.

17. CIA, Inspector General, "Report: Guatemala, v. I," 33.

18. CIA, "Statement of Honorable John Deutch on Guatemala," September 29, 1995, copy in author's files.

19. Dick Cheney with Liz Cheney, *In My Time: A Personal and Political Memoir* (New York: Simon & Schuster, 2011), quoted p. 335.

20. Jose A. Rodriguez, Jr., with Bill Harlow, *Hard Measures: How*

Aggressive CIA Actions after 9/11 Saved American Lives (New York: Threshold Editions, 2012); versus John Kiriakou with Michael Ruby, *The Reluctant Spy: My Secret Life in the CIA's War on Terror* (New York: Bantam Books, 2009).

21. George H. Tenet with Bill Harlow, *At the Center of the Storm: My Years at the CIA* (New York: HarperCollins, 2007), 240.

22. Ali H. Soufan with Daniel Freedman, *The Black Banners: The Inside Story of 9/11 and the War against al-Qaeda* (New York: W. W. Norton, 2011), 375–376.

23. Rodriguez, *Hard Measures*, 54–60, 85–86. Compare with Soufan, *The Black Banners*, 373–435. It is worth noting that one argument Rodriguez makes is that CIA was focused on the future—intelligence to disrupt the next attack—while the FBI method was backward-looking. Yet the evidence the CIA man cites to demonstrate the value of "senior Al Qa'ida detainee[s']" intelligence is the number of footnotes that trace to them in the 9/11 Commission Report (*Hard Measures*, 93). But the Commission's report was an historical account of the September 11 plot—by definition backward-looking.

24. Tenet, *At the Center of the Storm*, 241.

25. United States Congress (110th Cong., 2nd sess.), Senate Armed Services Committee, *Report: Inquiry into the Treatment of Detainees in U.S. Custody* (November 20, 2008), xv.

26. Condoleezza Rice, *No Higher Honor: A Memoir of My Years in Washington* (New York: Crown Publishers, 2011), 117.

27. Rodriguez, *Hard Measures*, 65.

28. Department of Justice, Office of Professional Responsibility, *Report: Investigation into the Office of Legal Counsel's Memoranda Concerning Issues Related to the Central Intelligence Agency's Use of "Enhanced Interrogation Techniques" on Suspected Terrorists*, July 29, 2009, copy in author's file (hereafter cited as "OPR Final Report"). Two prior drafts of this report, the responses from John Yoo and Jay S. Bybee, and Attorney General Mukasey's reflections after a final meeting with the investigators (put in a January 19, 2009, memorandum) are key records in this matter. See also the extensive commentary by legal experts at a Senate hearing in May 2009, in United States Congress (111th Cong., 1st sess.), Senate Judiciary Committee, *Hearing: What Went Wrong: Torture and the Office of Legal Counsel in the Bush Administration* (Washington, DC: Government Printing Office, 2009), passim.

29. CIA, "Congressional Notification Title" List, undated;

"Interrogation Briefings to the Hill," undated (both declassified April 15, 2010). These are among the documents released as a result of an FOIA lawsuit brought by the American Civil Liberties Union. These will be cited hereafter as "ACLU documents." CIA, Letter, Leon V. Panetta–Silvestre Reyes, May 5, 2009, with accompanying list, "Member Briefings on Enhanced Interrogation Techniques," no date (unclassified), copy in author's files.

30. Rodriguez, *Hard Measures*, 64.

31. Porter J. Goss, "Security over Politics," *Washington Post*, April 25, 2009, A15.

32. In addition, former senator Bob Graham, vice-chairman of the Senate Select Committee on Intelligence, found that the CIA record listed him at briefings he had not attended and added that his briefing on interrogation methods had not mentioned waterboarding. One entry on the CIA list included the name of a staffer who had merely accompanied members to the room, and another noted the presence of a staff aide no longer employed by the oversight committees. Paul Kane, "Democrats Defending Pelosi," *Washington Post*, May 20, 2009, A4. In addition, a briefing for Senate committee staff on May 6, 2004, was left off the list, in that case possibly because the discussion centered on the CIA's lack of involvement with the abuses at Abu Ghraib prison in Iraq.

33. Soufan, *The Black Banners*, 378.

34. Cheney, *In My Time*, 357–358. Note the discrepancy with Jose Rodriguez's claims of FBI incompetence versus CIA mastery.

35. CIA, Cable, Headquarters–Field, April 27, 2002 (declassified April 15, 2010), ACLU documents.

36. CIA, Cable, Headquarters–Field, "EYES ONLY," May 6, 2002 (declassified April 15, 2010), ACLU documents.

37. Rodriguez, *Hard Measures*, 84.

38. CIA, Office of the Inspector General, "Special Review: Counterterrorism Detention and Interrogation Activities (September 2001–October 2003)," 2003-7123-IG, May 7, 2004 (declassified), pp. 25, 31–32, 36–38, ACLU documents. Hereafter cited as "Helgerson Report."

39. CIA, Record of Interview with Office of the Inspector General, June 18, 2003 (declassified April 15, 2010), ACLU documents.

40. Helgerson Report, 37.

41. CIA, Stanley Moskowitz, Memorandum for the Record,

"Member Briefing, 02/04/2003," no date (declassified ca. February 2010), ACLU documents; Rodriguez, *Hard Measures*, 187.

42. As with so much else, Jose Rodriguez also disputes the number of recorded waterboardings of Zubaydah, which has been repeatedly stated in official documents from both inside and outside the CIA. These figures, the spy chieftain declares, were "in the mind of the IG" (*Hard Measures*, 177).

43. Glenn L. Carle, *The Interrogator: An Education* (New York: Nation Books, 2011), 171–175, 181–182.

44. Department of Justice, OPR Final Report, 22.

45. Rice, *No Higher Honor*, 120.

46. Rodriguez, *Hard Measures*, 127.

47. Department of State, Embassy, Athens, Memorandum, Robin Quinville–Ambassador Charles P. Ries, "Briefer for Your Breakfast Meetings with John Bellinger," April 10, 2008, http://www.state.gov /documents/organization/125139.pdf (accessed May 25, 2012).

48. Rodriguez, *Hard Measures*, 189.

49. Ibid., 118–119.

50. Dana Priest, "From Ex-CIA Official, a Blunt Defense of Harsh Interrogation," *Washington Post*, April 25, 2012, C1, C9.

51. Dana Priest, "CIA Holds Terror Suspects in Secret Prisons," *Washington Post*, November 2, 2005, A1.

52. CIA, Cable, "EYES ONLY," Immediate, [Deleted]–Director, 080304Z, November 2005 (declassified April 15, 2010), ACLU documents.

53. Rodriguez, *Hard Measures*, 119, 192–194.

54. CIA, Cable, "EYES ONLY," Headquarters–[Deleted] Station, 081855Z, November 2005 (declassified April 15, 2010), ACLU documents.

55. Rodriguez, *Hard Measures*, 193.

56. CIA, e-mail, [Deleted]–Executive Director Kyle D. Foggo, November 10, 2005, 5:48 p.m. (declassified April 15, 2010), ACLU documents. Jose Rodriguez (*Hard Measures*, 195) contends that he had only one conversation about destroying the tapes—in August 2005—and that the exchange regarding who would take the heat took place during the course of that discussion. The declassified CIA document is quite clear as to the date and context—and the remarks were recorded by an agency officer other than Rodriguez, further attesting to their authenticity.

CHAPTER 6. ASSASSINATION

1. Harrison E. Salisbury, *Without Fear or Favor: An Uncompromising Look at* The New York Times (New York: Times Books, 1980), 536–539; Daniel Schorr, *Clearing the Air* (New York: Berkley Books, 1978), quoted p. 145.

2. Schorr, *Clearing the Air*, quoted pp. 145, 147.

3. Kathryn S. Olmstead, *Challenging the Secret Government: The Post-Watergate Investigations of the CIA and FBI* (Chapel Hill: University of North Carolina Press, 1996), 59.

4. Nicolas Dujmovic, "Ronald Reagan, Intelligence, William Casey, and CIA: A Reappraisal," CIA Paper (Center for the Study of Intelligence, April 2011), 7–8.

5. White House, James A. Wilderotter, Memorandum for the Record, April 16, 1975, Gerald R. Ford Library, Ford Papers, White House Operations (hereafter abbreviated GRFL, GRFP, WHO), Robert K. Wolthius Files, Subject Series, box 2, folder "Intelligence Investigations: Church Committee (2)."

6. David W. Belin, *Final Disclosure: The Full Truth about the Assassination of President Kennedy* (New York: Charles Scribner's Sons, 1988), 172.

7. Commission on CIA Activities within the United States (Rockefeller Commission), "Summary of Facts: Investigation of CIA Involvement in Plans to Assassinate Foreign Leaders," no date (June 5, 1975 [declassified May 24, 2000]), GRFL, GRFP, WHO, Richard Cheney Files, Intelligence Series, box 7, folder "Report on CIA Assassination Plots (1)," p. 86.

8. Loch K. Johnson, *A Season of Inquiry: The Senate Intelligence Investigation* (Lexington: University Press of Kentucky, 1985), 48.

9. CIA, Letter, William E. Colby–President Gerald Ford, October 20, 1975 (declassified May 24, 2000), GRFL, GRFP, WHO, Richard Cheney Files, Intelligence Series, box 7, folder "Report on CIA Assassination Plots (2)."

10. Ibid., quoted p. 116.

11. Gerald R. Ford, News Conference, June 9, 1975, *Weekly Compilation of Presidential Documents* 11, no. 24 (1975): 611.

12. United States Congress (94th Cong., 1st sess.), Senate, Select Committee to Study Governmental Operations with Respect to Intelligence Activities, *Interim Report: Alleged Assassination Plots*

Involving Foreign Leaders (Washington, DC: Government Printing Office, 1975), 282–283, 289–290.

13. White House, Executive Order 11905, "United States Foreign Intelligence Activities," February 18, 1976, Section 5 (g), *Weekly Compilation of Presidential Documents* 12, no. 8 (February 23, 1976).

14. White House, Executive Order 12036, "United States Foreign Intelligence Activities," January 24, 1978, Section 2-305, copy in author's files.

15. White House, Executive Order 12333, "United States Intelligence Activities," December 4, 1981, Section 2.11, *Federal Record*, 46 FR 59941, 3FR, 1981 Compilation, pp. 200 et seq.

16. Dana Priest, "Covert CIA Program Withstands New Furor," *Washington Post*, December 30, 2005, quoted p. A11.

17. United States Congress (110th Cong., 1st sess.), Senate Select Committee on Intelligence, *Hearings: Nomination of John A. Rizzo to Be General Counsel of the Central Intelligence Agency* (Washington, DC: Government Printing Office, 2008), 19, 21, 32.

18. Greg Miller, "John Rizzo: The Most Influential Lawyer in CIA History," *Los Angeles Times*, June 29, 2009, A1.

19. CIA, George Tenet, "Written Statement for the Record of the Director of Central Intelligence before the National Commission on Terrorist Attacks upon the United States," March 24, 2004, 11, copy in author's files.

20. Tara McKelvey, "Inside the Killing Machine," *Newsweek* magazine, February 13, 2011, http://www.thedailybeast.com /newsweek/2011/02/13/inside-the-killing-machine.print.html (accessed November 25, 2012), quoted p. 3.

21. Ibid., quoted p. 4.

22. Rizzo nomination hearing, 42.

23. CIA, Statement to Employees from Acting Director Michael Morell: "Zero Dark Thirty," December 21, 2012, https://www.cia .gov/mobile/pr-statements/2012/message-from-the-acting -director-zero-dark-thirty.html (accessed January 12, 2013).

24. Richard Cheney Interview, Cable News Network, *State of the Union*, October 2, 2011.

25. Scott Shane, "CIA Reviewing Its Process for Briefing Congress," *New York Times*, July 10, 2009, A17; Paul Kane and Ben Pershing, "Secret Program Fuels CIA-Congress Dispute," *Washington Post*, July 10, 2009, A1; Greg Miller, "Cheney Linked to Secrecy of CIA

Program," *Los Angeles Times*, July 12, 2009, A1; Associated Press, "Dick Cheney Kept Congress in Dark over CIA Counterterrorism Action," *The Guardian*, July 12, 2009; Joby Warrick and Ben Pershing, "CIA Had Program to Kill Al Qaeda Leaders," *Washington Post*, July 14, 2009, A2; David Ignatius, "The CIA's 'Hit Team' Miss," *Washington Post*, July 23, 2009, A21.

CHAPTER 7. CLOAKING THE DAGGER

1. The standard sources on the CIA and media in this conventional sense begin with the seminal series reported by John M. Crewdson and Joseph B. Treaster and written by Crewdson in the *New York Times* in 1977 ("The CIA: Secret Shaper of Public Opinion," December 25, 26, 27, 1977); and Carl Bernstein's article "The CIA and the Media" (*Rolling Stone*, October 20, 1977). Political scientist and Church Committee staffer Loch K. Johnson provided a more refined view in his paper "The CIA and the Media" (*Intelligence and National Security* 1, no. 2 [May 1986]: 143–169). For the CIA's cultural Cold War see Frances Stonor Saunders, *Who Paid the Piper? The CIA and the Cultural Cold War* (London: Granta, 1999 [this book appeared under a different title in a U.S. edition]), and, more recently, Hugh Wilford, *The Mighty Wurlitzer: How the CIA Played America* (Cambridge, MA: Harvard University Press, 2008).

2. Harrison Salisbury, *Without Fear or Favor* (New York: Times Books, 1980), 477–483; as well as Gruson's obituary, Eric Pace, "Sydney Gruson, 81, Correspondent, Editor and Executive for New York Times, Is Dead," *New York Times*, March 9, 1998, A18. The CIA's documents on the Gruson affair were released in 2003.

3. James Scott, telephone interview with author, June 29, 2007.

4. Central Intelligence Agency, Memorandum, John McCone–John F. Kennedy, "Subject: Dr. Bernard B. Fall," no date (handwritten notation indicates "1962"). This redaction was declassified on April 1, 1976 (Vietnam Center [Texas Tech University], Glenn Helm Collection, box 2, file 21). I believe the document resides in Kennedy's papers as well, but I do not have that citation immediately at hand. A June 21, 1962, note from General Edward Lansdale to Secretary of Defense Robert S. McNamara notes the "recent" presidential inquiry about Fall (Memo, Edward Lansdale–Robert McNamara, June 21, 1962, declassified June 5, 2000, FOIA 87-0346).

5. Dorothy Fall, *Bernard Fall: Memories of a Soldier-Scholar*

(Washington, DC: Potomac Books, 2006), 189–202. At the time she wrote, Dorothy Fall remained unaware of the CIA position on her husband or the memo that McCone forwarded to President Kennedy (Prados conversation with Dorothy Fall, April 3, 2008).

6. PDB for "President's Daily Brief," the highly classified intelligence report series prepared for presidents' personal information. In actuality, in 1963 this type of report was called the "President's Intelligence Checklist" (PICL), but because the PDB designation was already in use by the time of The Family Jewels and continues to be used today, for purposes of consistency and because this is likely to be familiar to more readers, the designation PDB will be used here throughout.

7. CIA, John McCone, Memorandum for the Record, November 29, 1963 (declassified April 21, 1998), Lyndon Baines Johnson Library, Lyndon Baines Johnson Papers, National Security File [hereafter cited as LBJL, LBJP, NSF], John McCone Memos Series, box 1, folder "Meetings with the President 23.11.63–27.12.63."

8. CIA, John McCone, Memorandum for the Record, December 9, 1963 (declassified August 26, 1999), LBJL, LBJP, NSF, John McCone Memos Series, box 1, folder "Meetings with the President 23.11.63–27.12.63." The subject was the canceled SAMOS satellite, the leak of which McCone suspected had come from the air force, but this set his top satellite expert and the head of the National Reconnaissance Office to "go into this."

9. CIA, John McCone, Memorandum for the Record, January 5, 1964 (declassified March 4, 1998), LBJL, LBJP, NSF, John McCone Memos Series, box 1, folder "Meetings with the President, 4.1.64–24.4.65."

10. CIA, John McCone, Memorandum for the Record, April 2, 1964 (declassified October 9, 1999), LBJL, LBJP, NSF, John McCone Memos Series, box 1, folder "Meetings with the President, 4.1.64–24.4.65."

11. Salisbury, *Without Fear or Favor*, 515; Grogan's memorandum, which leaked to the newspaper, is quoted on pp. 519–520; the full account is on pp. 514–528.

12. The account here follows what is probably the most detailed analysis of the *Ramparts* case, that of Angus Mackenzie in *Secrets: The CIA's War at Home* (Berkeley: University of California Press, 1999), 15–25.

13. John Prados, *Safe for Democracy: The Secret Wars of the CIA* (Chicago: Ivan Dee Publisher, 2006), quoted p. 370.

14. For details on the National Student Association scandal, see Prados, *Safe for Democracy*, 368–375; Mackenzie, *Secrets*, 19–23; and Richard M. Helms with William Hood, *A Look over My Shoulder: A Life in the CIA* (New York: Random House, 2003), 343–350.

15. Wilford, *The Mighty Wurlitzer*, 143.

16. CIA, Briefing Paper, "CIA and Illicit Drugs," July 19, 1972, reprinted, U.S. Congress (95th Cong., 1st and 2nd sess.), House of Representatives, Permanent Select Committee on Intelligence, *Hearings: The CIA and the Media* (Washington, DC: Government Printing Office, 1978), 347.

17. David Wise and Thomas B. Ross, *The Invisible Government* (New York: Random House, 1964).

18. United States Congress (95th Cong., 2nd sess.), Select Committee on Assassinations, *Hearings, v. IV* (Washington, DC: Government Printing Office, 1979), 23.

19. David Binder, "Measuring the Years in Terms of CIA Directors," *New York Times*, August 10, 1988, 12.

20. CIA, John McCone, Memorandum for the Record, May 20, 1964 (declassified August 26, 1999), LBJL, LBJP, NSF, John McCone Memoranda Series, box 1, folder "Meetings with the President 3.4.64–20.5.64." McCone's session with Wise and Ross took place on May 15, 1964.

21. Joseph Burkholder Smith, *Portrait of a Cold Warrior* (New York: Ballantine Books, 1981), 425.

22. Haynes Johnson, *The Bay of Pigs: The Leaders' Story of Brigade 2506* (New York: W. W. Norton, 1964). See also John Prados, *William Colby and the CIA: The Secret Wars of a Controversial Spymaster* (Lawrence: University Press of Kansas, 2009), 242. This book was published in hardcover by Oxford University Press in 2003.

23. Mark Lane, *Rush to Judgment: A Critique of the Warren Commission's Inquiry into the Assassination of President John F. Kennedy, Officer J. D. Tippet, and Lee Harvey Oswald* (New York: Holt, Rinehart & Winston, 1966).

24. William Manchester, *Death of a President: November 20–November 25, 1963* (New York: Harper & Row, 1967). The book's publication date was New Year's Day.

25. Alfred W. McCoy, with Cathleen B. Read and Leonard P. Adams

II, *The Politics of Heroin in Southeast Asia* (New York: Random House, 1972).

26. Alfred W. McCoy, telephone interview with author, March 12, 2008.

27. John Prados, *William Colby and the CIA*, 244–245. Alfred W. McCoy, telephone interview with author, October 25, 2007. The McCoy ploy goes curiously unrecorded in Cord Meyer's own memoir, *Facing Reality: From World Federalism to the CIA* (New York: Harper & Row, 1980).

28. Edward G. Lansdale, *In the Midst of Wars: An American's Mission to Southeast Asia* (New York: Harper & Row, 1972). Lansdale's final text focused almost entirely on his help to South Vietnamese leader Ngo Dinh Diem during 1954–1955, but even there passed over lightly the clandestine missions into North Vietnam for which he was responsible, and most directly, major features of the CIA's role in the 1955 Saigon infighting through which Diem consolidated his power.

29. Author interview with Michael Getler, October 20, 2010.

30. Jack Anderson with George Clifford, *The Anderson Papers* (New York: Random House, 1973).

31. Jack Anderson with Daryl Gibson, *Peace, War, and Politics: An Eyewitness Account* (New York: Tom Doherty Associates, 1999), 233–241, quoted p. 241.

32. Bob Thompson, "The Hersh Alternative," *Washington Post Magazine*, January 28, 2001, quoted p. 13.

33. CIA, Memorandum, Director of Central Intelligence–Deputy Director for Intelligence, May 11, 1983 (declassified August 5, 2008), National Archives and Records Administration, CIA CREST series, job no. RDP88B0443R001404050075-8.

34. Richard Aldrich, "Tad Szulc and the CIA," paper presented at the conference of the Society of Historians of American Foreign Relations, Washington, DC, June 24, 2011.

35. Tad Szulc testimony, House Permanent Select Committee on Intelligence, *The CIA and the Media*, 103.

36. For example, in May 1976 the Russian weekly journal *Literaturnaya Gazeta*, accurately or not, named journalists Christopher S. Wren (*New York Times*), George Krimsky (Associated Press), and Alfred Friendly, Jr. (*Newsweek*) as CIA assets (United Press International, "Paper in Moscow Links 3 U.S. Correspondents to the C.I.A.," *New York Times*, May 26, 1976). All the news organizations involved denied the charge. Regardless of the accuracy of Soviet claims,

however, there can be little doubt that American journalists in Moscow did talk to the CIA.

37. Frank Snepp, *Decent Interval: A CIA Insider's Account of Saigon's Indecent End Told by the CIA's Chief Strategy Analyst in Vietnam* (New York: Random House, 1978), passim.

38. For example, Matthew Jones, "Cyrus L. Sulzberger, Harrison E. Salisbury and the CIA: The *New York Times*, Journalistic Integrity, and the End of a Friendship," paper presented at the conference of the Society of Historians of American Foreign Relations, Washington, DC, June 24, 2011.

39. Duane R. Clarridge with Digby Diehl, *A Spy for All Seasons* (New York: Scribner, 1997), 156.

40. HPSCI, *The CIA and the Media*, passim.

41. Carl Bernstein, "The CIA and the Media: How America's Most Powerful News Media Worked Hand in Glove with the Central Intelligence Agency and Why the Church Committee Covered It Up," *Rolling Stone*, October 20, 1977, 55–67.

42. David Atlee Phillips testimony, HPSCI, *The CIA and the Media*, 68.

43. Frank Snepp, *Irreparable Harm: A Firsthand Account of How One Agent Took on the CIA in an Epic Battle over Free Speech* (Lawrence: University Press of Kansas, 2001), 72.

44. Bob Woodward, *VEIL: The Secret Wars of the CIA, 1981–1987* (New York: Pocket Books, 1988), 587–588.

45. Central Intelligence Agency, Regulation HR 7-lc(8) (l) Sections 2(b), (c), issued by Stansfield Turner, November 30, 1977, in HPSCI, *The CIA and the Media*, reprinted pp. 523–524.

46. CIA, 1961 Covert Action Staff paper, in United States Congress, Senate (94th Cong., 2nd sess.), Select Committee to Study Governmental Operations with Respect to Intelligence Activities (Church Committee), *Final Report: Book I: Foreign and Military Intelligence* (Washington, DC: Government Printing Office, 1976), quoted p. 193.

47. John Barron, *KGB: The Secret Work of Soviet Secret Agents* (New York: Reader's Digest Press, 1974).

48. John Barron, *MIG Pilot: The Final Escape of Lieutenant Belenko* (Englewood Cliffs, NJ: McGraw-Hill, 1980).

49. Conversation with David Martin, March 28, 2012; David C. Martin, *A Wilderness of Mirrors* (New York: Harper & Row, 1980).

50. Conversation with Edward Epstein, March 28, 2012.

51. Edward Jay Epstein, *Legend: The Secret World of Lee Harvey Oswald* (New York: Reader's Digest Press, 1978).

52. Jerrold L. Schecter and Peter Deriabin, *The Spy Who Saved the World: How a Soviet Colonel Changed the Course of the Cold War* (New York: Charles Scribner's Sons, 1992).

53. Evan Thomas, *The Very Best Men / Four Who Dared: The Early Years of the CIA* (New York: Simon & Schuster, 1995).

54. Peter Grose, *Gentleman Spy: The Life of Allen Dulles* (Boston: Houghton Mifflin, 1994); and *Operation Rollback: America's Secret War behind the Iron Curtain* (Boston: Houghton Mifflin, 2000).

55. Benjamin Weiser, *A Secret Life: A Polish Colonel, His Covert Mission, and the Price He Paid to Save His Country* (New York: Public Affairs Press, 2004).

56. United States District Court for the Eastern District of Massachusetts, *Douglas Valentine v. Central Intelligence Agency*, 92-30025-F. The documents quoted (officials' identities redacted) are a CIA/Publications Review Board (PRB) memorandum for the record of July 31, 1986, a PRB letter of April 7, 1987, a PRB letter (only referred to) of December 24, 1987, a memorandum from the PRB associate legal advisor to Directorate of Operations management staff of April 8, 1988, and an undated note (only referred to) from an employee of the Office of the Inspector General.

CHAPTER 8. PLUGGING THE DIKE

1. Victor Marchetti and John D. Marks, *The CIA and the Cult of Intelligence* (New York: Knopf, 1974).

2. Angus Mackenzie, *Secrets: The CIA's War at Home* (Berkeley: University of California Press, 1999), 46.

3. White House, Memorandum, John D. Ehrlichman–Richard M. Nixon, "C.I.A. vs. Marchetti," May 30, 1972, Richard M. Nixon Library, Nixon Papers, President's Office File, Handwriting File, box 17, folder "President's Handwriting, May 1972."

4. CIA, Letter, Richard Helms–John D. Ehrlichman, May 23, 1972, Richard M. Nixon Library, Nixon Papers, President's Office File, Handwriting File, box 17, folder "President's Handwriting, May 1972."

5. Philip Agee, *On the Run* (Secaucus, NJ: Lyle Stuart, 1987), quoted p. 36.

6. Joseph B. Smith, *Portrait of a Cold Warrior* (New York: Ballantine Books, 1981), 412.

7. Frank Snepp, *Irreparable Harm: A Firsthand Account of How One Agent Took on the CIA in an Epic Battle over Free Speech* (Lawrence: University Press of Kansas, 2001), 81.

8. CIA, Memorandum, Stansfield Turner–Zbigniew Brzezinski, October 23, 1978, Jimmy Carter Library (declassified RAC NLC-43-8-4-4-8), CIA CREST series.

9. CIA, Letter, George V. Lauder–Stansfield Turner, June 30, 1986, CIA Electronic Reading Room, Document 0001356702.pdf (accessed April 15, 2012).

10. CIA, Public Affairs Office, DCI Weekly Report, March 16, 1984 (declassified October 16, 2008), National Archives and Records Administration, CIA CREST series, job no. RDP86M00886R002700030008-5.

11. Stansfield Turner, *Secrecy and Democracy: The CIA in Transition* (Boston: Houghton Mifflin, 1985), x–xi.

12. CIA, Letter, George V. Lauder–Gene Cryer, July 9, 1985, CIA Electronic Reading Room, document 0001356720.pdf (accessed April 15, 2012).

13. CIA, Letter, George V. Lauder–Frank Davies, July 10, 1985, CIA Electronic Reading Room, document 0001356743.pdf (accessed April 15, 2012).

14. Ibid.

15. William Hood, *Mole* (New York: W. W. Norton, 1982).

16. Russell Jack Smith, *The Unknown CIA: My Three Decades with the Agency* (Washington, DC: Pergamon-Brassey's, 1989).

17. Scott D. Breckinridge, *CIA and the Cold War: A Memoir* (Westport, CT: Praeger, 1993).

18. Tom Gilligan, *CIA Life: 10,000 Days with the Agency* (Guilford, CT: Foreign Intelligence Press, 1991).

19. Orrin Deforest and David Chanoff, *Slow Burn* (New York: Simon & Schuster, 1990).

20. Richard Bissell with Jonathan E. Lewis and Frances T. Pudlo, *Reflections of a Cold Warrior: From Yalta to the Bay of Pigs* (New Haven, CT: Yale University Press, 1996).

21. Miles Copeland, *The Game Player: Confessions of the CIA's Original Political Operative* (London: Aurum Press, 1989), ix.

22. Duane R. Clarridge, *A Spy for All Seasons: My Life in the CIA* (New York: Scribner, 1997).

23. John H. Hedley, "Reviewing the Work of CIA Authors: Secrets,

Free Speech, and Fig Leaves," *Studies in Intelligence*, Spring 1998, 75–83.

24. CIA, Memorandum, "Publications Review Board Standards" (OIM 00-0359), April 5, 2000, copy in author's files. (It is worth noting that this never-secret set of administrative rules bears the CIA declassification number MORI 1512162 and contains deletions that would supposedly damage national security.)

25. Richard L. Holm, *The American Agent: My Life in the CIA* (London: St. Ermin's Press, 2003).

26. Robert Baer, *See No Evil: The True Story of a Ground Soldier in the CIA's War on Terrorism* (New York: Crown Books, 2002).

27. Ted Shackley with Richard A. Finney, *Spymaster: My Life in the CIA* (Dulles, VA: Potomac Books, 2005).

28. Frank Holober, *Raiders of the China Coast: CIA Covert Operations during the Korean War* (Annapolis, MD: Naval Institute Press, 1999).

29. Floyd L. Paseman, *A Spy's Journey: A CIA Memoir* (St. Paul, MN: Zenith Press, 2004).

30. Stuart Methven, *Laughter in the Shadows: A CIA Memoir* (Annapolis, MD: Naval Institute Press, 2008).

31. Larry Devlin, *Chief of Station, Congo: Fighting the Cold War in a Hot Zone* (New York: Public Affairs Press, 2007).

32. David W. Doyle, *True Men and Traitors: From the OSS to the CIA, My Life in the Shadows* (New York: John Wiley's Sons, 2001).

33. Milt Bearden and James Risen, *The Main Enemy: The Inside Story of the CIA's Final Showdown with the KGB* (New York: Random House, 2003).

34. Robert Gates, *From the Shadows: The Ultimate Insider's Story of Five Presidents and How They Won the Cold War* (New York: Simon & Schuster, 1996), 4.

35. George Tenet with Bill Harlow, *At the Center of the Storm: My Years at the CIA* (New York: HarperCollins, 2007).

36. Richard Helms with William Hood, *A Look over My Shoulder: A Life in the Central Intelligence Agency* (New York: Random House, 2003), 452.

37. T. J. Waters, *Class 11: Inside the CIA's First Post-9/11 Spy Class* (New York: Dutton, 2006).

38. John F. Sullivan, *Gatekeeper: Memoirs of a CIA Polygraph Examiner* (Washington, DC: Potomac Books, 2007).

39. Melissa Boyle Mahle, *Denial and Deception: An Insider View of the CIA from Iran-Contra to 9/11* (New York: Nation Books, 2004), x.

40. Associated Press, "New Rules to Govern Publications by CIA Officers," *USA Today*, January 11, 2005.

41. Antonio and Jonna Mendez with Bruce Henderson, *Spy Dust: Two Masters of Disguise Reveal the Tools and Operations That Helped Win the Cold War* (New York: Atria Books, 2002), 282. This book was the sequel to Antonio's *The Master of Disguise: My Secret Life in the CIA* (with Malcolm McConnell) (New York: William Morrow, 1999). There, too, Mendez was happy with the result.

42. James M. Olson, *Fair Play: The Moral Dilemmas of Spying* (Washington, DC: Potomac Books, 2006).

43. Robert Wallace and H. Keith Melton with Henry R. Schlesinger, *Spycraft: The Secret History of the CIA's Spying from Communism to Al Qaeda* (New York: Dutton, 2008), xix–xxi.

44. Ishmael Jones, *The Human Factor: Inside the CIA's Dysfunctional Intelligence Culture* (New York: Encounter Books, 2008).

45. U.S. District Court, Eastern District of Virginia, *United States of America v. Ishmael Jones, a pen name*, 1:10cv765 (GBL/TRJ), *Complaint*, July 9, 2010, 7.

46. Henry A. Crumpton, *The Art of Intelligence: Lessons from a Life in the CIA's Clandestine Service* (New York: Penguin Press, 2012), 325.

47. Gary C. Schroen, *First In: An Insider's Account of How the CIA Spearheaded the War on Terror in Afghanistan* (New York: Ballantine Books, 2007), xi–xii.

48. Gary Berntsen with Ralph Pezzullo, *Jawbreaker: The Attack on Bin Laden and Al Qaeda, a Personal Account by the CIA's Key Field Commander* (New York: Crown Publishers, 2005), ix–x.

49. John Kiriakou with Michael Ruby, *The Reluctant Spy: My Secret Life in the CIA's War on Terror* (New York: Bantam, 2009), xi.

50. Glenn L. Carle, *The Interrogator: An Education* (New York: Nation Books, 2011), 291–292.

51. Valerie Plame Wilson, *Fair Game: How a Top Spy Was Betrayed by Her Own Government* (New York: Simon & Schuster, 2008).

52. Steven Lee Myers, "U.S. Envoy Puts Match to Bridges with Iraq Tell-All," *New York Times*, October 7, 2011. The book is Peter Van Buren, *We Meant Well: How I Helped Lose the Battle for the Hearts and Minds of the Iraqi People* (New York: Henry Holt and Company, 2011).

53. Scott Shane, "C.I.A. Fighting Memoir of 9/11 by F.B.I. Agent," *New York Times*, August 26, 2011, quoted p. A16.

54. Ali Soufan with Daniel Freedman, *The Black Banners: The Inside Story of 9/11 and the War against al-Qaeda* (New York: W. W. Norton, 2011), xi.

55. Conversation with Ali Soufan, April 15, 2012.

CHAPTER 9. CIRCLING THE WAGONS

1. Loch K. Johnson, *A Season of Inquiry: The Senate Intelligence Investigation* (Lexington: University Press of Kentucky, 1985), quoted p. 47.

2. Stanley Kutler, *Abuse of Power: The New Nixon Tapes* (New York: Free Press, 1997).

3. CIA, Vernon Walters, Memorandum for the Record, June 28, 1972, in Gerald Gold et al., eds., *The Watergate Hearings: Break-in and Cover-up* (New York: Bantam Books, 1973), reprinted pp. 786–787.

4. Ibid., pp. 787–788.

5. Vernon A. Walters, *Silent Missions* (Garden City, NY: Doubleday, 1978), 588–589.

6. CIA, Memorandum, Richard Helms–Vernon Walters, June 28, 1972, in Robert M. Hathaway and Russell Jack Smith, *Richard Helms as Director of Central Intelligence* (CIA: Center for the Study of Intelligence/History Staff, 1993; declassified July 2006), quoted p. 193.

7. CIA, Vernon A. Walters, Memorandum for the Record, July 6, 1972, in Gold, *The Watergate Hearings*, reprinted pp. 790–792.

8. White House, Memorandum, Brent Scowcroft–Gerald R. Ford, "Award of the National Security Medal to Lieutenant General Vernon A. Walters," June 8, 1976, Gerald R. Ford Library, Ford Papers, White House Central Files, Agency Files, box 20, folder "FG 6-2: CIA, 6/1/76–1/20/77."

9. CIA, Morning Staff Meeting Notes, June 19, 1972, *Family Jewels Documents*, p. 296.

10. CIA, Morning Staff Meeting Notes, June 20, 1972, *Family Jewels Documents*, p. 296.

11. During the Watergate investigations it would be disputed by some whether White House domestic affairs counsel John D. Ehrlichman had actually telephoned Cushman on cooperation with Hunt. It is worth noting that Cushman's reason for mentioning Hunt at the CIA director's staff meeting was to report his phone conversation with Ehrlichman (*Family Jewels Documents*, 286).

12. Senate Watergate Committee, Senator Howard Baker,

"Minority Report on CIA Involvement," reprinted in *The Senate Watergate Report* (New York: Dell Books, 1974), 752–755.

13. Cord Meyer, *Facing Reality: From World Federalism to the CIA* (New York: Harper & Row, 1980), 150.

14. William E. Colby with Peter Forbath, *Honorable Men: My Life in the CIA* (New York: Simon & Schuster, 1978), quoted p. 321.

15. Robert M. Hathaway and Russell Jack Smith, *Richard Helms as Director of Central Intelligence, 1966–1973* (CIA: Center for the Study of Intelligence/History Staff, 1993; declassified July 2006), 187.

16. Ronald Reagan, "Remarks on Signing the Immigration Reform and Control Act of 1986," November 6, 1986, *Public Papers of the President: Ronald Reagan 1986*, vol. 2, 1521–1522.

17. Ronald Reagan, "Remarks and an Informal Exchange with Reporters Prior to a Meeting with David Jacobsen," November 7, 1986, *Public Papers of the President: Ronald Reagan 1986*, vol. 2, 1533–1534. Also see Peter Kornbluh and Malcolm Byrne, eds., *The Iran-Contra Scandal: The Declassified History* (New York: New Press, 1993), 305, which quotes presidential press secretary Ari Fleischer as commenting that Reagan knew all these statements were false at the time.

18. Ronald Reagan Diary, entries for November 7, 8/9, 10, 11, and 12, 1986, in Douglas Brinkley, ed., *The Reagan Diaries: Unabridged* (New York: HarperCollins, 2009), vol. 2, 655–657.

19. Reagan Diary, November 13, 1986, vol. 2, 657.

20. Ronald Reagan, "Address to the Nation on Iran Arms," November 13, 1986, *Public Papers of the President* (http://www.presidency.ucsb.edu/ws/index.php?pid=36728 [accessed January 20, 2013]). The president's citation of "boatloads" of weapons was actually a veiled reference to the "Danish sailor" reported in his diary. Actually the comment *was* correct, but from the Danish seamen's union, not a sailor, except that the ship had carried weapons to Central America. A second shipment had been en route in October when diverted to a U.S. port because statutes had changed to make it legal for the U.S. military to accept weapons for onward shipment to the *contras*. And on the day of Reagan's speech, the Panamanian-flagged ship *Angelique* departed Setubal, Portugal, for Iran with a shipment of weapons. This was apparently part of an ongoing program of Portuguese arms sales to Iran, not Reagan's Iran-Contra initiative. The Danish sailor would come up again at President Reagan's news conference on November 19.

21. Ronald Reagan Diary, November 17 and 19, 1986, in Brinkley, *Reagan Diaries*, vol. 2, 658, 659.

22. Theodore Draper, *A Very Thin Line: The Iran-Contra Affairs* (New York: Hill & Wang, 1991), 482.

23. Ronald Reagan, "The President's News Conference," November 19, 1986; and "Statement on the Iran Arms and Contra Aid Controversy," November 19, 1986, in *Public Papers of the President* (respectively, http://www.presidency.ucsb.edu/ws/index.php?pid=36748 and http://www.presidency.ucsb.edu/ws/index.php?pid=36749 [accessed January 20, 2013]).

24. CIA, Letter, William J. Casey–Ronald Reagan, November 23, 1986, in Lawrence E. Walsh, et al., *Final Report of the Independent Counsel for Iran/Contra Matters: Investigations and Prosecutions* (United States Court of Appeals for the District of Columbia Circuit, August 4, 1993), quoted vol. 1, 215.

25. Robert M. Gates, *From the Shadows: The Ultimate Insider's Story of Five Presidents and How They Won the Cold War* (New York: Simon & Schuster, 1996), 402–403. It follows from this, Gates argues, that the notion Casey was running an "Enterprise" with the private benefactors in Central America is incorrect. My view is that the off-the-shelf covert operation was quite real. Unlike for the diversion, there is a huge weight of evidence from North's notebooks, guarded channel CIA (KL-43) communications traffic, and testimony from Iran-Contra figures that Bill Casey was moving pieces around the Central American chessboard in exactly the manner of an active operation.

26. James McCullough, "Coping with Iran-Contra: Personal Reflections on Bill Casey's Last Month at CIA," *Studies in Intelligence*, Summer 1995, pp. 27–44.

27. Gates, *From the Shadows*, 410.

28. Ibid., 315, 394–395, quoted on 400–401.

29. David Gries, "Coping with Iran-Contra: Commentary," *Studies in Intelligence*, Summer 1996, https://www.cia.gov/library/center-for-the-study-of-intelligence/csi-publications/csi-studies/studies/96unclass/gries.htm (accessed January 13, 2013).

30. Lawrence E. Walsh, *Firewall: The Iran-Contra Conspiracy and Cover-up* (New York: W. W. Norton, 1997), 50.

31. Oliver North, *Taking the Stand: The Testimony of Lieutenant Colonel Oliver L. North* (New York: Pocket Books, 1987), 507.

32. Ronald Reagan Diary, August 8, 1987, in Brinkley, *Reagan Diaries*, vol. 2, 762.

33. Draper, *A Very Thin Line*, 24–25.

34. Dick Cheney with Liz Cheney, *In My Time: A Personal and Political Memoir* (New York: Simon & Schuster, 2011), 143.

35. United States Congress (100th Cong., 1st sess.), *Report of the Congressional Committees Investigating the Iran-Contra Affair* (Washington, DC: Government Printing Office, 1987), 437.

36. Mark Mazzetti, "CIA Destroyed Tapes of Interrogations," *New York Times*, December 6, 2007, A1.

37. George W. Bush, *Decision Points* (New York: Crown Books, 2010), 180.

CHAPTER 10. CLARITY

1. Harry Howe Ransom, *Can American Democracy Survive Cold War?* (New York: Doubleday & Company, 1963). The citation that follows is to the Anchor Press edition, which appeared in 1964.

2. Ibid., 166.

≡ INDEX ≡